Praise for *Unlikely Friends*

"At its core missiology is the study of transformation; its roots in the preaching of the gospel, its effects in history, and the means by which it occurs. *Unlikely Friends* honors Dana Robert by following a course she plotted in examining how friendship plays a role in transformation beyond personal relationships. It is a welcome addition and enlargement of the tools available to missiologists. And a fulsome relief from decades of focusing on ideological analysis that often loses sight of the human dimension of mission. At the least it should send us all back to the archives to re-examine friendships forgotten or ignored and quite possibly discover where transformation really begins."

—ROBERT HUNT, Director of Global Theological Education, Perkins School of Theology, Southern Methodist University

"As one of Dana Robert's early doctoral students, I have been blessed directly by her scholarship and intellect, care and companionship, for close to four decades. The authors' contributions in this festschrift reflect the breadth and depth of her mentorship and faithfulness to companions on the way. *Unlikely Friends* is a fitting tribute to Dana Robert whose friendship has significantly advanced God's mission of restoration and reconciliation in the academy and the global church."

—IAN T. DOUGLAS, Bishop, The Episcopal Church in Connecticut

"This remarkable collection honors and extends Dana Robert's work on friendships in world Christianity—friendships that embrace diversity and transform societies. The authors present luminous narratives based in detailed research and vivifying the many faces of friendship. They reveal hidden histories as well as surprising transformations in widely different contexts, times of conflict and crisis, interfaith communities, culturally conflicted contexts, the transnational deaf community, and so much more. This book will inspire and transform you."

—MARY ELIZABETH MOORE, Dean Emeritus and Professor of Theology and Education, Boston University School of Theology

"Sometimes simple truths have profound implications. That is the testimony of the essays in *Unlikely Friends*. Human friendships, which cross boundaries, are the crucible for understanding the practice of world mission. With skilled academic insight, these essays testify to the incarnational power of human relationships. These well-researched stories of friendship not only illumine the past, but also point the way forward, given the polarizing nature of modern cultures. Further, the wisdom found here suggests pathways for our ecumenical calling within world Christianity and beyond."

—WESLEY GRANBERG-MICHAELSON, member of the international committee for the Global Christian Forum

Unlikely Friends

July 26, 2021

To John, on your birthday.

May your friendships sustain
you at this time.

Love, peace, joy, bless you
on your day!

With friendship,

Michele

Yes, Amen and
Amen. May you be all the more
in God's reality in the years
ahead. With admiration and thanks
for all you give to us at St. John's. Sam

Unlikely Friends

How God Uses Boundary-Crossing Friendships
to Transform the World

edited by
David W. Scott
Daryl R. Ireland
Grace Y. May
Casely B. Essamuah

PICKWICK *Publications* · Eugene, Oregon

UNLIKELY FRIENDS
How God Uses Boundary-Crossing Friendships to Transform the World

The photo on page 146 appears courtesy of the Mennonite ChurchUSA Archives. It comes from Africa Inter-Mennonite Mission Records, 1911–2018, X-68, Mennonite ChurchUSA Archives, Elkhart, Indiana.
The photo on page 224 appears courtesy of Boston University. It was taken by Dave Green for Boston University Photography.
Scripture quotations marked NRSV are taken from New Revised Standard Version Bible, copyright © 1989 National Council of the Churches of Christ in the United States of America. Used by permission. All rights reserved worldwide.
Scripture quotations marked MSG are taken from THE MESSAGE, copyright © 1993, 2002, 2018 by Eugene H. Peterson. Used by permission of NavPress, represented by Tyndale House Publishers. All rights reserved.

Pickwick Publications
An Imprint of Wipf and Stock Publishers
199 W. 8th Ave., Suite 3
Eugene, OR 97401

www.wipfandstock.com

PAPERBACK ISBN: 978-1-7252-8637-5
HARDCOVER ISBN: 978-1-7252-8638-2
EBOOK ISBN: 978-1-7252-8639-9

Cataloguing-in-Publication data:

Names: Scott, David W., editor | Ireland, Daryl R., editor | May, Grace Y., editor | Essamuah, Casely B., editor.

Title: Unlikely friends : how God uses boundary-crossing friendships to transform the world / edited by David W. Scott, Daryl R. Ireland, Grace Y. May, and Casely B. Essamuah.

Description: Eugene, OR: Pickwick Publications, 2021 | Includes bibliographical references.

Identifiers: ISBN 978-1-7252-8637-5 (paperback) | ISBN 978-1-7252-8638-2 (hardcover) | ISBN 978-1-7252-8639-9 (ebook)

Subjects: LCSH: Friendship—Religious aspects—Christianity. | Missions—Study and teaching. | Robert, Dana Lee.

Classification: BV4647.F7 U55 2021 (paperback) | BV4647.F7 (ebook)

07/01/21

To Dr. Dana L. Robert, teacher and friend

Contents

SECTION II: THE PROBLEMS WITH FRIENDSHIP

SECTION III: THE PRACTICE OF FRIENDSHIP

SECTION IV: FRIENDSHIP AND DANA L. ROBERT

List of Contributors

Soojin Chung, Assistant Professor of Intercultural Studies, California Baptist University

Casely B. Essamuah, Secretary, Global Christian Forum

Anicka Fast, Representative for Burkina Faso, Mennonite Central Committee

Ada Focer, Research Affiliate of the Center for Global Christianity & Mission, Boston University

Margaret Eletta Guider, OSF, Associate Professor of Missiology and Chair of the Ecclesiastical Faculty, Boston College School of Theology and Ministry

Daryl R. Ireland, Research Assistant Professor of Mission and Associate Director, Center for Global Christianity & Mission, Boston University

Tyler Lenocker, Visiting Researcher, Center for Global Christianity & Mission, Boston University

Bonnie Sue Lewis, Professor Emeritus of Mission and World Christianity, University of Dubuque Theological Seminary

Grace Y. May, Director of the Women's Institute and Associate Professor of Biblical Studies, William Carey International University

Kendal P. Mobley, Associate Professor of Religion and Coordinator of the Spiritual Life Center, Johnson C. Smith University

Mark Noll, Francis A. McAnaney Professor of History Emeritus, University of Notre Dame

Angel Santiago-Vendrell, E. Stanley Jones Associate Professor of Evangelism, Asbury Theological Seminary

David W. Scott, Mission Theologian, Global Ministries, The United Methodist Church, and Visiting Researcher, Center for Global Christianity & Mission, Boston University

Michèle Sigg, Executive Director, Dictionary of African Christian Biography (DACB.org), Boston University

Brian Stanley, Professor of World Christianity, University of Edinburgh

Kirk VanGilder, Associate Professor of Religion, Gallaudet University

Preface

This edited volume is conceived as a way to honor Dana L. Robert on her sixty-fifth birthday in 2021. A volume dedicated to using friendship as a lens to understand mission seems in several ways an especially appropriate topic by which to honor her.

First, this volume seeks to extend Robert's own scholarship, which, as the story recounted at the beginning of the Introduction highlights, has often used friendship as a way to better understand mission. Friendship as a theme recurs throughout Robert's work, but works of Robert's that centrally address the significance of friendship in understanding mission include her book *Faithful Friendships: Embracing Diversity in Christian Community* and her articles "Cross-Cultural Friendship in the Creation of Twentieth-Century World Christianity" and "Global Friendship as Incarnational Missional Practice." Robert has led the way in helping the scholarly world understand the importance of friendship in mission. This volume attempts to take her insights and extend them beyond the work of one scholar to have them embraced by an entire scholarly community.

The topic of friendship is further a fitting one with which to honor Robert because, like her work on many topics, friendship as a concept transcends the divide between history and theology. The late David Bosch wrote that mission is "the mother of theology."[1] While Robert intentionally chose to subtitle her book *American Women in Mission: A Social History of Their Thought and Practice*, the truth of the matter is that she not only recounted and analyzed assiduously the contributions of women leaders in mission, she was doing theology by considering how theology shaped their narratives and how their lived experiences impacted their thoughts and strategies. In

---

1. Bosch, *Transforming Mission*, 16.

her inimitable way, Robert was setting a high bar for mission theology that demanded careful and rigorous attention be paid to the historical context in which missionaries practiced their theology. What is more, Robert discovered the theological reflections of women leaders, not only in books, but in personal correspondence stored in attics, missions committee minutes in churches, and reports and articles in denominational archives. In so doing, she was able to uncover the theology that both enveloped these leaders and emerged from them. Whether it was in "Women's Work for Women" or missions in the remotest regions of the earth, women's voices and theology deserve to be heard. Robert has shown how the connection between history and theology applies to the topic of friendship as well, and we hope this book engages the topic in the same spirit.

As any good mission theologian will tell you, good theology must speak to the historical context in which it is written. As her biography later in this volume makes clear, Robert has consistent proved her ability to speak to her time, or to "evangelize the inevitable," as she puts it. Here again, a volume on friendship seems a fitting way in which to honor this aspect of her scholarship. The present historical context appears to be a moment when we as a global society are moving toward conflict rather than convergence. While fluctuation between these two poles can be a cyclical movement, there is something lost each time the pendulum swings. During a moment of convergence, the prophet needs to be able to imagine a different future and help people see those who have been frozen out of the consensus, despite the appearance of contentment. Now, as we move in the other direction, it is time to remind people that in the midst of fractured relationships, we must not turn entirely against one another. Friendship is a kind of glue that can overcome the forces that repel. But these cannot be ordinary friendships—the kind that bind us closer to people like us. They need to transcend that rule of homogeny. Robert once said something to one of us that left a deep impression. If we cannot have true friendships that cross boundaries, then Jesus is a liar. In essence, she was making boundary-crossing friendships a test of the veracity of the gospel. We think she is right, and we think the present moment calls for this type of theological and historical reflection, which we hope this volume provides.

The nature of the community that contributed to this volume is another way in which friendship is a fitting topic by which to honor Robert. This book is composed of chapters written by her friends. These friends include colleagues and peers who are widely recognized as experts in their fields. It also includes chapters by friends from among her seventy-some PhD students. The book also includes a compilation of commendations of Robert by her peers, colleagues, students, and yes, friends. The range of voices included here is indicative of how extensive Robert's influence has been in the field of contemporary mission studies, not just as a scholar, but also as a teacher and a friend.

We the editors and contributors have learned much about mission from our friendships with Dana Robert. In addition, crafting this volume has brought us together in friendship across age, race, and gender, giving us a taste of the fruit of missional friendship. We hope you, too, will taste the goodness of the fruits of such boundary-crossing friendships through this volume and thereby be motivated to cultivate your own friendships across boundaries.

DAVID W. SCOTT
DARYL R. IRELAND
GRACE Y. MAY
CASELY B. ESSAMUAH
Boston, Massachusetts

BIBLIOGRAPHY

Bosch, David J. *Transforming Mission: Paradigm Shifts in Theology of Mission.* Maryknoll, NY: Orbis, 1991.

Robert, Dana L. *American Women in Mission: A Social History of Their Thought and Practice.* Macon, GA: Mercer University Press, 1998.

———. "Cross-Cultural Friendship in the Creation of Twentieth-Century World Christianity." *International Bulletin of Missionary Research* 35.2 (2011) 100–107.

———. *Faithful Friendships: Embracing Diversity in Christian Community.* Grand Rapids, MI: Eerdmans, 2019.

———. "Global Friendship as Incarnational Missional Practice." *International Bulletin of Missionary Research* 39.4 (2015) 180–84.

Acknowledgments

Books are always cooperative projects, and edited volumes especially so. This book would not have been possible without the strong collaboration and gracious friendship shared among the editors, the eager participation and diligent work by the contributing authors, and the gracious sentiments shared by those offering commendations of Dr. Dana L. Robert. In addition, Morgan Crago, Research Fellow at Boston University School of Theology, and Kara Jackman, Archivist at the Boston University School of Theology Library, labored meticulously to put together the bibliography of Robert's works featured in this book.

This book, though, comes out of a larger community of Robert's friends, students, and colleagues, and we are conscious that there were many who participated in the development of this book, even if they did not author a chapter. In particular, we would like to recognize those who participated in two panels at the 2018 Annual Meeting of the American Society of Missiology that served as a test run for the idea of an edited volume on friendship. These who presented were Anicka Fast, Ben Hartley, Steve Lloyd, Kip Mobley, Myung Soo Park, Eva Pascal, and Titus Pressler. The genesis of this book came in a discussion of a still larger group of Robert's then-current and former students at the 2017 Annual Meeting of the American Society of Missiology. Those who participated in that conversation and subsequent email discussions include Laura Chevalier, Soojin Chung, Rich Darr, Charles Farhadian, Anicka Fast, Ben Hartley, Chris James, Tyler Lenocker, Kip Mobley, Travis Myers, Sung-Deuk Oak, Ruth Padilla DeBorst, Titus Pressler, Michèle Sigg, Anneke Stasson, Doug Tzan, Zhongxin Wang, Bruce Yoder, and Gina Zurlo. All of these friends helped make this book possible.

Finally, we would like to acknowledge the Boston University Center for Global Christianity and Mission (and its donors) for underwriting the typesetting costs associated with this book and for serving as an administrative hub and central node for connecting those associated with this book. The Center was, of course, founded by Robert and her husband, Inus Daneel, so it seems fitting that it has played a role in this effort at honoring her.

Introduction

Understanding Mission through Friendship

DAVID W. SCOTT AND DARYL R. IRELAND

The story of the origins of Chilean Pentecostalism usually begins with the preaching of Rev. Willis C. Hoover. Hoover was an American missionary with the Methodist Episcopal Church who underwent a Pentecostal experience and eventually left the Methodist Episcopal Church to found a Pentecostal group that would become one of the largest Protestant denominations in Chile, the Methodist Pentecostal Church of Chile.

Yet, as Dana L. Robert has shown, it is possible to start the history of Chilean Pentecostalism somewhere else: with a friendship.[1] In this case, it is the friendship between Mary Hilton Hoover, Willis's wife, and Minnie Abrams. Mary and Minnie were classmates at the Chicago Training School for City, Home, and Foreign Missions, and they had become friends there. Mary married Willis and went as a missionary to Chile; Minnie stayed single and went as a missionary to India. They kept in touch, though, as friends do.

While in India, Minnie Abrams worked with Pandita Ramabai at Ramabai's Mukti Mission, where in 1905, a Pentecostal revival broke out. This experience led Abrams to write one of the early books of Pentecostal theology, *The Baptism of the Holy Ghost & Fire*. Abrams proceeded to send copies of the book all over the world, including to her friend Mary Hoover. Mary shared it with her husband Willis, who was led to seek his own Pentecostal experience as a result. The rest, as they say, is history.

Most of the scholarship on Chilean Pentecostalism since then has focused on Willis and either his American background or his divine

1. Robert, *American Women in Mission*, 244–48.

1

inspiration and spiritual leadership in introducing Pentecostalism to Chile. But by focusing on friendship, Dana Robert was able to flip the dominant gender narrative of this moment in mission history and add new understandings of how beliefs and practices were shared through international networks of missionaries and indigenous Christians. Moreover, Robert showed that such beliefs and practices flowed not just in a center-periphery relationship between the United States and the countries in which its missionaries worked, but between many spots in the globe. Rather than the story of a heroic and divinely inspired American man and his bold preaching, the origins of Chilean Pentecostalism turn out to be a story about female friendship, letter writing, and the influence of a leader from the Global South (Ramabai). This reframing of the origins of Chilean Pentecostalism thus sheds new insights on gender, the agency of Christians from the global South, mission networking, and more. All because of a focus on friendship.

This volume seeks to answer the question: If paying attention to friendship in this one instance has transformed our understandings of mission, what can be accomplished by paying more thorough attention to friendship as a means for understanding mission in a variety of contexts? How can we better understand and practice mission by focusing on the power, the problems, and the practice of mission friendship, especially friendships that cross boundaries of gender, nationality, race, class, and culture? And how does paying attention to such boundary-crossing friendships allow us to discover the sometimes-surprising ways God works in the world?

THE NATURE OF FRIENDSHIP

Though difficult to define precisely, friendship is a basic form of human relationship. Categories, models, rules, and expectations for friendship vary across time and culture, but the experience of people bound together by mutual affection recurs throughout human experience. Whether this mutual affection exists instead of or in addition to other bonds and relationships, it is at the heart of friendship.

Friendship is often presumed to be built on similarities. Aristotle argued in the *Nicomachean Ethics* that friendship was the supreme exercise of virtue. The basis of such a relationship was similarity. Good friends were alike in status, wealth, and purpose. For Confucius, too, friendship presumed equality in station—the only one of the five fundamental social relations that did so. Research in psychology, anthropology, and sociology has borne out these philosophers' claims. Friends generally share similar ages, health, education, religion, family background, social status, political views and even levels of attractiveness.

But a dissenting minority within the human experience points to vital friendships that transcend the rule of homogeneity. These friendships occur not between those alike in almost every way. Instead, they cross boundaries of race, ethnicity, class, gender, nationality, religion, social location, etc. These boundary-crossing relationships do not mirror Aristotle's description, but they may come closest to his ideal. Because of the challenges of differences, transcultural friendships demand and develop virtues like few other relationships. In a world riven by nationalism, ethnicity, and religion, transcultural friendships stand out as a counter-witness to division among groups and antipathy toward the Other.

Such boundary-crossing friendships do not just happen. They require significant dedication and effort. They also depend upon certain practices of friendship. In her book *Faithful Friendships: Embracing Diversity in Christian Community*, Dana L. Robert has identified four dimensions of the practice of boundary-crossing friendship: remaining, exile, struggle, and joy. By remaining, Robert suggests the commitment entailed in friendship to stay with another, even over long times and throughout great difficulties. Exile connotes the way in which commitments to boundary-crossing friendships can take people away from their homes, families, and communities of origin. Struggle incorporates the factors, both internal and external to a friendship, that arise to challenge the strength and commitment of that friendship. Finally, Robert emphasizes the joy that comes from the experience of boundary-crossing friendships. Robert's work thus suggests the perils, but also the promise, of the pursuit of such friendships.

BOUNDARY-CROSSING FRIENDSHIP
AND CHRISTIAN MISSION

Although boundary-crossing friendships have existed in many realms, Christian mission has been a particularly fertile ground for the formation of such friendships. Christian mission inherently involves crossing boundaries.[2] In the process, some missionaries, as this book demonstrates, have been able to establish relationships that cross boundaries, too. They have extended their affection to others despite dissimilarities and have found that affection reciprocated. They have formed friendships.

Yet such examples of cross-boundary friendships are not just interesting anecdotes from the personal lives of missionaries and their associates.

2. See Scott, *Crossing Boundaries.*

They have impacts beyond the bounds of the friendships. Friendship can motivate people to bridge differences and to work together. Friends learn from one another and reshape their thinking based on ideas received from one another. Friendships build global networks and community. While Robert has cautioned that friendship is not a missionary strategy, mission friendships have nonetheless shaped mission in important ways, and it has led to significant mission outcomes. To overlook these relationships is to ignore something absolutely essential to mission and world Christianity.

Thus, mission friendships need to be documented and analyzed so that those interested in cross-cultural and other boundary-crossing mission can better understand the spiritualities, theologies, and practices of mission that lead to and follow from mission friendships. We need to know more about how such friendships arise, how they are shaped, their limitations and conditions, and their impact, both on the friends involved and on their broader contexts.

This book aims to take up the project of using friendship as a lens through which to understand mission. Using twelve essays, it will examine the nature and effects of cross-boundary friendships in mission. It will address such questions as the following: What roles do Christian theology and piety play in developing friends' ability to cross seemingly unbridgeable gaps? How do race, class, and gender shape these relationships? How do transcultural friends negotiate the different meanings of friendship across cultures? What effect do differences of power have on a friendship—is it still a friendship? How has friendship—both as a concept and an experience—shaped the ways in which Christians have understood and practiced mission? How have friendships supported the work of mission, and how has the work of mission formed friendships? What convictions emerge because of transcultural friendships? What are the promises—and limitations—of mission friendship as a means to heal the fractures in our world?

THE OPPORTUNITIES AND CHALLENGES OF STUDYING MISSION FRIENDSHIP

There is much to be gained by using friendship as a lens to better understand mission, both through and beyond this collection of essays. Studying friendship yields new insights into what mission is and how mission has been and should be practiced. It gives us new questions about mission and suggests new answers to old questions.

That friendship offers such opportunities is in part true because it has so infrequently been a subject of investigation for missiologists. Regularly,

Robert has called friendship "the hidden dimension of mission." One reason friendship has remained hidden is because of the challenges of documenting and uncovering friendships. Mission records are much more concerned with the institutional rather than the personal. We know that such relationships exist, but they are seldom written about in business minutes or appear in institutional histories. Yet, just as mission historians have learned to re-read documentary evidence to uncover and recover the voices and perspectives of indigenous Christians, women, and other marginalized persons, so too can these same sources be re-read to uncover and recover the threads of friendship that bound missionaries, their indigenous coworkers, and their supporters together.

There is perhaps also a challenge of values, especially within the Western academy, that has led traditional approaches to mission history and theology to overlook the significance of friendship. Both Western culture, with its valorization of individualism, and academia, which is predicated upon a mythos of scholars as solo producers of knowledge, have too often overlooked and undervalued relationships and their fruits. Yet just as the fields of mission studies, World Christianity, and theology are being reshaped by the theological and historical visions of scholars from around the world, so too can the adoption of friendship as a scholarly lens be another means by which we move beyond traditional understandings of mission in ways that deepen and extend our collective knowledge. Friendship thus offers an opportunity to bring in more voices from women, non-Westerners, practitioners, and others overlooked in traditional accounts of mission.

Not only is the adoption of friendship as a perspective on mission possible, it is necessary. At a moment when nations are turning inward to blood-and-soil ethnic nationalisms and are divided by identity politics, it is imperative to foreground transcultural friendships as a central witness to the good news of a God who reconciles all people to himself through Christ. Whether it is Indian independence leader Mohandas Gandhi's bond with missionaries including C. F. Andrews from England and E. Stanley Jones from the United States, American missionaries' devotion to Mozambican revolutionary Eduardo Mondlane,[3] the friendship formed over household chores between American missionary Edna Kensinger and future Congolese church founder Kazadi Matthieu,[4] or the friendships Douglas Hall formed with George Bullock and Eldin Villafañe in urban Boston,[5] transcultural

---

3. See chapter by Ada Focer on pp. 25–39.

4. See chapter by Anicka Fast on pp. 144–62.

5. See chapter by Tyler Lenocker on pp. 90–105.

friendships have demonstrably overcome the centrifugal forces of colonialism, racism, and nationalism that push people apart.

By befriending someone different, even a presumed enemy, transcultural friends generate narratives, movements, and institutions that build global community. Adopting friendship as a lens for understanding mission is not just an interesting intellectual exercise but an affirmation of a moral vision in which difference can be met with love and not enmity. Thus, the essays in this volume seek to not only provide an academic accounting of mission friendships in the past, but to suggest insights for those who would seek to cultivate such friendships today.

MISSION FRIENDSHIP IN THIS VOLUME

This volume opens with a series of essays exploring the power of mission friendships. These essays examine the ways in which friendships, of different sorts and in different historical settings, have contributed to forming new theologies of mission, accomplishing specific mission projects, and changing attitudes and understandings on a variety of topics, including race and politics. The volume begins with an essay by Mark Noll, exploring what a focus on friendship adds to a series of biographical snapshots of Christian leaders around the world. The first section then proceeds with additional snapshots of the impact of friendship in various historical contexts covering a variety of continents—Africa, Asia, Europe, Latin America, and North America. Ada Focer describes in the second chapter how a network of friendship was forged among missionaries working towards postcolonial liberation in Southern Africa. Soojin Chung writes in the third chapter about how American Christians promoted interracial adoption of Asian children as a means to advance world friendship. The fourth chapter, by Michèle Miller Sigg, demonstrates how a friendship between two female leaders in the French Protestant *Réveil*, Émilie Mallet and Albertine de Broglie, pushed them to generate a defense of women's mission leadership. In the fifth chapter, Angel Santiago-Vendrell traces a series of teacher-to-student friendships that shaped the development of Protestant liberation theology in Latin America. Tyler Lenocker shows in the sixth chapter how a series of friendships with other Christian leaders shaped the work and the theology of Douglas and Judy Hall and the Emmanuel Gospel Center in Boston. In the process, the authors suggest different ways of understanding mission friendship. Noll offers a description of various types of friends: those emerging from patron-client relationships, goal-oriented friendships, and deeper levels of connection and solidarity. Focer describes friendship as a practice of solidarity among a group of friends, even through difficult times. Chung writes about friendship as a rhetoric and ideal. Sigg offers a theological grounding for friendship in the person of Christ. And Santiago-Vendrell and Lenocker show friendship as a bond between pairs of individuals.

While tensions of race, nationality, and gender are evident in this first set of essays, the second section of the book examines the problems with friendship by paying closer attention to how race, nationality, gender, and other elements of difference have complicated and challenged the practice of mission friendship historically. Brian Stanley's recounting of friendship in the first years of the Serampore Mission of the Baptist Missionary Society shows how an early emphasis on friendship among the first generation of missionaries broke down as the mission progressed. Kendal P. Mobley details the racial tensions that characterized a series of friendships between the African American mission educator Charlotte Hawkins Brown and various white supporters of her school in North Carolina. In Anicka Fast's chapter on the friendship between American missionary Edna Kensinger and her Congolese helper, Kazadi Matthieu, this friendship is embedded within a larger network of relationships marked by tension and distance along lines of nationality.

The third set of chapters is on the practice of friendship. In contains reflections on mission friendship that have arisen out of various experiences of friendship by the authors. Bonnie Sue Lewis recounts her experiences of interfaith friendship with others living in a small city in Iowa. Kirk VanGilder explains the power of DEAF-SAME to form transnational friendships among Deaf people brought together by mission. Margaret Eletta Guider offers a defense of mentoring, missional colleagueship, and friendship in the Lord based on her own experiences as a mentor and mentee.

The fourth section of the book connects the theme of friendship to the life and work of Dana L. Robert as a way of paying tribute to her. In addition to advancing the academic study of mission friendship, this book is also a *festschrift* for Robert, and the materials in this section honor her scholarship and teaching. A series of commendations by colleagues and former students demonstrates how Robert has combined friendship with her own path-setting scholarly work and extensive mentoring of doctoral students. A biographical essay by Daryl R. Ireland recounts the ways in which Robert has "evangelized the inevitable" by pioneering new fields and forms of scholarship, including a focus on mission friendship. A bibliography of Robert's writings directs interested readers to this rich collection of insights into and reflections on missiology and World Christianity.

This volume is built on the conviction that one of the best ways to honor Robert's legacy is to continue her work. Thus, we the editors hope that this volume succeeds on two fronts: We hope it will give adequate testimony to the impact of Robert on the fields of missiology and World Christianity. But we also hope it will extend her emphasis on friendship as an important dimension of analysis in missiology and World Christianity and that it will encourage others to do so as well. Proverbs 27:17 says, "As iron sharpens iron, so one person sharpens a friend" (CEB). Our understanding of mission has been sharpened by Dana L. Robert. May this book in turn sharpen the understanding of others.

BIBLIOGRAPHY

Abrams, Minnie F. *The Baptism of the Holy Ghost & Fire*. Kedagon: Pandita Ramabai Mukti Mission, 1906.

Aristotle, *Nicomachean Ethics*. Translated by Terence Irwin. 3rd ed. Indianapolis: Hackett, 2019.

Robert, Dana L. *American Women in Mission: A Society History of Their Thought and Practice*. Macon, GA: Mercer University Press, 1997.

————. *Faithful Friendships: Embracing Diversity in Christian Community*. Grand Rapids, MI: Eerdmans, 2019.

Scott, David W. *Crossing Boundaries: Sharing God's Good News through Mission*. Nashville, TN: Wesley's Foundery, 2019.

SECTION I

The Power of Friendship

"Give Us Friends"

Varieties of Friendship in the Christian Mission

MARK NOLL

The premise of this book is that the Christian mission, both past and present, rests substantially on personal relationships, connections between specific individuals, and networks of shared interest drawing people into common action. Beginning with the Gospel accounts of Jesus' commitment to his twelve disciples and through the many person-to-person stories that figure centrally in the Book of Acts, the original narrative of the Christian faith was largely a record of personal encounters. That Christian faith, in turn, appeared as an outgrowth of an older story in which Yahweh dealt personally with Abraham, Isaac, and Jacob, and with Moses and the prophets, as the means for engaging the entire nation of Israel.

The recent reorientation of the worldwide history of Christianity has been propelled by a number of voices, including Dana Lee Robert as one of the most important.[1] With encouragement from Robert and others who insist on viewing Christianity as a global reality, I was led to re-think my own understanding of the history of Christianity—not as a matter of "the West to the rest" but as a dynamic global system of mutual influences flowing back and forth across vast regions, immense periods of time, and cultures of great diversity. Yet until her stress on the connection of individuals to individuals—on friendship—as foundational to the Christian faith itself, I did not recognize how crucially cross-cultural friendship has functioned in the dynamic development of Christian faith around the world.[2]

1. Robert, *Christian Mission*; *Gospel Bearers*.
2. Robert, *Faithful Friendships*.

This chapter seeks to probe more deeply into what such friendships have meant. It draws on an earlier book that I prepared as a co-author with Carolyn Nystrom, entitled *Clouds of Witnesses*.[3] That work was intended as an introduction for American readers to seventeen Christian leaders from the recent history of Africa and Asia whose stories have been largely unknown outside their native regions. The book had been long finished before Robert's emphasis on "cross-cultural and cross-ethnic relationships" raised a question in my mind about the role of friendship in the lives of these seventeen significant leaders.[4] As it turns out, for at least nine of the seventeen, friendship across imposing cultural barriers meant a great deal—in some cases, a very great deal—for their lives and ministries.

This chapter focuses on the meaning of those friendships—first, by simply noting their importance for the recent expansion of Christianity in both geographical reach and spiritual depth, but, second, to suggest that meaningful cross-cultural friendships have appeared in considerable variety. The common denominator was close, open, affirmative personal relationships, but developed in several different ways. Often, they seem to have grown from what were originally patron-client relationships. Even deeper friendships have flourished in goal-directed collaborative labor. And in at least a few instances, friendships have become even more—for John Chilembwe in Nyasaland (now Malawi) a pathway to love characteristic of families, for Pandita Ramabai in India and England a source of creative conflict, and for V. S. Azariah in India an inspiration for profound theology.

FROM PATRON TO FRIEND

The route from patronage to friendship has been often recorded because it regularly appears in accounts written by Western missionaries or their biographers. In such accounts it can be difficult to discern if and when the asymmetrical exercise of authority moves on to respectful mutuality. That move, however, seems to have taken place in the life of Bernard Mizeki (c. 1861–1896), the pioneering evangelist of Mashonaland, which is now part of northern Zimbabwe.[5] Mizeki was born in Portuguese East Africa (Mozambique), but most of his education took place in Cape Town, South Africa. There his main teacher was Paula Dorothea von Blomberg, a missionary from Germany who directed Zonnenbloem College. This college was itself distinctive for instructing African, European, and mixed-race (colored)

---

3. Noll and Nystrom, *Clouds of Witnesses*.

4. Robert, *Faithful Friendships*, 3.

5. See Noll and Nystrom, *Clouds of Witnesses*, 21–32.

boys and young men together. During Mizeki's five years at the college, the Anglicans with whom Mizeki would eventually serve regarded him as only an "average" convert with no particular distinction. Fräulein Blomberg saw something more. She discovered that Mizeki possessed a remarkable capacity for African languages and that he could be an effective speaker in the trips she organized into outlying villages. Details are scarce, but it appears that by the time Mizeki took up his duties assisting the Anglican mission to the Shona and Ndebele peoples, he had been thoroughly prepared. As Dana Robert has herself shown, Mizeki's life, ministry, and martyrdom laid the foundation for extraordinary Christian expansion in that region.[6] Significantly, much of this missionary success came from his own unusual ability to make friends across the often dangerous lines of tribal conflict. That ability seems to have come about, at least in part, from the mutually supportive personal relationship that developed when an unmarried female from Germany moved from her role of teacher to something closer to friendship with a young African whom other Europeans simply took for granted.

The modern history of Christianity in China includes many instances when Western patronage blossomed into cross-cultural friendship, perhaps because so many Chinese believers possessed the kind of intelligence and initiative that missionaries valued among themselves. The life of Shi Meiyu (or Mary Stone, 1873–1954) records such an event.[7] She was the daughter of first-generation Methodist converts who pushed back against Chinese traditions consigning daughters to bound feet and minimal education. Instead, they chose to educate her at a missionary school conducted by Gertrude Howe, who had indicated her flexibility toward cultural barriers by adopting a Chinese orphan girl as her own child. Howe's careful instruction of Shi Meiyu and her adopted daughter prepared the two young women for medical training in the United States (nearly a first for Chinese female students). When the fully certified women doctors returned to China, Gertrude Howe became a co-worker at the hospital they established in Jiujiang. A patron had become a colleague and presumably also a friend.

And this particular story went on. During her decades of medical service, Mary Stone's closest colleague, friend, and companion was an American missionary, Jennie Hughes, who arrived in China shortly after Stone returned from her medical training. With sponsorship first from American Methodists and then from independent fund-raising circles, she developed with Stone, Hughes coordinated the evangelistic outreach, spiritual training, and general education at the complex of institutions where Mary Stone

---

6. Robert, *Christian Mission*, 167–70.

7. See Noll and Nystrom, *Clouds of Witnesses*, 201–13.

oversaw the medical work. Together the two friends also took in twenty children whom they raised as their own. After the women moved their operations to Shanghai, they began an outreach known as "the Bethel Bands," teams of evangelists led by Chinese Christians, but also including Western participants, who were responsible for some of the most effective evangelistic efforts anywhere in the world during the first half of the twentieth century. Even in decades when many Westerners looked upon the Chinese as barbaric and many Chinese reciprocated by considering Western missionaries imperialists, the friendships of Shi Meiyu and Gertrude Howe, and then of Shi and Jennie Hughes, represented notable signs of contradiction. They also indicated how helpful such friendships could be for promoting evangelism and practical good works.

GOAL-ORIENTED COLLABORATION

Friendship growing from shared tasks has probably been even more common in the recent history of Christianity than from patrons transformed into friends. One of the most often quoted passages from C. S. Lewis's *The Four Loves* has been his description of how "friends" differ from "lovers." Where the latter "are normally face to face, absorbed in each other," friends are found "side by side, absorbed in some common interest." Lewis wisely expanded on that description of side-by-side friendship by noting that two individuals sharing a common task can easily expand such a friendship to include others who are similarly absorbed in the same "common interest."[8] Once realizing the analytical value of Lewis's insight for the small group of non-Western believers we had researched, it was obvious we had stumbled upon at least two instances of just that kind of friendship.

The East African Revival was one of the great works of long-lasting importance in the twentieth-century history of Christianity. Thankfully this event—a source of intra-tribal strife, adjustment to modernity, and an East African political force, as well as a landmark of evangelism—is now beginning to receive serious historical attention.[9] Yet even as serious studies multiply, one feature of the story remains prominent in almost all accounts, the friendship between Simeon Nsibambi (1897–1978) and Joe Church (1899–1989).[10]

Dr. Joe Church had come out to work at a hospital in Rwanda under the sponsorship of the Anglican Church Missionary Society. Early in his

8. Lewis, *Four Loves*, 91.

9. Such studies include MacMaster and Jacobs, *Gentle Wind of God*; Ward and Wild-Wood, *East African Revival*; Peterson, *Ethnic Patriotism*.

10. See Noll and Nystrom, *Clouds of Witnesses*, 99–110.

service, he experienced serious discouragement for physical and administrative, but mostly spiritual, reasons. He later wrote about the critical turning point that occurred when, in the summer of 1929, he visited the Anglicans' Namirembe Cathedral in nearby Kampala, Uganda: "I had been praying for a long time that God would lead me to one really saved African with whom I could have deep fellowship. God was answering that prayer that Sunday morning, when something happened that changed the course of my missionary career."[11] The "something" was his meeting with Simeon Nsibambi, a second-generation Ugandan Christian in his early thirties who had shortly before experienced what he called a special in-filling of the Holy Spirit. After they met in Kampala, Church and Nsibambi spent two days studying the Scriptures together, especially for what it meant to live what Church described as a victorious, Spirit-filled life. In the months and years that followed, Nsibambi organized groups of Africans for fellowship, prayer, and then itinerant preaching; Church brought a widening circle of missionaries into connection with the Africans Nsibambi recruited. Soon lengthy evangelistic trips followed when a few Europeans joined more Africans in preaching aimed at conversion, but even more at encouraging baptized believers into lives of active Christian witness. A significant feature of the Revival was the public confession of sin, which became most memorable when white missionaries took their turn in confessing their faults before the Africans.

Nsibambi and Church soon stepped back as others with strong preaching gifts came to the fore. Yet they continued to provide, individually and together, calming counsel to a movement prone to judgmental excess. The history of the East African Revival is worthy of extended analysis in itself. Crucial for its initiation and for much of its ongoing importance was the bridge of friendship that in 1929 enlisted two individuals with strikingly different backgrounds into a common spiritual effort.

Less well known than the Nsibambi-Church friendship is the story of Byang Kato (1937–1975) and the friends, both African and European, with whom he partnered to aid what was then a mostly Nigerian denomination called the Evangelical Church of West Africa (ECWA).[12] While still a youth, Kato, who was born into a Hausa-speaking family in central Nigeria, heard the Christian message from Mary Hass, a missionary sponsored by the Sudan Interior Mission. Later Kato would be trained, apprenticed, sponsored, and educated (in Nigeria, England, America, and France) with the

11. Church, *Quest for the Highest*, 66.

12. See Noll and Nystrom, *Clouds of Witnesses*, 80–95. Personal quotations in what follows are from personal interviews conducted by Carolyn Nystrom.

assistance of the mission, which was renamed SIM International in 1980. But also from an early age, he displayed remarkable initiative as a teacher and youth leader in Nigeria, an organizer of relief efforts during the Biafran Civil War (1967–1970), a short-term missionary in Alaska during his time of study in the United States, a speaker at the American InterVarsity's triennial Urbana Missionary Conference (1970), an ordained pastor and sought-after speaker in the ECWA, and finally as the general secretary of the Association of Evangelicals in Africa and Mozambique. Kato's promising career was cut short when, in 1975, he drowned off the Kenyan coast while on a family vacation. Before his untimely demise, Kato had outlined an ambitious agenda for African church life and theological education, including plans to promote theological literature produced by Africans, new schools of theology, a theological journal managed by Africans, and an accrediting system to upgrade standards of theological education.

Crucially for his full program of personal activity and his ambitious plans, Kato was joined by SIM missionaries who very early in his short life had been transformed from assisters to assistants. In the process of that transition, the dark-skinned Nigerian and white-skinned missionaries were no longer merely co-workers. Not long before he died, Kato wrote to Harrold Fuller, SIM's deputy director for West Africa, "Dear Harold, I cannot thank the Lord enough for knitting our hearts together." SIM's director of Nigerian Christian education, Jim Plueddemann, already considered himself Kato's deputy. Years later, after Plueddemann became the international director of SIM, he said of his boss, "Byang is my best friend." Today the ECWA, which Kato so ably served with his missionary friends, is an African-directed denomination known as the Evangelical Church Winning All; its more than six thousand congregations, with two and a half million adult members and ten million regular attenders, are found throughout the world.[13]

STILL DEEPER LEVELS

To discover consequential cross-cultural friendships arising from the shared work of ministry, it is only necessary to look for them. Even a little searching, however, shows that shared labor can sometimes inspire an even deeper level of friendship. The remarkable intertwined lives of John Chilembwe (c. 1870–1915) and Joseph Booth (1851–1932) reveal an especially poignant story of cross-ethnic friendship evolving into a familial kind of love.[14] Joseph Booth came to the Zambezi region of Nyasaland (now Malawi) in 1892

13. ECWA, "History."
14. See Noll and Nystrom, *Clouds of Witnesses*, 33–49.

as a forty-one-year-old maverick. Booth's Unitarian English home had given him a strong ethical conscience, but he found his distinctive combination of orthodox Baptist theology and ardent pacifism on his own. After working as a sheep farmer in New Zealand and a chef in Australia, and while serving as a deacon in his Melbourne Baptist church, he experienced a call to missionary service. When the China Inland Mission rejected Booth's application because of his age, he struck out for Africa on his own. His goal was to follow the commitment of his model, Dr. David Livingstone, to both evangelism and economic development of the evangelized. Booth arrived in Nyasaland when the region was in turmoil as Britain solidified its colonial rule. He and his two young children (his wife had died in Australia) soon desperately needed help.

After employing several house servants who specialized in ripping off the family, the Booths took on a yard man of about twenty years of age who spoke only a little English but had told Booth he heard they were looking for a cook, translator, and general factotum. John Chilembwe had been introduced to the English language and to Christian faith at a Church of Scotland mission in Blantyre, the new British administrative center south of Lake Nyasa. Immediately life improved for the Booths because of Chilembwe's skill at managing the household and his quiet but winning personality.

Circumstances soon drew the native Yao-speaker closer to this English-Australian family. Booth experienced a severe illness during which Chilembwe faithfully cared for him and the children. When Booth's teenaged son became seriously ill, Chilembwe transported the lad through floods to the coast in what proved a vain effort to reach medical attention (the young man died soon thereafter). When health returned to the family, Chilembwe became the star pupil in the school Booth established and then a crucial facilitator in Booth's Zambezi Industrial Mission, an enterprise that promoted Booth's ideal of Christian economic development. In January 1897, Chilembwe joined Booth, another English missionary, and another African leader in forming the "African Christian Union." Its purpose was "to unite together in the name of Jesus Christ such persons as desire to see full justice done to the African race and are resolved to work towards and pray for the day when the African people shall become an African Nation."[15]

Despite objections from British colonial officials, who opposed his plans for African economic independence, Booth persevered, with expanded opportunities for Chilembwe. In 1897, after hard work raising funds, Booth and Chilembwe traveled to America. Booth published a book, *Africa for the Africans*, that he hoped would aid fund-raising for his Zambezi

15. Quoted in Shepperson and Price, *Independent African*, 531–32.

mission. He also encouraged Chilembwe to attend the Virginia Theological Seminary and College in Lynchburg that had been recently established by African American Baptists. Chilembwe studied for two years in Lynchburg, at the end of which time he was appointed a missionary for the National Baptist Convention, the United States' largest black denomination.

During their time in America, Chilembwe and Booth reached an amicable parting of the ways. Chilembwe now enjoyed support from the National Baptist Convention, as Booth took another ideological turn by becoming a Seventh-day Baptist and insisting that Christian worship should take place on Saturday.

Booth, however, remained a supporter from a distance as Chilembwe returned to Nyasaland and founded the Providence Industrial Mission. Its Christian, educational, and economic goals followed the path that Booth had begun with his Zambezi Mission. Until the European outbreak of war in 1914 scrambled affairs in Africa, Chilembwe enjoyed considerable success. The Mission expanded to seven sites training over one thousand children and almost that many adults. Its experiments in raising crops for the market (tea, cotton, coffee, rubber, and pepper) moved some Africans closer to economic independence. Chilembwe also continued to preach as he oversaw the construction of a stately new church.

The crisis of war came on the heels of harsh impositions from British colonial officials and white landowners. When tens of thousands of Africans were drafted to do the dirty work supporting Britain's attack on German East Africa (modern Tanzania), it was the last straw.

In November 1914, Chilembwe wrote a letter to the *Nyasaland Times* calling the colonial government to task. Two months later, he led an armed revolt against the colonial government that resulted in the death of three British settlers. Retribution came swiftly. Chilembwe's followers were dispersed, and he was killed in early February 1915. In the wake of the rebellion, Joseph Booth was also expelled from his new home in South Africa despite having had little contact with Chilembwe for several years.

Booth and his daughter Emily, whom Chilembwe had cared for during her own severe illness, did not forget their friend. She later wrote a memoir that expressed personal gratitude for how Chilembwe had helped the family. For his part, Booth wrote one of the most moving tributes ever to have graced the record of cross-cultural Christian friendship:

> Poor kindhearted Chilembwe, who wept with and for the writer's fever-stricken and apparently dying child; nursed and fed the father with a woman's kindness during 10 months of utter prostration; wept, labored with and soothed the dying hours of

my sweet son John Edward at the close of a 2 month's toilsome journey to the ocean post, for food and goods, in flood time of rainy season, 1894. . . . Yes, dear Chilembwe, gladly would I have died[,] by my own countrymen shot, to have kept thee from the false path of slaying.[16]

The friendship between Pandita Ramabai (1858–1922) and Sister Geraldine (1843–1917) of the Community of St. Mary the Virgin may have been as affectionate as the relationship of John Chilembwe and the Booth family, but instead of tenderness, it was marked by contention.[17] Sister Geraldine met Ramabai Saraswati after she went out to India in 1878 from the Community of St. Mary's home base in Wantage, England. Their relationship, sustained until the Sister's death nearly forty years later, is particularly illuminating for a book focusing on cross-cultural Christian friendship. Close friends they certainly were, but in a friendship marked by the proverbial iron sharpening iron (Prov 27:17).

Ramabai Saraswati won her title as "the Pandita" as a young adult because of her mastery of the Sanskrit-language texts of Hindu religion. (By the age of twenty she could recite eighteen thousand verses from these texts and also discourse on them learnedly.) That mastery created a sensation because of the settled Hindu tradition that reserved serious religious training for men. Ramabai's father, who taught his wife, who then instructed their daughter, broke from that tradition. Ramabai's recognition was also extraordinary because, before she was twenty-four years old, all of her familial supporters died—father, mother, a beloved brother, and a husband with whom she had given birth to a daughter. Before her husband died in early 1882, they had been introduced to Christianity though contact with missionaries, though she was not much impressed. Her opinion began to change, however, after meeting regularly with a Brahman Anglican convert and the Anglican sisters of the Community of St. Mary the Virgin. At the same time, she was gaining further notoriety for denouncing India's treatment of women—child marriage, illiteracy, and the sometimes-fatal suffering of high-caste widows. The Anglican sisters encouraged Ramabai to seek further education in England. They hoped to instruct her in the Christian faith; she hoped to pursue training to become a physician. Always fiercely independent, Ramabai published a book, *Morals for Women*, so that she could maintain herself in England through its royalties.

The friendship that had begun in India flourished when Ramabai settled in England near the Wantage Community to which Sister Geraldine

16. Quoted in Shepperson and Price, *Independent African*, 358.
17. See Noll and Nystrom, *Clouds of Witnesses*, 127–40.

had returned for reasons of her health. At first stand-offish to a personal Christian profession, Ramabai asked to be baptized after the traumatic death of an Indian woman friend who had accompanied her to England. But the baptism, which cemented the connection between Ramabai and the Community of St. Mary, took place under circumstances that anticipated the contentions of later years—Ramabai made a sincere profession of faith but refused to follow the Sacrament of Penance that the Anglo-Catholic sisters normally required of adult converts.

Ramabai was frustrated in pursuit of a medical career because of problems with her hearing. But undaunted, she continued to study, to engage Sister Geraldine and other Anglican leaders in serious conversation, and to take part in the Community's philanthropic activities among the poor that especially impressed the young Indian scholar. Eventually Ramabai resolved to return to India via an extended visit to the United States, which she financed through the publication of another book, *The High-Caste Hindu Woman*, a devastating exposé of India's mistreatment of women and of the Hindu underpinning for that mistreatment. On her return to India in 1889, she founded a home and school for high-caste widows, an enterprise that expanded over the years to a vast complex of schools, clinics, refuges, and retreats. She eventually established the Mukti (= "freedom") Mission east of Bombay/Mumbai, a flourishing site of holistic ministry that exists to this day. Ramabai's enterprises were Christian, but with the same kind of independence she had always shown. In 1905, the Mukti Mission experienced a memorable season of Pentecostal-typed revival that Ramabai guided peacefully. She devoted much of her later years to translating the entire Bible into Marathi, the local language.

And until Sister Geraldine died in 1917, Ramabai maintained a remarkably frank, open, but also fond correspondence with Sister Geraldine. The Sister usually opened her letters with "My dear Ramabai"; Ramabai usually replied with "My dear old Ajeebai" or "Dearest old Ajeebai" (the Marathi word of respect for an older person). These two strong-willed women differed in much—how to understand the Trinity, whether women should be teaching men, what kind of authority the Western churches should exercise in India, how to provide Ramabai's daughter with a proper education, and more.

Ramabai once explained at length to Sister Geraldine why she put so little stock in the ecclesiastical traditions that meant so much to the Community of St. Mary the Virgin. Yet she began the letter with a sincere show of kindness: "Now my dearest Ajeebai, you know that I love you and respect you as my own mother and I shall never forget your love and kindness and care. I cannot but love you and be grateful to you—always. And I do hope that you will forgive me and Mano [her daughter] if we have been wrong and forget all our shortcomings. I shall never be happy unless I know that you have forgiven us."[18] For her part, Sister Geraldine penned a retrospective of their relationship shortly before she died. It began by acknowledging "Ramabai's wonderful and noble life," but did not hesitate to criticize what she called her "great mistakes." This late memoir included a meandering, but also perceptive account of a distinctive kind of friendship: "I believe Ramabai had strong affections, but as a friend, she was very exacting and wrong-headed and strained friendship almost to breaking point, but in the long run her higher nature asserted itself and though she had by unwise friendship woven a web around herself which she would feign have broken through and could not, there were times when she strongly realized what our friendship had meant for her and her child and she did not shrink from making a public declaration of her feelings."[19] For these strong Christians, friendship meant most of all the liberty to speak freely to each other across the cultural divides that remained very real for both of them.

The intertwined lives of Chilembwe and Booth, as well as the Pandita and the Sister, illustrate how deep personal friendships have flourished in the cross-cultural spread of the Christian message. In the reflections of Vedanayagam Samuel Azariah (1874–1945), the first indigenous Anglican bishop in India, we can also observe how friendship—both emulated and explained—can lead to a firmer grasp of Christian faith itself.[20]

At the great World Missionary Conference held at Edinburgh in 1910, Azariah was one of the very few non-Western speakers called to the platform. In the closing paragraphs of his powerful address, he explained succinctly the ultimate value at stake in a conception of the faith as a worldwide reality:

> The exceeding riches of the glory of Christ can be fully realized not by the Englishman, the American, and the Continental alone, not by the Japanese, the Chinese, and the Indians by themselves—but by all working together, worshipping together, and learning together the Perfect Image of our Lord and Christ. It is only "with all the Saints" that we can "comprehend the love of Christ which passeth knowledge, that we might be filled with all the fulness of God."

18. Ramabai to Sister Geraldine, November 25, 1896, in Shah, *Letters and Correspondence*, 335.

19. Shah, *Letters and Correspondence*, 393, 415.

20. See Noll and Nystrom, *Clouds of Witnesses*, 141–56. Our work here relied almost entirely on Harper, *In the Shadow of the Mahatma*.

Then he ended by specifying one requirement for reaching this supernal goal: it would "be possible only from spiritual friendship between the two races." He was thinking of Western culture and Indian culture, but his scope included all missionary efforts. Azariah took pains to praise the Western missionary movement for its "heroism and self-denying labours." But his final words pleaded for more: "You have given your bodies to be burned. We also ask for *love*. Give US FRIENDS!"[21]

Behind Azariah's dramatic speech lay a remarkable personal history in which experiences of friendship across high cultural barriers played a central part. Azariah grew up in a first-generation Christian home where he received faithful instruction and where his parents saw to their son's education in schools run by the Church of England and the Church of Scotland. After showing great promise as a student, Azariah made the fateful career choice to serve with the Young Men's Christian Association (YMCA), which had come to India only in 1890. During Azariah's service for the YMCA from 1895 to 1909, he experienced personally the friendships across cultural divides about which he spoke at Edinburgh.

Azariah enjoyed a number of close relationships with British and especially American missionaries in the YMCA, particularly with Sherwood Eddy (1871–1963).[22] Eddy was an energetic young American who had studied at Yale, Union Seminary, and Princeton Seminary. He had been drawn to the YMCA and a sister organization, the Student Volunteer Movement for World Missions, by attending summer sessions at Dwight L. Moody's Northfield Conferences in Massachusetts. Shortly after he arrived in India as a YMCA worker, he met Azariah. The two seemed to have connected immediately. Eddy, who retained the down-home values of his Midwestern upbringing in Kansas, lacked the class consciousness that characterized most British and many East Coast American missionaries. His freedom in working comfortably with all sorts of Indians paralleled Azariah's life-long resistance to India's traditions of caste. Through several years of ceaseless activity—traveling, lecturing, evangelizing, debating, organizing concerts and social gatherings, setting up reading rooms, and more—the two first worked together closely and then built a deep friendship that survived through the decades that followed. Remarkably, it remained firm even as Eddy drifted to more liberal theological convictions while Azariah retained the evangelical beliefs of his early life.

---

21. Azariah, "Problem of Co-Operation," 315.

22. Excellent on the Azariah-Eddy friendship are Harper, *In the Shadow of the Mahatma*; Nutt, *Whole Gospel*.

Eddy provided particularly important assistance as Azariah proceeded toward what had become the stated, though not always implemented, three-self goal of the Western missionary movement. That is, missionaries were to exist only until they were succeeded by self-governing, self-propagating, and self-funding local churches. When Azariah and his Indian associates founded the Indian Missionary Society of Tinnevelly for the southern part of the sub-continent in 1903 and then the National Missionary Society in 1905, Eddy enthusiastically did all he could to help. A little later he may have assisted Azariah in writing his 1910 speech for Edinburgh.[23]

In that speech, Azariah took to task the unwillingness of many Western missionaries to share meals with their Indian colleagues or to visit them in their homes. He paused, though, to note an important exception. He had begun his address with the blunt assertion, "the problem of race relations is one of the most serious problems confronting the Church today." But then as he documented the patronizing attitude of Western missionaries, he noted, "In the Young Men's Christian Association we have a body that stands foremost in having successfully solved the problem."[24] Azariah's profound friendship with Eddy, and more casual connections with other YMCA workers, explained the exception.

Azariah's stellar career after ending his work with the YMCA was marked by unusually effective outreach across India's extremely strict caste divisions. During his thirty-two years as the Anglican Bishop of Dornakal, he was particularly effective as a lower-caste Indian himself in reaching out with manifest love to his diocese's untouchables (Dalits). He also worked effectively with Brahmans and the other higher castes. Azariah's stance in the world Anglican fellowship was much more complicated than in the YMCA, since he met there a great deal of patronizing suspicion as well as a few instances of notable cross-cultural acceptance.

Azariah rooted his vison of a worldwide church communicating "the Perfect Image of our Lord and Christ" in the gospel record concerning Jesus himself. At Edinburgh he began the body of his address by expositing John 15:15: "The relationship between Him and His Immediate disciples and followers was not only one of Teacher and pupils, Master and disciples, but, above all, that of Friend and friends."[25] Friendship, as he described it, involved personal, administrative, and spiritual dimensions. Together they defined, not only a relationship crucial for cross-cultural Christian advance, but a God-given possibility foundational for the Christian faith itself.

23. Nutt, *Whole Gospel*, 72.

24. Azariah, "Problem of Co-Operation," 306–7.

25. Azariah, "Problem of Co-Operation," 307–8.

CONCLUSION

Records of friendship in the history of Christianity provide much more evidence for many more varieties than outlined in this short chapter. Yet the ones sketched here can suggest the importance of that relationship for every expression of the faith. By pointing out that significance and then illustrating it so forcefully in her writings and her circle of students-become-friends, Dana Robert has enriched the historical record but also deepened understanding of the religion that itself began with friendship extended from God to humanity.

BIBLIOGRAPHY

Azariah, V. S. "The Problem of Co-Operation between Foreign and Native Workers." In vol. 9 of *World Missionary Conference, 1910: The History and Records of the Conference*, 306–15. New York: Fleming H. Revell, 1910.

Church, J. E. *Quest for the Highest: An Autobiographical Account of the East African Revival.* Cape Town: Oxford University Press, 1981.

Evangelical Church Winning All (ECWA). "History." Online. https://www.ecwausa. org/history-of-ecwa-church.

Harper, Susan Billington. *In the Shadow of the Mahatma: Bishop V. S. Azariah and the Travails of Christianity in British India.* Grand Rapids, MI: Eerdmans, 2000.

Lewis, C. S. *The Four Loves.* New York: Harcourt, Brace, Jovanovich, 1960.

MacMaster, Richard K., and Donald R. Jacobs. *A Gentle Wind of God: The Influence of the East African Revival.* Scottdale, PA: Herald, 2006.

Noll, Mark A., and Carolyn Nystrom. *Clouds of Witnesses: Christian Voices from Africa and Asia.* Downers Grove, IL: InterVarsity, 2011.

Nutt, Rick L. *The Whole Gospel for the Whole World: Sherwood Eddy and the American Protestant Mission.* Macon, GA: Mercer University Press, 1997.

Peterson, Derek R. *Ethnic Patriotism and the East African Revival.* New York: Cambridge University Press, 2012.

Robert, Dana L. *Christian Mission: How Christianity Became a World Religion.* Malden, MA: Wiley-Blackwell, 2009.

———. *Faithful Friendships: Embracing Diversity in Christian Community.* Grand Rapids, MI: Eerdmans, 2019.

———, ed. *Gospel Bearers, Gender Barriers: Missionary Women in the Twentieth Century.* Maryknoll, NY: Orbis, 2002.

Shah, A. B., ed. *Letters and Correspondence of Pandita Ramabai, Compiled by Sister Geraldine.* Bombay: Maharashtra State Board for Literature and Culture, 1977.

Shepperson, George, and Thomas Price. *Independent African: John Chilembwe and the Origins, Setting and Significance of the Nyasaland Native Rising of 1915.* Edinburgh: Edinburgh University Press, 1958.

Ward, Kevin, and Emma Wild-Wood, eds. *The East African Revival: History and Legacies.* 2012. Reprint, New York: Routledge, 2017.

Friendship and Solidarity in Southern Africa

ADA FOCER

In August of 1964, Gail Hovey was a newlywed spending the summer in Waverly, Ohio, before entering her final year at Union Theological Seminary in New York. Leaving her new husband for the first time, she traveled to Chicago for the National Student Christian Federation (NSCF) annual meeting. There she heard Hank Crane, the Africa Secretary at the World Student Christian Federation (WSCF), tell the gathered students, "If you care about what's happening in civil rights in the United States, you also have to care about what's happening in Southern Africa, because the US is on the wrong side of every single struggle that is going on right now."[1]

At the time, Gail knew as little as most other Americans, even very powerful ones, about Africa. It was not taught in schools. News from there only rarely and briefly appeared in American media. But Gail had spent her junior year at a women's college in Beirut, Lebanon, through a Presbyterian Church (PCUSA) program. She had made friends with people who had a level of political sophistication about the world beyond anything she had ever witnessed in her classmates back home. She aspired to it. She was also active in the civil rights movement. So, when Hank Crane threw down his challenge, Gail picked it up, as did others. The causes of self-determination and majority rule in Southern Africa became a central passion of her life. Her compatriots in this long struggle became people she could count on no matter what.

---

1. Gail Hovey, interview with author, Haverstraw, NY, 2009.

For this chapter, "friendship" will be defined as just that—being able to count on each other no matter what—and "solidarity" will be understood as the mutual support people gave each other through the decades of the long struggle for the liberation of the Portuguese colonies and the transfer of power to the majority populations of Rhodesia (now Zimbabwe) and South Africa. These factors, I will argue, were the reason why this group of people stayed the course when other groups supportive of African liberation that they sometimes allied with, like the Students for a Democratic Society (SDS), did not. Their politics were deeply embedded in their relationships.

But it was definitely not a soft and sentimental kind of friendship that held these people together through the years. Three of the four married couples who will be profiled here eventually divorced. There were deaths that broke their hearts. Year in and year out, there were fierce arguments about strategy and purpose and the next right thing to do. Equally fierce, though, was their commitment. They were held together not just by their relationships to each other and to the wider network of liberation activists, but also their relationships to elders in the resistance to the injustices being perpetrated in Southern Africa, like Hank Crane. Behind them was a tradition and a supranational Christian community that had come into being and played an enormously important role in the world over the previous hundred years.

THE MISSIONARIES VERSUS THE COLD WARRIORS

Hank Crane was a missionary kid, but to say that does not say nearly enough about what he represented for the students gathered at the NSCF meeting in Chicago in 1964 nor for those who ended up devoting their lives to Southern Africa. He spoke from first-hand experience at a time when authenticity counted for just about everything with youth. He was born in the Kasai River region of what was then the Belgian Congo in 1921 to Southern Presbyterian missionaries Charles and Louise Crane, who had arrived in 1912. His future in-laws, Roy and LeNoir Cleveland, arrived two years later in 1914. Their daughter and Hank's future wife, Abie (Anne Boyd) Cleveland, was born a few months after he was in 1922. By 1964, Hank and his family had collectively spent fifty years in the Congo. The struggle there against colonial domination was their struggle.[2]

But even before the arrival of the Cranes and the Clevelands, missionary resistance to the grim conditions they discovered was already well underway. The mission was founded in 1891, only a few years after the

2. Anne Crane, interview with author, Jamaica Plain, MA, 2019.

European powers divided Africa among themselves in 1884–1885. The Europeans were rapidly industrializing, and Africa had the raw materials those industries demanded. The Congo had rubber. Africans were being captured and forced to gather it under nightmarish conditions. Over ten million of them eventually died in the process.[3]

So, the missionaries in the Kasai region tried to intervene. They used animals like goats to buy the freedom of the enslaved from traders who traversed their area. Some of those freed chose to return to their homes; others chose to remain at the mission and became some of the first converts and evangelists. The missionaries also pleaded with the Belgians to institute more humane working conditions, to no avail. In 1909, one of the mission founders, William Sheppard, an African American from Virginia, was tried for defaming the Kasai Company, the major rubber producer, after writing an article describing and criticizing its inhumane practices in a publication distributed in the United States. The charges were eventually dropped, but the case got attention around the world.[4]

All this began before Hank and Abie Crane were even born, but it shaped the mission and them. A photo in the possession of Anne Crane, their daughter, taken not long after the Cranes and Clevelands arrived, shows a racially mixed group reflective of the actual make-up of the mission at that time: African American, African, and white American. By 1940, the Belgians forced the Presbyterians to withdraw the African American missionaries, thinking, wrongly, that would eliminate what they saw as the troublemakers. Rather, the commitment to justice for, and solidarity with, the Congolese people got passed across racial lines and from generation to generation.[5] At the NSCF meeting in Chicago, Hank Crane was recruiting yet another generation to join the resistance in all of Southern Africa.

The Cold Warriors running the US government, by contrast, knew almost nothing about Africa. Close friendships with Africans were unheard of. Africa is entirely missing from most of the voluminous biographies of the people who constructed the Cold War against the Soviet Union and advanced it in the "third world" countries caught in the crosshairs of this conflict. Their primary relationships were with the war-weary and near-broke European colonizers—the country's NATO allies—who were fighting tooth and nail to retain at least economic if not total control.[6]

3. Hochschild, *King Leopold's Ghost*; Minter, *King Solomon's Mines Revisited*.

4. Anne Crane, interview with author, Jamaica Plain, MA, 2019.

5. Anne Crane, interview with author, Jamaica Plain, MA, 2019.

6. Isaacson and Thomas, *Wise Men*, 29; Westad, *Global Cold War*, 5.

Theoretically, the United States, a former colony itself, supported self-determination, but its bureaucratic organization told a different tale. The US State Department had no bureau of African Affairs until 1958. Before that, colonies were handled through their European colonizers, functionally granting them veto power over American policymaking. The CIA finally created an African Division in 1959 but had no direct reporting from the Congo until July 1960, right before they got involved in the assassination of the first elected Congolese prime minister, Patrice Lumumba.[7]

What substituted for direct engagement with actual Africans for American officials were abstract ideologies that justified their continued control. Belief in a racial hierarchy with white people at the top and black people at the bottom was foundational. Also commonplace was a belief that the world was progressing to a more civilized state, defined as more like what Northern European countries and the United States already exhibited. Therefore, those northern and whiter countries had a responsibility to "tutor" the African nations, even after independence, to be more like them. Redefining those countries as "underdeveloped" contained that same assumption, that the "developed" nations had a responsibility to help them progress.[8]

Two other beliefs pertained directly to the Cold War with the Soviet Union. Cold Warriors first made up, then came to believe, a myth that the Soviet Union had a plan for world domination.[9] Much more concrete was the fear that communists would gain control of those African countries so rich in the raw materials the West relied on to fuel its economy, thus destroying the American way of life. Anticommunism became the central organizing idea—perhaps even the only one that mattered—of postwar American life.[10]

Because of all these factors and others, US policy ended up either supporting continued control and repression on the part of European colonial powers, most egregiously Portugal, which refused to relinquish any control of its colonies, or the white minority rulers in places like Rhodesia and South Africa. If attempts at control through existing rulers did not work, the CIA covertly intervened themselves to get rid of them and install new leaders they chose in order to make sure Africa was controlled by people friendly to the United States.

---

7. Halberstam, *Best*, 83; Kinzer, *Brothers*, 267; Prados, *Safe for Democracy*, 273–97.
8. Hunt, *Ideology*, 46–91, 125–70; Rist, *History of Development*.
9. Leffler, *Soul of Mankind*, 56; Spalding, *First Cold Warrior*, 54.
10. Williams, *Tragedy*, 198–201; Leffler, *Soul of Mankind*, 64.

Even the Protestant theologian, Reinhold Niebuhr, possibly the most prominent public intellectual of the time, got on the anticommunism bandwagon with no more concrete knowledge about the emerging post-colonial nations in Africa than anyone in the government.[11] He, too, was a Europeanist who bought into most of the same beliefs as everyone else.[12] "The chief effect of his [Niebuhr's] writing and sermonizing in the 1950s was to wed American Protestantism to America's anticommunist struggle for the world," wrote Union Theological ethicist Gary Dorrien.[13]

THE SOUTHERN AFRICA COMMITTEE IS BORN

Against the monolith of those fictions and fears that relegated the hopes of the Southern African people for self-determination to some far, future time, came the Southern Africa Committee of the National Student Christian Federation that was created several months after the Chicago NSCF meeting. Gail Hovey's field work her senior year at Union Theological Seminary (UTS), in 1964–1965, was staffing the new committee. Another UTS student, Bill Minter, who had relatives at the Kasai mission in the Congo, succeeded her in that role the following year.[14]

From the beginning, the Committee "studied, produced study materials, held conferences, helped organize demonstrations and other protests, and lobbied within the National Council of Churches for action on this issue." Perhaps most notable in the context of this discussion is that they sought out information from direct contact with people involved in the nationalist movements. Concrete information about particular situations provided by actual human beings began to fill what Bill called "the information gap."[15] In the spring of 1965, when a group of them met with a Chase Manhattan banker in advance of a planned protest, they were amazed to discover they knew more about Chase's involvement in South Africa than he did. Mobilizing careful, grassroots research as a foundation of action characterized the group from the beginning.

In late 1965, concerned about the lack of information available in the United States about the new Unilateral Declaration of Independence (UDI) from Great Britain by the white minority in Rhodesia, two other founding members of the Southern Africa Committee, David Wiley, a doctoral

11. Hulsether, *Protestant Left*, 34–42.

12. Fox, *Reinhold Niebuhr*, 225.

13. Dorrien, *Soul in Society*, 129.

14. Gail Hovey, email message to the author, 2019.

15. Minter, *Action Against Apartheid*.

student at Princeton, and Marylee Crofts, who were then married, put together a newsletter, the *Rhodesian News Summary*, aimed at Protestant leaders whose churches were involved in Southern Africa. Over the next three years, it evolved into *Southern Africa Magazine* and continued in print for the next fifteen years, until 1983, providing a critical source of information directly from Southern Africa to its approximately four thousand activist subscribers. It helped bind them together.[16]

FRONTIER INTERNSHIP IN MISSION: EMBEDDED IN AFRICA

By that time, Dave and Marylee had already spent two years (1961–1963) in Southern Rhodesia as participants in an experimental new mission program sponsored by the Presbyterian Church (PCUSA), Frontier Internship in Mission (FIM). The brainchild of Margaret Flory, the director of Student World Relations for the PCUSA, its purpose was to put new college or seminary graduates on the "frontiers" where the church was supposedly absent or irrelevant. These selected frontiers were defined by racial tensions, new nationalism, militant non-Christian faiths, modern secularism, displaced, rejected and uprooted peoples, communism, technological upheaval, the university world, and responsibility for statesmanship. Most of them clearly spoke to contemporary struggles in the emerging post-colonial world.

Unintentionally overlooked by this claim that the church was absent or irrelevant in these struggles was the ample evidence to the contrary from the 1955 and 1959 Student Volunteer Movement (SVM) Quadrennials, where the foundation of the FIM was laid. Traditional missionaries wrote conference study books; missionary kids like Hank Crane and African Student Christian Movement (SCM) leaders like Bola Ige from Nigeria helped organize and lead them; international students made up over one third of the three thousand plus participants at each event. These Christians were already very much at work on these frontiers. What the FIM was really about then was making it possible for young Americans to go to these places for several years, to live with and learn from the people already active there, and to take their place in the struggle for justice already underway. Solidarity—being Christian together with others—in this struggle became the point.

Dave Wiley and Marylee Crofts headed to Southern Rhodesia in 1961 as part of the first class of Frontier Interns.[17] Both of them were from the

---

16. Wiley, email message to the author, 2019; Hovey, *Media for the Movement.*

17. Marylee Crofts, interview with the author, Raleigh, NC, 2009; David Wiley, interview with the author, East Lansing, MI, 2008.

Midwest and very involved in the Student Christian Movement (SCM) and World Student Christian Federation (WSCF). At the time they arrived in Southern Rhodesia, between 6 and 7 percent of the country's population was European and white, yet this small minority controlled the government and allocated its resources to its own benefit. Everything was strictly segregated, except the university where they worked with the student Christian association. Outside of that, they took courses and taught them. Marylee got active in the YWCA, one of the few places where mixed race groups of women congregated. Dave connected with some African Independent Churches (AICs) and preached sometimes.

Most important of all, Dave said, were the relationships. "Through the FI program and our work there, we were cast into all these relationships with African students, pastors, and ordinary people. Those were wonderful enriching relationships, and I think that's in the core and character of these African societies. . . . There were levels of social integration and comradeship that I had never before experienced here in the US."[18]

At the university, students told them they wanted interracial activities to begin to get to know each other and support for their political protest against the colonial regime. In response, Marylee and Dave ran work camps in the African townships where the groups lived in unfinished concrete huts and got to know each other while doing projects together. A particularly memorable protest they helped with was on the Opening Day of Parliament. During the National Anthem, when everyone was standing at attention, they held up protest signs they painted earlier at their cottage. That gave them sixty seconds or so of exposure for their anticolonial message before they ran.

Marylee and Dave were not the only Americans on this "frontier." One of the others, United Methodist Bishop Ralph Dodge, also supported that protest by letting them stash their signs in his nearby office until the last minute before the Opening Day ceremony. He was a great friend and mentor during their internship. He and his wife arrived in Angola as missionaries in 1936 and had worked tirelessly after that to build the church and support for the cause of liberation both in the Southern African countries and back in the United States. Like them, he was often frustrated with the desire of many in the missionary community to maintain the status quo, but he had the power to promote Africans anyway and did. The predominantly African leadership of his Conference by the 1960s reflected that effort.[19]

18. David Wiley, interview with the author, East Lansing, MI, 2008.

19. Dodge, *Revolutionary Bishop*, 115–17, 186–88.

Bishop Dodge was expelled by the government in 1964, a year after Dave and Marylee were.

When Gail Hovey and her then-husband, the late Don Morlan, finished their last year at UTS in 1965, they, too, applied to be Frontier Interns representing the Southern Africa Committee (SAC) in South Africa.[20] Margaret Flory and her friends, Swiss missionaries François (also a missionary kid) and Molly Bill, proposed an internship that appeared so traditional to the authorities—Don was to be the chaplain at a school, Lemana, and Gail's role was "wife"—that they would grant them visas. Although Gail and Don were initially distressed at being in such a remote place three hundred miles from Johannesburg, it turned out to be a better situation to get to know Africans.

It was also a good time and place to learn about repression. Nelson Mandela and many of his associates were jailed right before they arrived in 1964. The chilling effect on political activity was total. Ordinary channels of communication were completely blocked. Their students, they discovered, knew virtually nothing about South Africa's past or its present struggles. Although uncomfortable with the role at first, Gail discovered she could begin to fill that void, telling them about important South Africans they had never heard of or raising questions about situations that were taken for granted.

Gail recalled preaching about the crucifixion one day at required chapel: "We had to speak in biblical language to say what we meant. . . . The idea I was putting out there was that the people with the most power are the most responsible. Kids don't listen in chapel, but they were listening. . . . I often found myself in that weird position of being a white American telling Africans about stuff in their history or about American history that I shouldn't be having to tell them. . . . It was very complicated."

But the fundamental lesson for this future editor of *Southern Africa Magazine* was that even when it appears that all channels for the flow of information are blocked, information, like water, can find alternate paths. She came to understand herself as one of those alternate paths.

Back at Union Theological in New York, current students Bill Minter and Ruth Brandon were deeply involved in the struggle for civil rights in the United States. Bill spent ten years of his childhood on a cooperative interracial farm in Mississippi, and both of them participated in the Student Interracial Ministries in Raleigh, North Carolina, one summer and with a Student Non-Violent Coordinating Committee (SNCC) project in southwestern Georgia the next. Neither were they strangers to African colonialism. Bill had participated in the Presbyterians' West African summer study

20. Gail Hovey, interview with the author, Haverstraw, NY, 2009.

seminar then spent his junior year at university in Nigeria. Ruth was raised in Vermont, but her mother regularly corresponded with a close friend who was a missionary in Angola. By 1966, when Eduardo Mondlane, the leader of FRELIMO, the liberation party in Mozambique, came to speak at Union, Bill was working for the Southern Africa Committee.

While superficially Mondlane's position with FRELIMO, the party justifying violent revolution against the Portuguese in order to win liberation from them, seems like it should have put him beyond the circle of Protestant interest or support, Eduardo Mondlane was, in almost every way, deeply embedded in the same networks the Frontier Interns were. He had gone to mission schools, including Lemana, where Gail and Don lived and worked; he attended Oberlin, as Ruth Brandon had; he attended dozens of Student Christian Movement conferences while a doctoral student at Northwestern, a professor at Cornell, and on the staff of the Trusteeship Council at the United Nations, just like they had. He even attended the Athens Student Volunteer Movement (SVM) Quadrennial in 1959, rooming with Hank Crane. He had known Margaret Flory since 1953.[21]

So, when Bill and Ruth heard him speak at Union and say that FRELIMO was starting a middle school in Tanzania for the Mozambican young people in exile, they were immediately interested in teaching there. What was necessary to make that happen was Mondlane convincing others in FRELIMO that they were not American spies, since the United States, a NATO ally of their enemy Portugal, was therefore also an enemy. The church, too, was considered an enemy since the Roman Catholic Church was bound to the Portuguese colonialists by a concordat with Rome. The government appointed the priests. But Mondlane, as FRELIMO leader and a Protestant, said he would vouch for them and welcome them if they could find funding elsewhere. Enter Margaret Flory and the Frontier Intern program. Margaret said "yes."

Being present on the frontier of new nationalisms was their FIM assignment. They taught middle school students—Bill, math, and Ruth, geography—in the Portuguese they learned by total immersion, and after the school had to close part way through 1968, at the end of their internship, they taught teachers. When they could, they sent information back to New York for dissemination to friends of the movement. Eduardo Mondlane and his American wife, Janet, lived nearby and became good friends.

Probably at the behest of Margaret Flory, in 1967 Hank Crane invited the Frontier Interns then in the region to his home at the Zambian Mindolo

---

21. Ruth Brandon, interview with the author, Bellbrook, OH, 2009; William Minter, interview with the author, Washington, DC, 2009; Faris, *Liberating Mission*; Flory, *Moments in Time*, 83; Parrott, "Struggle for Solidarity," 254.

Ecumenical Retreat Center for a meeting. Gail, Don, Bill, and Ruth were still in their internships in South Africa and Tanzania, respectively, so were able to attend. Dave and Marylee were back, living in Zambia, while Dave did his dissertation research, so they were also in attendance. Several other people, including Methodist missionaries Carolyn and Charles Wilhelm and Frontier Intern Dave Robinson, also came.

Ruth Brandon describes the group that emerged from that meeting as "a non-residential intentional community" that was more a network of relationships rather than a formal organization. They called themselves the Zambia Group and for almost twenty years they wrote to each other quarterly and met annually on retreat to talk through where things stood in Southern Africa and debate what the appropriate action for the coming year should be. They contributed to a common financial fund and decided where it should be directed. Dave Wiley recalls they also spent considerable time in career discernment.[22]

Over the course of that first meeting in Zambia, attendees produced a document analyzing the situation in Southern Africa as they by then understood it, then outlined a series of goals and strategies to guide their action going forward. Most of all, they wanted to change the kneejerk Cold War anticommunism underlying the reactionary American foreign policy into active support for locally controlled socialist nation building in places like Southern Africa. They outlined a grassroots strategy to make that happen.[23]

The mountain that they would have to climb to accomplish this was enormous. A measure of just how high might be the 1967 trip to Southern Africa taken by George Kennan, the author of the Cold War containment policy and an international relations heavyweight. Its purpose, he wrote in his journal, was "to cure my ignorance since I'd never been there." Indeed, his extensive notes indicate he travelled widely and was deeply unsettled by what he learned about conditions, particularly in apartheid South Africa. But ultimately, he concluded that supporting liberation movements or a rapid shift to majority rule did not make sense. It was simply not America's business. His host was a friend with extensive mining interests there, counterevidence Kennan did not seem to notice.[24]

Yet, if Kennan was the Goliath in foreign policy circles, there were yet more Davids at work on the margins. New Frontier Interns and recent

22. Ruth Brandon, Marylee Crofts, Gail Hovey, William Minter, and David Wiley, email messages to the author, 2019.

23. Parrott, "Struggle for Solidarity," 267–71. A complete set of Zambia Group records has been donated to Yale Divinity School Library and will be available for use in 2025.

24. Gaddis, *George F. Kennan*, 603–5.

Duke graduates Tami Hultman and Reed Kramer arrived in South Africa that year for a two-year internship that involved research on behalf of the pension funds of the churches into the involvement of American corporations in supporting the apartheid regime. The funds' boards provided them with letters of introduction that corporate managers interpreted as normal due diligence and so welcomed them.[25] Reed recalled,

> We didn't go in to lecture. That wasn't our role. We went in to ask questions and we expressed genuine interest and we never argued with anything they told us. We just asked them for the information and in most cases we had as much access as we could possibly hope for and then we usually were able to meet with the unions or representatives of workers who were glad to tell their side of the story. It wasn't difficult to get to them. It was just a matter of being willing to ask.[26]

And what they discovered was that the American companies were much more conservative in their labor policies and much more reactionary than the South African ones in general because they did not want to get kicked out. When Tami and Reed got back to New York in 1969, they compiled and published the results of their research. That report then served as the foundation for the divestment movement. Then they returned home to Durham, North Carolina, and founded the Southern Africa Committee South and *All-Africa News* to disseminate African journalism in the United States.

A SEASON OF DEATH

In the late 1960s, the Southern Africa activists entered the season of death. "It's hard to say what factors build lasting connections between people, but surely the deaths of those engaged in a common struggle must count among the most powerful," Bill Minter wrote recently.[27] In March 1968, back in New York, the Methodist missionary and Zambia Group member Charles Wilhem, an age-peer, died of cancer. The next month, April, Martin Luther King Jr. was assassinated, and in June so was Robert Kennedy. Gail Hovey and Don Morlan, who had recently returned to New York from their South Africa FI assignment, were concerned that Carolyn Wilhelm not be alone with another death and so went to her place for dinner that night. Together

---

25. Tami Hultman, interview with the author, Washington, DC, 2009.

26. Reed Kramer, telephone interview with the author, 2010.

27. Minter et al., *No Easy Victories*, 9.

they remembered and took strength from Kennedy's speech to the youth of South Africa when he visited there: "I believe that in this generation those with the courage to enter the moral conflict will find themselves with companions in every corner of the world."[28]

They had companions, but the deaths kept coming. The day FRELIMO FIs, Bill Minter and Ruth Brandon, arrived back at Bill's parents' house in Tucson, in February 1969, they got a phone call from Gail telling them that Eduardo Mondlane had been assassinated by a letter bomb, not long after he dropped them off at the airport. "That was very, very deep for us," Ruth recalled, "because we were essentially his protegées. . . . It probably also reinforced our commitments to hang in there with the people."[29]

And then in November 1970, Hank Crane died of cancer at forty-nine. His daughter Anne had been deeply impacted by his work. When she was growing up, at family prayer time Hank would lead them in reading Bible stories in the context of what was going on around them. Anne lapped it up. After his death, she entered the University of Wisconsin as a graduate student in African Studies, lived with Dave Wiley and Marylee Crofts, and, although younger than the others, became part of the Zambia Group, too.[30]

There was, yet, one more death that mattered deeply, not of a person but of the entire century-old tradition that spawned these Southern Africa activists. At the end of February 1969, the General Committee of the University Christian Movement (UCM), since 1966 the successor to the NSCF, voted itself out of existence.

The people in this chapter were all connected in some way with the YMCA and its offshoots, the student Christian associations and the WSCF that federated them and the SVM, which recruited people like Ralph Dodge and perhaps the Cranes and Clevelands to go to work for denominational mission boards. Bill Minter's father and uncle were YMCA activists in the 1930s. These and related organizations were also the avenues to programs like the ones sponsored by Margaret Flory's office. It is how Marylee, Dave, Gail, Don, Bill, Ruth, Tami, and Reed all got connected with Southern Africa and each other. People on this network around the world were potential friends and collaborators. When the UCM voted itself out of existence, most of the entry points to this world and these potential friends vanished, too. Rising generations would not be able to opt in like the FIs profiled here were.

In many places and to many people in the churches, the government, and in business, the UCM was not mourned. The global friendships that

28. Gail Hovey, interview with the author, Haverstraw, NY, 2019.

29. Ruth Brandon, interview with the author, Bellbrook, OH, 2009.

30. Anne Crane, interview with the author, Jamaica Plain, MA, 2019.

developed in the context of this global YMCA-spawned network provided both a backchannel avenue for information about what was true and a context for ethical reflection on policy, what was right. These channels subverted the ordinary reliance of citizens on those in power to tell them what was going on in the world and what it meant. It sometimes persuaded them to take a public stance in opposition to mainstream power brokers when they concluded their actions were unjust. It manufactured "troublemakers." The question was: trouble for whom?

IN FOR THE LONG HAUL

The Southern Africa Committee outlived the University Christian Movement, its organizational parent, by decades. Bill Minter said they had learned from Eduardo Mondlane "that one continues to do one's work in any case," an approach very much tied to his leadership. "There was a narrative of social justice which included opposition to racism, colonialism and apartheid, but also included a long term perspective that even if those things won that won't be the end of it." They forged ahead.[31]

Historian R. Joseph Parrott, in his comprehensive history of how a diverse group of Southern Africa activists, including the Zambia Group, created a solidarity movement, showed how they successfully cultivated the support of key Congressional leaders and fundamentally challenged Cold War anticommunist interventionism. Part of that effort included the successful campaign of the SAC/Zambia Group activists to move the National Council of Churches further to the left on this issue.[32]

In 2008, Bill Minter, Gail Hovey, and Charles Cobb published their own remarkable history of the solidarity movement on behalf of Southern Africa, *No Easy Victories: African Liberation and American Activists Over a Half Century, 1950–2000*. Combining their first-hand knowledge with their extraordinary talents as researchers and journalists, decade by decade, the book chronicles why the movement had the success that it did. Another critical contribution to the effort to preserve the record of exactly how this movement worked is the African Activist Archive (africanactivist.msu. edu) established at Michigan State University by David Wiley, the longtime director of the African Studies Center there. Bill Minter and Marylee Crofts are also scholars of Africa. Marylee took numerous groups of educators to Africa on learning trips, a contemporary manifestation perhaps of Margaret Flory's "summer study seminars." Bill still regularly publishes the

31. William Minter, interview with the author, Washington, DC, 2009.

32. Parrott, "Struggle for Solidarity."

AfricaFocus Bulletin, an electronic newsletter. Past issues are archived along with other resources at AfricaFocus.org. Tami Hultman and Reed Kramer continue to publish AllAfrica.com, which distributes eight hundred news items daily aggregated from one hundred forty African news sites and combined with new stories produced by their own reporters based in six field offices.

Ruth Brandon lived in Mozambique for extended periods two more times. The third time she was invited by the church, pastored a new church there, and taught in a seminary. Her experience in the solidarity movement prompted her to think deeply about what it all means.

> In America, our concept is that [to be human] is to develop your own uniqueness as fully and completely as possible, and to stand up for what you are called individually to be and do. That is the American way. The African concept is: if that's all you do, you aren't human yet. You are only fully human when you are in relationship. So you have to find the community of which you are an authentic part, and build that relationship, and when you are thoroughly related there, then you have the capacity to be fully human.[33]

In this context, friendship and solidarity take on even deeper meanings. Joseph Parrott credits the success of the movement through the years to the way they bound together people and groups that disagreed about so much but agreed about the goal of self-determination for the Southern Africa people. These groups were in relationship with each other, and relationships presume difference. At a divisive time, this kind of human community turned out to be radical and powerful enough.

BIBLIOGRAPHY

Bilheimer, Robert S. *Breakthrough: The Emergence of the Ecumenical Tradition.* Grand Rapids, MI: Eerdmans, 1989.

Dodge, Ralph E. *The Revolutionary Bishop: Who Saw God at Work in Africa.* Tucson, AZ: Wheatmark, 1986.

Dorrien, Gary. *Soul in Society: The Making and Renewal of Social Christianity.* Minneapolis: Fortress, 1995.

Faris, Robert. *Liberating Mission in Mozambique: Faith and Revolution in the Life of Eduardo Mondlane.* Eugene, OR: Pickwick, 2014.

Flory, Margaret. *Moments in Time: One Woman's Ecumenical Journey.* New York: Friendship, 1995.

Fox, Richard Wightman. *Reinhold Niebuhr: A Biography.* New York: Pantheon, 1985.

33. Ruth Brandon, interview with the author, Bellbrook, OH, 2009.

Gaddis, John Lewis. *George F. Kennan: An American Life.* New York: Penguin, 2011.

Halberstam, David. *The Best and the Brightest.* New York: Ballantine, 1992.

Hochschild, Adam. *King Leopold's Ghost: A Story of Greed, Terror, and Heroism in Colonial Africa.* Boston: Houghton Mifflin Harcourt, 1998.

Hovey, Gail. "Media for the Movement: Southern Africa Magazine." In *No Easy Victories: African Liberation and American Activists Over a Half Century, 1950–2000,* edited by William Minter et al., 110–12. Trenton, NJ: Africa World, 2007.

Hulsether, Mark. *Building a Protestant Left: Christianity and Crisis Magazine, 1941–1993.* Knoxville: University of Tennessee Press, 1999.

Hunt, Michael H. *Ideology and US Foreign Policy.* New Haven, CT: Yale University Press, 1987.

Isaacson, Walter, and Evan Thomas. *The Wise Men: Six Friends and the World They Made.* New York: Simon & Schuster, 1986.

Kinzer, Stephen. *The Brothers: John Foster Dulles, Allen Dulles, and Their Secret World War.* New York: Henry Holt, 2013.

Leffler, Melvyn P. *For the Soul of Mankind: The United States, the Soviet Union, and the Cold War.* New York: Hill and Wang, 2008.

Minter, William. "Action Against Apartheid." In *Reflections on Protest: Student Presence in Political Conflict,* edited by Bruce Douglas, 179–88. Richmond, VA: John Knox, 1968.

———. *King Solomon's Mines Revisited: Western Interests and the Burdened History of Southern Africa.* New York: Basic, 1988.

Minter, William, et al., eds. *No Easy Victories: African Liberation and American Activists Over a Half-Century, 1950–2000.* Trenton, NJ: Africa World, 2007.

Parrott, Raymond Joseph. "Struggle for Solidarity: The New Left, Portuguese Africa Decolonization, and the End of the Cold War Consensus." PhD diss., University of Texas at Austin, 2016.

Prados, John. *Safe for Democracy: The Secret Wars of the CIA.* Chicago: Ivan R. Dee, 2006.

Rist, Gilbert. *The History of Development: From Western Origins to Global Faith.* London; New York: Zed, 2014.

Spalding, Elizabeth Edwards. *The First Cold Warrior: Harry Truman, Containment, and the Remaking of Liberal Internationalism.* Lexington: University Press of Kentucky, 2006.

VanDusen, Henry P. *They Found the Church There: The Armed Forces Discover Christian Missions.* New York: Scribner's Sons, 1945.

Westad, Odd Arne. *The Global Cold War: Third World Interventions and the Making of Our Times.* Cambridge: Cambridge University Press, 2007.

Williams, William Appleman. *The Tragedy of American Diplomacy.* New York: Norton, 2009.

How Missionaries Fostered World Friendship through Transnational Adoption

SOOJIN CHUNG

From 1882 through the end of the 1940s, East Asians were regarded in both official US policy and widespread public opinion as unassimilable aliens unfit for citizenship in the United States. The American media painted dehumanizing portraits of the so-called Orientals, doing everything from calling them names to spreading negative stereotypes. In the early 1950s, however, Christian missionaries started to adopt mixed-race children, inspiring thousands of families across the nation to seek out Asian children to adopt.

What these mission activities had in common was the theme of world friendship through transnational adoption. Pearl Buck, a beloved novelist and ecumenical missionary, used the term friendship more symbolically and broadly—she believed that mixed-race children could be a positive bridge between the East and the West, alleviating the racial tension and ignorance so prevalent in the United States. Commenting on Jessie Bennett Sams's *White Mother*, in which Sams described her experience as a black woman who had been raised by a white woman in the South, Buck argued that such love and friendship could be a solution to racial conflict. Helen Doss used the term friendship more literally, to refer to an equal relationship centered around love and care for one another. Doss published *All the Children of the World* and *Friends Around the World* to teach children about world friendship. Introducing the concept of adoption, Doss emphasized that God's boundary-less love for all children should also propel the readers to seek transcultural friendship.

The efforts of these missionaries eventually led to the end of racial matching, a philosophy that governed non-relative adoption during the early twentieth century. Transnational adoption was not merely a personal and private act, but also a profoundly communal and public act that could actualize world friendship and reconciliation. By adopting mixed-race children and demonstrating that such unexpected friendship was possible among families, the missionaries championed world friendship and transcultural families.

AMERICAN RACISM BASED ON THE EUGENICS MOVEMENT

From 1900 to 1940, the notion of "bad blood" was a universally accepted principle in the domestic adoption landscape. Advocates of the eugenics movement believed that so-called "bad blood" (genetically inferior people in terms of physical attributes, illness, psychological disorders, and/or race) must be eliminated through sterilization and controlled breeding (negative eugenics). Thousands of women of color and those who suffered from illness and poverty were involuntarily sterilized during the first half of the twentieth century. Eugenicists argued that genetically superior people's reproduction, by contrast, must be encouraged (positive eugenics).[1] The movement was mostly supported by American intellectuals of virtually all political parties prior to the eugenics movement's negative association with Nazi Germany.

Fears and anxiety about "bad blood" spread widely beyond psychologists and biologists and were shared by social workers engaged in setting adoption policy. The eugenics movement that circulated among the elites pointed to the larger American context of racism. Popular media and literature also echoed the ideology that negative hereditary traits such as feeble-mindedness were innate. Moreover, ordinary Americans believed that negative hereditary traits included race and ethnicity, betraying the racial attitude of the time. Racism had a deep and extensive impact on adoption policies. Social workers and policy makers believed it was a social crime to place "inferior" or "defective" children for adoption. Professionals used intelligence tests and investigated elaborate genealogies before placing children in adoptive homes.

1. Quiroz, "From Race Matching," 250.

Eugenicists' definition of "racial improvement" entailed not only discouraging the procreation of people of color but also filtering people in terms of ethnicity and religion. In 1924, majorities in the House and Senate passed the Immigration Act, which virtually eliminated the flow of immigrants into the United States. President Calvin Coolidge noted, "America must be kept American. Biological laws show . . . that Nordics deteriorate when mixed with other races." Eugenicists zealously acclaimed and supported the new law. The "other races," according to the eugenicists, meant not only people of color, but Jews, southern Europeans, and other non-Nordic people.[2]

Especially prominent in the 1950s adoption landscape were anxieties about miscegenation in transracial and transnational adoption. Due to lingering effects of eugenics from previous decades, there was a prevailing view of the inferiority of people of African descent. Many professionals believed that mixing the races in marriage would destroy the purity of each race and lead to "mongrelization."[3] Moreover, the fear of "race suicide," the notion that non-whites would come to outnumber whites, was reflected in various immigration laws and welfare reforms. Consequently, it was against the social welfare system to place non-white children in white American homes. "Scientific" racism of trained professionals and everyday racism of ordinary people led to the perception that children of color were poor in temperament and feeble-minded, prone to emotional instability, insanity, and violence. This led to the strict policy of racial matching, an attempt to create fictitious biological kinship without blood.

The ideal form of matching entailed not only racial matching, but also perfect matching in terms of religious background, intelligence, and physical resemblance. In other words, adoptive parents wanted a baby who could pass as their own child. In an attempt to artificially create kinship without blood, both adoptive parents and professionals produced a paradoxical result: ironically, matching validated the notion that blood was thicker than love, which inherently made adoption inferior to blood kinship. The 1950s obsession with the nuclear family turned adoption into a practice that served infertile couples' needs. Healthy white babies were in high demand, and prospective parents who wished for children who resembled them desperately attempted to prove their parental worthiness to adoption agencies.[4]

2. Kevles, *In the Name of Eugenics*.

3. May, *Barren in the Promised Land*, 103–10.

4. May, *Barren in the Promised Land*, 144–45.

PEARL BUCK'S VISION FOR GLOBAL FRIENDSHIP

In this landscape of strict racial matching and racial hostility, in 1949, Pearl Sydenstricker Buck founded Welcome House, the first transracial and transnational adoption agency in America, marking the beginning of the transnational adoption of mixed-race "Amerasian" children (a term she coined).[5] She defied the conventional matching system and invented "special needs" adoption. Her firm belief in racial equality and global friendship—traits that represented the ecumenical movement—prompted her to advance transracial and transnational adoption.

The birth story of Welcome House shows Buck's personal connection to the adoption movement.[6] On an ordinary December day in 1948, she received an unexpected letter that changed her life. As she was sorting through piles of mail, she found a long white envelope from an adoption agency. The letter inquired, "Can you help us?" It was a Christmas card from an adoption agency about Robbie, a mixed-race fifteen-month-old baby who needed a home.[7] His mother was a young American "missionary kid," and his father was an Indian man. The young woman's missionary parents forbade marriage, and she was brought to America in haste; the child was immediately given up for adoption.[8]

The agency wrote that they considered Robbie the "finest child" they had ever had in the agency, but he proved unadoptable because of his darker skin. It was also social welfare policy at the time to place all children with matched parents—in this case, Indian American adoptive parents. Robbie had stayed in several foster homes and moved five times during his fifteen months. In an effort to find him a home, the agency inquired throughout the country and even in Hawaii, but none was found. Agency employees even reached out to the Indian embassy, only to receive the caustic reply that there were thousands such children and the embassy could not be responsible for them. The agency decided it could no longer keep the child—the only alternative place for him was an African American orphanage.[9]

Buck and her husband were infuriated at blatant injustice and took Robbie in themselves until they found a permanent home for him. Initially,

5. Chung, "Transnational Adoption," 52–58.

6. Chung, "Transnational Adoption."

7. The name of the baby is inconsistent in Pearl Buck's writings. In *Children for Adoption* she used the name Robbie, while in other unpublished manuscripts she called him Ved or David. She may have used a pseudonym to protect the child's identity.

8. Chung, "Transnational Adoption."

9. Buck, "Other/'A Case Study: Welcome House,'" 4052 [BM Box 64, Folder 265.12 XIX]; *Children for Adoption*, 79.

it was indignation that moved her to get on the phone. However, as she held Robbie, anxiously sucking his thumb with his eyes "huge and tragic," she felt her anger replaced with intense love. Within a week after she met Robbie, Buck was given a newborn, only nine days old. His name was Peter, born from a Chinese father and an American mother.[10] In the weeks that followed, Buck relentlessly approached adoption agencies to find homes for the babies. The attempt was fruitless. When she asked what would become of the children, she received only a simple shrug or the explanation that agencies could not afford to accept unadoptable children.[11] The reality was clear: nobody wanted to adopt mixed-race children. Upon this premise, she proceeded toward the first stage of her organization.

She started to persuade friends and local people in her county to help her establish an adoption agency specializing in mixed-race children. She lived in a small, quiet community founded upon the precepts of the Quakers and Mennonites. The county council listened attentively as she poured her heart out, describing the appalling treatment of the mixed-race children. She then proposed founding an agency that would place special needs children in adoptive families, and specifically mixed-race children. Her worries that the community would not accept such a proposal were quenched when one of the members exclaimed, in his stout Pennsylvania Dutch accent, "We not only want them, but we will be proud to have them."[12] As the multiracial family grew, Buck and some community volunteers formed a board of directors and made a formal application to the State of Pennsylvania to set up a private adoption agency. The cautious yet sympathetic officers had never heard of Amerasian children and decided to do an investigation to see if there was a real need for a special agency. The State Department of Welfare canvassed other states, and the answer was overwhelmingly in the affirmative. Many adoption agencies throughout the country replied that mixed-race children were the greatest problem faced by adoption agencies.

Welcome House Inc. was approved by the State and became the first adoption agency to specialize in the adoption of mixed-race, especially mixed-Asian, children. Welcome House was permitted to receive and place for adoption children from any state in the Union, born in America but of Asian or part-Asian ancestry. Through a "referral system," many agencies collaborated with Welcome House and referred mixed-race children

10. Here, too, the name is inconsistent. In *Children for Adoption*, Buck called him Peter; all other unpublished manuscripts named him Lennie. See, for instance, Buck, "Other/Welcome House Inc.," 4052 [BM Box 65, Folder 266.10 IX].

11. Buck, "Other/'A Case Study: Welcome House'" [BM Box 64, Folder 265.12 XIX].

12. Buck, *Children for Adoption*, 83.

to Buck.[13] Letters sent from various adoption agencies and social workers to Welcome House proved the dire necessity of an agency specializing in interracial adoption.[14]

One incident Buck repeatedly shared in her articles and her book *Children for Adoption* was the story of Lennie, a half-Japanese five-month-old. His mother, a young Japanese woman, died after giving birth to Lennie, and the heartbroken father placed his child for adoption because his own family would not receive him. It was Lennie who convinced Buck that mixed-race children could be adopted. In one of Buck's speaking engagements, she suddenly decided to appeal to the large crowd of well-dressed, intelligent people on behalf of Lennie. The next day, she received a letter from a young Presbyterian minister and his wife. Buck warned the minister that having a half-Japanese son could one day be a hazard to his career due to the narrow-mindedness of some Christians. The young couple did not care.

Buck ended the story by recounting that several years later, when the minister was applying for a church, he wrote a letter concerning his adopted son. The church replied: "We have reduced the applications to two, yours and another young man's. We see by your application, however, that you have adopted a little half-Japanese son. You are the man we want."[15] Buck remarked that while she was deeply disappointed in missionaries such as Robbie's biological grandparents, she still had hope in Christianity because Christians like Lennie's parents gave a glimpse of Christ-like love in this world.

For Buck, one of the most rewarding aspects of managing Welcome House was seeing the change in the outlook of American citizens, not by force or compulsion but by enlargement of perspective. Through interacting with mixed-race children, the small community in Pennsylvania became more global-minded. Through the children, the countries they regarded as foreign became no longer strange to them:

> Small Timmy brings Siam into our own family of nations because his maternal grandparents were citizens of Siam. We are less critical of India . . . because Ted and Philip are half Indian. We found our prejudices are shallow unless they have built upon early hostility. This, I believe, is the truth for any people. Prejudices can be changed.[16]

13. Buck, "Other/'Welcome House Inc.'" [BM Box 65, Folder 266.10 IX].

14. Buck, "Other/Letters to Welcome House," 4052 [BM Box 65, Folder 266.16 XV].

15. Buck, *Children for Adoption*, 86–87; "Other/'A Case Study: Welcome House'" [BM Box 64, Folder 265.12 XIX].

16. Buck, "Other/'A Case History: Welcome House,'" 4052 [BM Box 65, Folder

It is noteworthy that Buck made the notion of friendship both personal and public. She formed deep friendships with mixed-race children on a personal level, yet also believed that global friendship on a collective level could ultimately solve the problem of communism, since the bridge formed between the West and the East could alleviate the tension and could potentially win Asia over.

She yearned for the adoption of mixed-race children to eliminate prejudice and bring about global friendship based on universal colorblindness. She argued that the key to eliminating prejudice was to understand that in spite of differences, all human beings were basically the same, created in the image of God. She contended that when prejudice was unresolved, it bore fear—fear of the unknown and the "other" that prevented the communication essential to peace and reconciliation in any community. Arguing that the "world is only a community," she envisioned harmony between the United States and Asia through mixed-race children.[17]

Her vision for global friendship and union propelled her to collaborate with a myriad of adoption agencies, religious groups, and charities across the world. Because she considered the happiness of children the most important goal of her work, she was able to work with any agency that was willing to commit to her mission. She was gratified that agencies that in the past had never accepted mixed-race children were open to placing them after working with Welcome House.[18]

Showing a positive view of religious pluralism, Buck believed that the spirit of true religion had no room for the religious division that was often combined with racial prejudice. She argued that the "divisive and possessive jealousies" of religious groups must be replaced with the spirit of true religion that granted the freedom to approach the Father God. She declared that all men were "brothers," that all humanity was God's children. Emphasizing that all human beings were equally created in the image of God, she argued that everyone must be united in the spirit of service to humanity. She further wrote that all professional social workers were "servants of humanity" and hence must be united as a community to get rid of the monstrous problems facing humanity.[19]

Pearl Buck, much like the missionaries who advocated global friendship and Christian internationalism, argued that the battle should not be against certain races or nations—the struggle against racism and prejudice

---

266.10 IX].

17. Buck, "Other/'A Case Study: Welcome House'" [BM Box 64, Folder 265.12].

18. Buck, "Other/'A Case History: Welcome House'" [BM Box 65, Folder 266.10 IX].

19. Buck, "Men as Beasts," 727 [BM Box 1, Folder 42].

was, according to her, against those who did not uphold the principle of human equality.[20] In a speech, which she gave as a commencement address at Howard University (a historically black university) on June 5, 1942, Buck beseeched the young African American students in her audience to not think of racism as a local issue, but as a global issue that affected all of humanity.[21]

Buck's belief in human solidarity and the transcendent character of love was hopeful, but not naïve. She admitted that while love was colorblind, people were not. She acknowledged that it was more difficult to break the racial barriers facing African American children than those facing other mixed-race children. Caucasian adoptive parents preferred Asian or Native American children, and the recalcitrant racial hierarchy of the time branded blackness as "unassimilable."[22] To further complicate the issue, several African American social workers opposed the placement of black children with white parents because transnational and transracial adoptions posed "a growing threat to the preservation of the black family."[23] Cenie J. Williams Jr., president of the National Association of Black Social Workers, insisted that even if institutionalization were the only alternative, black children must not be placed in white homes.

In one of her last articles, "I Am the Better Woman for Having My Two Black Children," Buck addressed this very issue. Depicting the lives of her adopted daughters Henriette and Cheiko, both half-African, she affirmed that their chances were better with love than without and that she considered them her treasures. She emphasized the unusual friendship she had with her children and that cross-cultural love was the basis of a true family.[24] She mourned the fact that whatever difficulty was associated with adopting transracially was a result of social stigma and suspicion, not biology.

In her article, Buck failed to provide a real answer to the troubling systemic racial hierarchy that persisted in transracial adoption. Her answer that a white mother could conquer racial prejudice is at worst imperialistic and at best idealistic. Although she rightly pointed out that any difficulty associated with adopting transracially was a result of social stigma and suspicion, not biology, she did not discuss how the social stigma surrounding black or half-black babies might be broken. However, by providing her own experience and expressing her personal commitment to half-black children,

20. Buck, "Breaking the Barriers of Race Prejudice."
21. Buck, "Breaking the Barriers of Race Prejudice."
22. Herman, *Kinship by Design*, 17.
23. Conn, *Pearl S. Buck*, 375.
24. Buck, "I Am the Better Woman."

she demonstrated that on a personal level, it is possible to overcome racial prejudice. To her, the adoption of her black German daughter represented not only her personal commitment but also a public statement against racial injustice. Her hope of expanding her personal experience to address more systemic, institutional racism was in sync with her rhetoric of motherhood and friendship.

Pearl Buck—a multiculturalist even before the phrase was popularized—paved the way for global friendship through special needs adoption. Through countless anecdotes and case studies, she proved that older children, children with mixed racial backgrounds, and children with deafness, heart conditions, palsy, or limited sight could become part of happy, loving families where global friendship could blossom. Although the theme of motherhood was prevalent in her adoption essays, the fact that she associated friendship with transnational adoption is significant. The relationship between parents and children has an innate power difference. To speak solely in those terms was to reproduce the paternalism Buck criticized in American mission history. She knew that when missionaries founded churches in Asia, the hierarchy between the missionaries and indigenous Christians was often framed with a father-child paradigm. If applied uncritically to transnational adoption, Westerners might appear, again, as the superior figures who condescended to look after the impoverished children of the world. Thus, Buck liked to characterize transnational adoption as a form of global friendship—a term that denoted equality and forwarded her commitment to anti-imperialism in mission. Her writings and speeches steadily changed the public's perception of special needs adoption by providing continuous evidence that such children were "adoptable."

HELEN DOSS'S ADOPTION AND FRIENDSHIP NARRATIVES

Helen Doss's popular narrative *The Family Nobody Wanted*, published in 1954, supplied the story component that was lacking in Pearl Buck's essays. While Buck's articles served as a corrective to American hypocrisy and racist rhetoric, Doss's narratives offered a strong antidote to the culture of secrecy by breaking the prolonged silence concerning transnational adoption. The stories also acted as a crucial tool promoting cross-cultural friendship and familial love. The book was so well received that Hollywood made two films out of it, and the Doss family appeared in numerous TV shows.

At a time when transnational adoption was just starting to gain a small amount of momentum, Doss's book was a refreshing reminder that transcultural friendship was possible. The Doss family was the kind of Christians Pearl Buck was looking for—people who were not just willing, but eager to adopt children who were labeled "unadoptable" by most adoption agencies. Moreover, the memoir demystified secretive adoption practices and broke the stigma of transnational adoption. At the time, a family consisting of children of different races was considered "inferior" to an adoptive family consisting of only white family members. By portraying a realistic picture of the joys, sorrows, challenges, and rewards of raising an international family, Helen Doss normalized the practice of transnational adoption.

After finally convincing adoption agencies that race made no difference to them, the Doss couple adopted twelve children of color: Indian, Native American, Filipino, Hawaiian, Balinese, Malayan, and Mexican, in diverse combinations. The public affectionately called Helen Doss's family the "United Nations Family" because it represented so many cultures and ethnicities. The Doss family story was well received because, despite the unique quality of being a multi-ethnic family, it struck common chords and evoked a sense of ordinariness, commonality, and normalcy. Although the twelve children varied significantly in cultural background and race, they otherwise lived everyday lives in mid-twentieth-century America. Moreover, the baby boom audience found the story of a mother raising twelve children a reinforcement of the value attributed to the nuclear family.

In an episode of a TV show called "You Bet Your Life" that aired on December 17, 1954, Helen exclaimed, "Children do not really realize [the racial difference] . . . they know they are theoretically different but doesn't make any difference. For instance, my two oldest boys always play cowboy and Indian. But the blonde, blue-eyed boy plays the Indian and the Indian boy plays the cowboy."[25] According to Helen, the Doss children were truly colorblind. When Donny (Caucasian) was eight and Alex (Japanese, Burmese, and Korean mixed-race) was one year old, Donny said as he fondly glanced at Alex, "If he was seven years older, and if I had black hair, everybody would think that him and me was twins!" Helen and Carl were proud that their children took it for granted that they were alike simply because they were a "really real family." The children appeared exotic and different as separate people, but together they were a collection of silly, adorable, and seemingly ordinary American siblings.[26] They became true friends with one another despite their physical differences.

25. Marx, "You Bet Your Life #54–14."
26. Doss, *Family Nobody Wanted*, 164, 119; Herman, *Kinship by Design*, 213.

However, Doss's narrative was not just a story about a happy, ordinary family. Her adoption narrative spoke directly against competing narratives that denied the validity of cross-cultural friendship. Rather than attacking American racism, Doss moved readers and convinced them with her poignant stories and funny episodes. Instead of hiding, she openly communicated her adoption stories to her children, her relatives, and the public. She promoted colorblind love, but not racial essentialism that disregarded distinctiveness. She championed openness and was vocal about her stories and her faith, but with discernment and gentleness. Ordinary Americans were drawn to her stories because of these paradoxes—a family that was unique yet ordinary; colorblind yet distinct; bold yet humble.

Like Pearl Buck, Helen Doss advocated colorblind love and anti-racist rhetoric, but in a narrative form. By providing stories about an unconventional international family that was both ordinary and unique, she abated the stigma surrounding adoption and softened the dominant images of American family that promoted only homogeneity. Stating that skin color was a superficial thing, Helen and Carl were eager to adopt mixed-race children. One social worker who indignantly opposed this idea exclaimed, "I would rather see a child raised in an orphanage, than by parents who look so *different*. Crossing racial lines is against all our *principles* of good social-work practice."[27] She was one of many social workers influenced by the residue of eugenics principles. In response to this comment, Helen wrote that all races were alike underneath, the same in "range of intellect and capacity for moral and spiritual growth."[28]

Helen and Carl continued to face problems as they sought to adopt mixed-race children. When they wanted to adopt Rita, a social worker compared her with Susie, who had fairer skin: "Susie not only belongs to the dominant race, but also has beautiful blue eyes and blonde hair. How will poor little Rita feel, when the neighbor girls invite Susie to their birthday parties, their dances and slumber parties, and Rita isn't asked?" Despite the softer language compared to that used in previous decades, the principle of eugenics still governed the social worker's understanding of the "dominant race." Helen wrote that their children did not regard themselves different from one another: "Naturally they could see that there were minor and inconsequential variations, that Rita had 'the blackest, shiniest hair,' that Teddy could toast browner in the sun than the rest, but persons bearing such unearned distinctions were polite enough not to gloat."[29]

27. Doss, *Family Nobody Wanted*, 29–31.

28. Doss, *Family Nobody Wanted*, 29–31.

29. Doss, *Family Nobody Wanted*, 61, 164.

The beauty of these stories was that they carried certain moral lessons without overtly criticizing the readers. Rather than *telling* the readers that racism was wrong, Helen *showed* why racial segregation and eugenics principles were absurd. Her efforts to tell stories continued with her writing of children's books dedicated to broadening children's perspective on race and ethnicity. In 1958 and 1959, she published *All the Children of the World* and *Friends Around the World*, respectively, to teach children about the "wonderful variety to be found in God's world, and among all God's children." She also introduced the concept of adoption, stating, "When a mother and father adopt a baby, they think that their baby is just right. They love everything about their baby. They are glad that their baby is different from every other baby." She concluded the short storybook by emphasizing God's boundary-less love for all children, who were equally created in the image of God.[30]

In *Friends Around the World*, Helen emphasized commonality more than distinctiveness. She wrote about various styles of living, food, work environment, and worship from India to Sweden. For example, in China, Pear Blossom "eats her rice and fish with chopsticks," and in Russia, Peter likes "a thick slice of dark wheat bread with his pork and cabbage soup." By doing so, Helen introduced various cultures around the world as distinctive and unique. However, her main objective was to demonstrate that despite cultural differences, children were fundamentally alike inside, and genuine cross-cultural friendship was possible:

> All around the world children are eating, sleeping, playing, learning, and worshipping, each in his own way. Anywhere you go in the world, when you meet other children, you can be friends with them. You can be friends because you are alike in so many ways. These are your friends, all around the world.[31]

In this and similar passages, she advocated the same principle promoted by ecumenists such as Pearl Buck: global friendship based on the understanding that all human beings were equally created in the image of God.

The greatest accomplishment of *The Family Nobody Wanted* was making race matters familiar, relatable, and believable. The characters in Helen's stories were common American people who could easily be anyone's neighbor—Rita's teacher, who assumed that Rita would *only* crave chili and hot tamales because of her Mexican heritage; neighbors who asked if Alex loved eating Asian chop suey; a white-haired lady who was surprised to

30. Doss, *All the Children of the World.*
31. Doss, *Friends around the World.*

find out about Helen's adoptive family after assuming that Susie (a blue-eyed, blonde-haired girl) was Helen's biological daughter.[32] These playful, innocuous episodes reminded the readers to reflect on their perspective and behavior and think again about race matters. The stories were relatable and familiar, not theoretical and abstract.

The Dosses reminded the readers of the radical nature of Christianity. The notion that all men and women were created equally in the image of God and that all men were brothers took a radical faith to genuinely believe in. This was the same radical Christianity that shaped the antislavery movement; the radical Christianity that advocated ecumenism focusing on global friendship; the radical Christianity that spearheaded the anti-racist movement among a myriad of missionaries. Helen further wrote that Americans were no better than communist saboteurs if they continued to step on others because of the color of their skin.

When the Dosses informed their relatives of their plans to adopt Gretchen, Carl's mother said, "Just don't be bringing her visiting to my house. . . . No [n-word] will call *me* Grandma!" Helen grieved the fact that even her friends tried to stop her. One well-intentioned friend commented that most white communities would never accept "a girl of Negro blood into the heart of their social doings, especially after she gets to be in her teens and close to marrying age." They even suggested that the Dosses disguise her African heritage and "label her as something else." Helen responded, "We're teaching our other children to be proud of their whole heritage. Have we the right to make her ashamed to be what she is?" The adoption of Gretchen eventually failed. Months passed after they filled out the releases and affidavits, but they never heard back from the agency. Lamenting the fact that prejudice was irrational and unpatriotic, they resented the bitter reality tainted with virulent racial hostility.[33]

In 1959, Helen Doss published *The Really Real Family*, an adoption narrative about Elaine and Diane, two girls from Hawaii who were adopted into the Doss family together. In a compassionate and compelling way, Helen narrated the story from Elaine's perspective. Putting herself in Elaine's shoes, she wrote, "We didn't have any daddy, and we missed not having a mother or a daddy like other children. . . . Wouldn't it be nice, to have a really *real* family, all our very own?"[34] In her typical storytelling fashion, Helen made the stories about sibling quarrels, the jealous sister, and funny episodes come alive. What Helen tried to portray throughout all her books

32. Doss, *Friends around the World*, 166, 42.

33. Doss, *Friends around the World*, 188–90.

34. Doss, *Really Real Family*.

was that her family was a *really real* family—neither superior nor inferior to the biological family, but *real* in every sense of the word. The children were *real* friends, no matter how different they appeared.

When asked if they would do the same thing—adopt the children—over again, the Dosses unabashedly replied that adopting the children was the single most enriching experience they had ever had. Through the title *The Family Nobody Wanted*, Helen Doss ultimately pointed out the irony that although outsiders imagined that their family was "made up of incompatible opposites," the Doss family emphatically consisted of children who were deeply wanted.[35] Toward the end of the book, she proved the title's falsehood and irony. The night before the adoption of their final children, Doss affirmed the central message of her narratives: "Our family was meant to be just this way."[36]

CONCLUSION

In addition to missionaries' focus on global friendship, secular programs promoting international friendship started to arise in the 1930s. One of the largest international friendship programs, the International Friendship League, was founded in 1936 by Edna MacDonough. The International Friendship League was the largest international pen pal matching service supported by the federal government. In the Cold War era, the theme of global friendship became solidified in the political realm. In 1956, the Eisenhower administration made capital of the popularity of international friendship organizations to promote the rebranding of America's image. In the mid-1950s, Americans sent 330 million letters abroad annually.[37]

The most significant difference between missionaries and secular cultural ambassadors, such as war veterans or agents employed through the United States Information Agency, was missionaries' reason for the emphasis on cross-cultural friendship. The ecumenical missionaries' promotion of global friendship was a form of Christian witness against colonialism and racism. Amid Christian internationalist language, many ecumenical Christians started to advocate for developing global friendship across divisions as a statement of unity and diversity in the kingdom of God. This was a welcome antidote to the traditional mission practice, tinged as it was with cultural imperialism and religious hierarchy. Rather than viewing missions

---

35. Doss, *Family Nobody Wanted*, 165.
36. Doss, *Family Nobody Wanted*, 266.
37. Helgren, *American Girls*, 59.

in terms of strategies or programs, ecumenists started to view missions as a lifelong practice of global friendship and Christian witness.[38]

Finally, the loving, maternal, and adoptive image of mothers nurturing an international family proved a popular alternative to combative discourses of masculinization and American imperialism in the Cold War context.[39] The expansionist discourse was softened by the imagery of women building a bridge across racial lines, all the while staying within the boundaries of the domestic sphere. Furthermore, the fact that female missionaries vocalized their Christian faith seemed restorative after decades of war and blood. The once-held confidence in Christendom had been eradicated, and the Christian West's morality had become dubious after decades of bloodshed. Amid this damage to the reputation of Western Christianity, missionaries' efforts in anti-imperialistic, anti-racist humanitarian projects offered hope to a cynical country.

Buck, Doss, and many other Protestant missionaries defended racial minorities and the principle of human equality at a time when the situation of minority groups was precarious in both the United States and abroad. This chapter has demonstrated that these ecumenical, internationalist Christians used an anti-racist, anti-imperialist rhetoric to promote global friendship and human equality. Through transnational adoption, they sought to spread a holistic and oppositional focus on racism and their penetrating disgust with American imperialism. Their Christian values were closely in sync with the ecumenical mission thought that flourished from the 1920s to the 1960s.[40] Their vision for global friendship and anti-racism stemmed from their lifelong philosophy that all human beings were equally created in the divine likeness. To them, then, transnational adoption was merely another extension of the Christian practice.

BIBLIOGRAPHY

Buck, Pearl S. "Breaking the Barriers of Race Prejudice." *The Journal of Negro Education* 11.4 (1942) 444–53.
———. *Children for Adoption*. New York: Random, 1964.
———. "I Am the Better Woman for Having My Two Black Children." *Today's Health*, January 1972.
———. The Pearl S. Buck Literary Manuscripts Collection [BM]. West Virginia & Regional History Center, Morgantown, WV.

38. Robert, *Faithful Friendships*.

39. Klein, *Cold War Orientalism*, 189.

40. Thompson, "Sherwood Eddy," 65–93.

Chung, Soojin. "Transnational Adoption: A Noble Cause? Female Missionaries as Pioneers of Transnational Adoption, 1945–1965." *Evangelical Missions Quarterly* 52.4 (2016) 52–58.

Conn, Peter. *Pearl S. Buck: A Cultural Biography*. Cambridge: Cambridge University Press, 1996.

Doss, Helen. *All the Children of the World*. Nashville, TN: Abingdon, 1958.

———. *The Family Nobody Wanted*. Boston: Northeastern University Press, 1954.

———. *Friends around the World*. Nashville, TN: Abingdon, 1959.

———. *The Really Real Family*. Boston: Little, Brown, 1959.

Helgren, Jennifer. *American Girls and Global Responsibility: A New Relation to the World during the Early Cold War*. Rutgers, NJ: Rutgers University Press, 2017.

Herman, Ellen. *Kinship by Design: A History of Adoption in the Modern United States*. Chicago: University of Chicago Press, 2008.

Kevles, Daniel J. *In the Name of Eugenics: Genetics and the Uses of Human Heredity*. Berkeley: University of California Press, 1985.

Klein, Christina. *Cold War Orientalism: Asia in the Middlebrow Imagination 1945–1961*. Berkeley: University of California Press, 2003.

Marx, Groucho. "You Bet Your Life #54–14." December 16, 1954. *YouTube* video, October 17, 2013. Online. https://www.youtube.com/watch?v=Gwm-Vn35oO4 &ab_channel=GrouchoMarx-YouBetYourLife.

May, Elaine Tyler. *Barren in the Promised Land: Childless Americans and the Pursuit of Happiness*. Cambridge, MA: Harvard University Press, 1995.

Quiroz, Pamela Anne. "From Race Matching to Transnational Adoption: Race and the Changing Discourse of US Adoption." *Critical Discourse Studies* 5.3 (2008) 249–64.

Robert, Dana L. *Faithful Friendships: Embracing Diversity in Christian Community*. Grand Rapids, MI: Eerdmans, 2019.

Thompson, Michael G. "Sherwood Eddy, the Missionary Enterprise, and the Rise of Christian Internationalism in 1920s America." *Modern Intellectual History* 12 (2014) 65–93.

Friends for Mission

Émilie Mallet and Albertine de Broglie

MICHÈLE MILLER SIGG

In 1832, a cholera epidemic ravaged Paris, shutting down the city, wreaking economic devastation, and causing the terrified population to barricade themselves in their homes or to flee. In April of that year, all the annual assemblies of the many voluntary societies that had been born from the vigor of the Evangelical Revival or *Réveil* in France were canceled. In the midst of the chaos of death and dying, Madame Émilie Mallet (*née* Oberkampf) set up a temporary infirmary in a large, refurbished building to care for the poor wretches that the overflowing hospitals could no longer take in. "There," wrote Marie-Pape Carpantier, "impervious to imaginary dangers and confronting real dangers with the most admirable simplicity, she served the sick, exhorted the dying, consoled the desperate, promised mothers to adopt their orphans, husbands to care for their widows, young men to provide for their aged mothers. . . . And she acquitted herself scrupulously of these sacred debts."[1]

In circumstances not unlike the coronavirus pandemic, extraordinary courage, commitment, and compassion drove Mallet to pioneer, despite her frequent ill health, numerous initiatives to alleviate desperate human needs. Some were temporary, like the one described above, others long lasting, but all were out of her love of Jesus, with the help of close friends.[2] A common

---

1. This quote is from an obituary notice in *L'Ami de l'Enfance* by Marie-Pape Carpantier, an early education pioneer, quoted/paraphrased in Merlin, "Mme. Jules Mallet," 95.

2. Her monumental legacy in early childhood education—just to mention one initiative—in France received little or no recognition until the end of the nineteenth century, when it was documented by Protestants such as Henriette de Witt-Guizot

56

thread in all of Mallet's endeavors was the presence of likeminded female friends who labored alongside her in the work of mission: rescuing street children and vulnerable women, advocating for female inmates, pioneering new forms of Christian education, distributing Bibles, raising funds, and creating awareness for international missions.[3] One secret to the enduring success of her many charitable projects was the fact that she was a self-effacing leader and sought to mentor young female friends. As an integral component of her work in mission, Mallet instinctively nurtured numerous friendships as she organized charitable endeavors across denominational and national boundaries with powerful, devout, likeminded individuals.[4]

Mallet's powerful Christian witness was a model of mission and friendship that offers inspiration for confronting many of the same social ills we face today in the long struggle of Christian holistic mission. Her ministry not only offered hope to her contemporaries suffering from poverty, ignorance, and marginalization but she and one of her friends, Albertine de Broglie, devised a theology of female leadership in mission that inspired and empowered a new generation of Christian women to be bearers of the good news, both at home and abroad.

---

and Frank Puaux. See Witt-Guizot, *Une belle vie*; Puaux, *Les œuvres du protestantisme français*. The "partial rediscovery" of Mallet continued in the late twentieth century thanks to the work of scholars like Catherine Duprat and Jean-Noël Luc Robert, "Mallet (Madame) Emilie Oberkampf," 233.

3. I use the terms mission/missionary for Mallet's works of social renewal and holistic outreach, whether at home or abroad, including her initiatives in education. However, she never would have described herself or her work using those words. The term "missionnaire" belonged only to the vocabulary of Catholic missions because of the history of Protestant persecution in which Catholic missionaries were sent to forcibly convert Protestants to Catholicism.

4. Mallet's diverse friends include prominent Catholic Marquise de Pastoret in the infant school movement, the Duchess Albertine de Broglie in the women's auxiliary of the *Société Biblique Protestante de Paris* [Protestant Bible Society of Paris] and the women's committee of the *Société des Missions Évangéliques de Paris* [Paris Evangelical Missionary Society], British Quaker and prison reformer Elizabeth Fry in the ladies' committee of St. Lazare (a women's prison in Paris), and Mme. Pelet de la Lozère in the founding of the deaconesses of Reuilly (one of the earliest deaconess communities in Europe). She corresponded with many prominent figures, both male and female. Internationally, she developed a close epistolary friendship with Catholic Fr. Lambruschini, who had been censured by the Catholic Church for his pedagogical methods, and with Swiss Protestant Mathilde Calandrini, both in the infant school movement in Italy.

MALLET'S IDEA OF MISSION AND FRIENDSHIP

Mission and Christian friendship were intimately connected in Mallet's life, the one growing out of the fertile soil of the other. Each friendship belonged to a relational triangle in which Mallet and her friend were united by a third person—Jesus—who called them to his service in the world. The two friends (human friendship), united by their love for Jesus (divine friendship), reached out in service to their neighbor (mission). Like a three-legged stool, this triangle of human friendship, divine friendship, and mission formed a stable foundation on which any work of compassion could rest and thrive. Today, one might even use the term "missional friendship" to capture the inextricable relationship between the witness of the gospel and the love of friends. Put otherwise, in this concept, the mission that Jesus calls his followers to always arises out of loving relationships in the Christian community—the community in which Jesus is the first and ultimate friend.

The First Friend: Jesus, Model of Ultimate Love and Human Friendship

Jesus speaks about the relationship between mission and friendship in his teaching about the "new commandment" in the Gospel of John:

> This is my commandment, that you love one another as I have loved you. No one has greater love than this, to lay down one's life for one's friends. You are my friends if you do what I command you. I do not call you servants any longer, because the servant does not know what the master is doing; but I have called you friends, because I have made known to you everything that I have heard from my Father. (John 15:12–15 NRSV)

Here Jesus expands on the new commandment that he introduced in John 13:34. It includes mutual love between disciples that is the mark that they belong to Jesus ("By this everyone will know that you are my disciples, if you have love for one another" [John 13:35 NRSV]) and ultimately the sacrificial, life-giving love that *is* the good news—Jesus' death on the cross ("No one has greater love than this, to lay down one's life for one's friends").

Mallet's writing offers a window into how her friendship with Jesus informed her relationships with her neighbors. Her love for him and her desire to imitate him gave her a deep sense of her many duties to different groups of people. In one of her family prayers, this list of "duties" appears as a series of spiritual disciplines: to God, she had the duty of "contemplation, prayer, constant recourse to Him"; to humanity, "charity, devotion, unwavering kindness, humility"; to parental authority, "submission, respect, obedience, love"; and to enemies, "patience, forbearance, forgiveness for insults."[5]

Mallet published *Christian Prayers for Families*, a book of morning and evening prayers based on Scripture, in 1836. Intended for family devotions, it became a classic among French Protestants and went through seven editions over the next five decades. This excerpt of one of her prayers, titled "Concerning the Example and Imitation of the Lord Jesus Christ," provides the key to the essential qualities of Christ-like friendship:

> Every instant of our life we must have in front of our eyes what you did, oh Jesus, in order to know what we must do. When we are tested, we must remember your patience that also makes us patient; when we are tempted, we must remember how and with which words you pushed back the Spirit of darkness; when we are discouraged, we must not forget that you called for your Heavenly Father's help with prayers and ardent supplications: in the hours of heart-wrenching anguish, we must say with you, "May it be, oh God, not what I want, but what you want." Finally, Lord, at the hour of our death, may we say with love and obedience, "Father, I release my spirit into your hands." We see in the holy Gospels the way the Lord Jesus often spent the night in prayer, on the mountains, far from commotion. Could we not benefit from this touching example, and spend significant time in prayer during the last moments of the day? Oh God, please help us, through your Spirit of prayer "may he pray himself in us" and may he be the one who pleads with you to grant our humble request. Amen.[6]

Here Mallet describes Jesus' patient dependence on God's help "in the hours of heart-wrenching anguish," his humble obedience to his Father's will ("not what I want, but what you want"), and his devotion to and faith in the Father ("I release my spirit into your hands"). This portrait expresses her admiration for Jesus' self-sacrificing ministry as a "model for what we must do" that inspired her to deeper devotion ("could we not benefit from this touching example?"). Mallet's description of Jesus' model provides the essential characteristics of her missional friendships: devout faith, sacrificial love, gentle dependence, humility, and mutual admiration and inspiration.

---

5. Mallet, *Prières Chrétiennes*, 133–34. The title of this prayer (Prayer LX) was "*Sur l'Exemple et l'Imitation du Seigneur Jésus-Christ* [Concerning the Example and Imitation of the Lord Jesus Christ]." Mallet's several written works, including this one, were published without identifying her as the author. N.B. All translations from the French are mine unless otherwise indicated.

6. Mallet, *Prières Chrétiennes*, 133–34.

Mallet lived with a tender sense of dependence on Jesus' everyday help in her most burdensome and lonely tasks. In the following letter, she speaks about the challenges she faced while raising money for infant schools and for the work with the deaconesses of Reuilly:[7]

> Last year [1848] . . . I suffered greatly in body and soul, while I witnessed so much misery, I exhausted myself in my efforts to try and remedy it, and I constantly had the feeling I was trying to lift an enormous boulder. . . .
>
> As I cannot reach Mr. de Falloux [minister of education], I constantly have to write to this person and that person to send them requests and comments, always regarding my poor [infant] schools.
>
> Now, I must find the means to support the new schools that I have opened and the additional ones I want to open. . . . Add to these interests those of the Protestant work of the faubourg Saint Marcel [house of deaconesses]; it is all connected. These are my worries; the details would be interminable. When it comes down to action, all I have done is to go every day, or almost every day, to the twelfth district, in the sole, invisible, and divine company of the Lord.[8]

The response to her prayers for God's guidance and blessing enabled her to persevere in spite of the heavy burdens that she carried: "From that

7. Infant schools were designed to teach small children between the ages of two and six, following a certain pedagogy, depending on the location. In France, they were originally conceived to care for poor children without parental supervision. Infant schools were precursors to kindergarten. The concept evolved differently in Britain and in France. In the early 1840s, Pastor Antoine Vermeil and Caroline Malvesin founded an order of Protestant deaconesses, the Deaconesses of Reuilly, in an effort to reignite the flames of revival among a very divided Protestant population. Mallet was part of the founding committee. Through her friendship with British Quaker and prison reformer Elizabeth Fry, Mallet began to work in prison reform to help female inmates at the infamous prison of St. Lazare. Mallet was a member of the St. Lazare Committee [*Comité de St. Lazare*]. The *Comité de St. Lazare* was started in 1839, after Fry's second visit to France. There were twenty women on the committee. They visited the Protestant female prisoners in the prison of St. Lazare. Mallet supported the founding of the Deaconesses because it was the solution to their wish to create a sort of "halfway house," that is, a place for the rehabilitation of former female prisoners.

8. Mallet, *Prières Chrétiennes*, 416–17. This letter (Text 14), dated April 16, 1849, was addressed to her friend Sophie Pelet de la Lozère (quoted in article by Jean-Noël Luc in *Femmes Pédagogues*). The twelfth district is where Mallet opened infant schools and where the work of the deaconesses was located. Mallet had to appeal to two successive ministers of education, both husbands of her friends—Mr. Guizot and Mr. Pelet de la Lozère—to defend the interests of the women's committee in the work of infant education.

moment on, I had complete peace; everything went as if [carried out] by an invisible hand."[9]

Learning from Human Example

Growing up, Mallet witnessed self-sacrificing love modeled by the lives of her parents. Born in 1794, Mallet was the daughter of famous businessman Christophe-Philippe Oberkampf, descendant of a long line of Lutheran dyers in Wurtemburg, and his second wife, Élisabeth Massieu, of Huguenot descent. In the town of Jouy-en-Josas where they lived, right outside of Paris, Mallet witnessed her father's deep compassion for the working masses. He sheltered many of these poor in his factory during the terrifying attacks and pillages that the Prussians made at the end of Napoleon's reign in 1814.

Oberkampf's textile factory, *la manufacture de Jouy,* in Jouy-en-Josas, became a thriving industry locally and nationally and was famous for its printed cottons. Its success revived the region for fifty years, starting in 1760. In 1791, Oberkampf was elected mayor of the town against his will, with thirty out of thirty-nine votes. In 1806, he was awarded the Legion of Honor by Napoleon. During the Napoleonic wars, he protected his workers and supplied their needs until he died of exhaustion and illness in October of 1815, followed by his wife a year later.[10] Émilie was twenty-one.

A fascinating literary allusion suggests that Mallet's father was widely remembered as a man of exceptional self-sacrificing devotion to the local people. In 1834, Victor Hugo rented a house in Jouy-en-Josas for his mistress Juliette Drouet.[11] Although it was many years after the death of Oberkampf, his reputation would no doubt have lived on in popular memory. In his magnum opus *les Misérables,* Hugo painted his Christ-like protagonist Jean Valjean as the benevolent inventor, entrepreneur, and mayor of Montreuil-sur-Mer, a town described as being close to Paris, like Jouy, whose factory renewed the local economy. Several details of Jean Valjean's life in Montreuil-sur-Mer bear an uncanny resemblance to that of Oberkampf in Jouy.

9. Mallet, *Prières Chrétiennes,* 416.

10. Labouchère, *Oberkampf,* 3, 4, 84, 157, 222, 225.

11. This is a well-known local fact, and Juliette Drouet's house is a tourist attraction today in Jouy. See Office du Tourisme, Jouy-en-Josas, "Bienvenue."

Finding New Faith during the Réveil

A few years after the closing of her father's factories, Émilie and her husband Jules Mallet moved to Paris. There she quickly developed a dynamic social life among the *Haute Société Protestante* [Protestant High Society] and enjoyed the company of many friends.[12] However, grief drove her to seek comfort in the reading of the Bible that contained "those great truths which were the strong rock of consolation to the persecuted Huguenots."[13] Bibles could not be purchased in Paris, so she had to order one from Geneva.

In 1826, as she read Scripture and eagerly listened to the sermons of revivalist pastor Frédéric Monod, she understood Christ's message of love and hope, and her heart awakened to a vibrant, new faith. From then on, her commitment to infant education and other charitable endeavors deepened, along with her sense of duty and her sense of her own sinfulness.[14] Her life went through a dramatic transformation: "The truths of the Gospel, hitherto either coldly accepted or carelessly neglected, became once more a living power."[15] As a result, "From that moment on, indeed, . . . the life of Madame Jules Mallet was nothing more than an act of love. . . . Charity invaded her soul!"[16] Her biographer, Henriette de Witt-Guizot, herself a product of the *Réveil* and well aware of the international character of the revival sweeping through France, described it this way:

> The eighteenth century thought it had for ever [sic] abolished Christianity through its philosophical discoveries; the Revolution had drowned it in blood, and the Directory in pleasures; nevertheless, in spite of repeated blows and the long reign of religious indifference, it had once more emerged from the ruin which crushed it, and arisen, alive and vigorous, before the very eyes of those who had seen it descend to the tomb. . . . In Germany, Switzerland and England the same revival was on foot, and was seen in the over-filled churches and chapels. In France, along with the old doctrines were revived the heroic memories of the past; charitable institutions sprang up on all sides, and the Société Biblique, although barely started, freely distributed copies of this precious but too often deprived inheritance amongst

---

12. The *Haute Société Protestante* included members of Protestant nobility and high bourgeoisie.

13. Witt-Guizot, *Christian Woman*, 33.

14. Luc, *Femmes pédagogues*, 388–89.

15. Witt-Guizot, *Christian Woman*, 34.

16. Carpantier, *Foi et Vie*, 95.

the families of the very men whose blood had been so freely shed in its defense.[17]

The *Réveil* breathed new life into the faith of many traditional Reformed Protestants. When it set Mallet's faith afire, it equipped her with exceptional strength for the work of mission. This strength grew in her love of Jesus and in the friendship of devout women in the family of God.

Finding Likeminded Friends among Female Philanthropists

Soon after she arrived in Paris, Mallet found a group of likeminded female friends—women involved in various forms of philanthropy and fundraising who were "striving to help and instruct the poor and the ignorant."[18] Mallet first joined the women's auxiliary of the Protestant Bible Society of Paris (*Société Biblique Protestante de Paris*) that began under the leadership of Sigismond Billing and Albertine de Broglie in April 1823. Of the eighteen women founders, at least two thirds would be involved in the women's committee of the Paris Evangelical Missionary Society, which began in 1825.[19] Mallet soon became a founder and leader of the infant school movement as well, which would be one of her most remarkable legacies.

The rise of female philanthropists came in response to the state of French society at that time. After the upheaval of the 1789 Revolution and the dismantling of the Catholic Church during the period of "dechristianization," the social reality of the family had suffered a terrible blow. Many families had collapsed under the weight of poverty, abuse, the loss of paternal authority, rising rates of cohabitation, and distressing numbers of abandoned children.[20] Beginning in the last decades of the eighteenth

17. Witt-Guizot, *Christian Woman*, 35.

18. Witt-Guizot, *Christian Woman*, 37.

19. Douen, *Histoire de la Société biblique protestante de Paris*, 323. In Appendix 1, titled "Société Biblique Auxiliaire des Dames de Paris," the eighteen founders included "de Broglie,* Gautier Delessert,* Dominique André,* Baronness Matthieu de Faviers, Mandrot, Kieffer,* Frédéric Monod,* Jules Mallet,* Stapfer,* Juillerat,* François Delessert,* Baronness Hottinguer, Baronness S. de Berckheim,* de Salvandy, Countess Rapp, Scherer, Bartholdi née Walther,* Mark Wilks.*" The starred names are those of future members of the Paris Mission women's committee or of spouses of Paris Mission executive members (sometimes they were both). Most of these women were members of the *Haute Société Protestante* (High Protestant Society).

20. Before 1830, somewhere between 22 and 27 percent of Parisians were considered indigent (the poorest of the poor). The number of poor and indigent Parisians in 1846 was around 635,000, or 67 percent of the population of the *département* of the Seine (that included Paris and its immediate suburbs). Between 1815 and 1841, in Paris alone, one child out of three was born out of wedlock. To make things worse, such

century, this crisis, in particular the plight of poor women and children, had inspired devout Parisian women, both Catholic and Protestant, to create philanthropic initiatives to provide secure housing and education for them.

Mallet and her friends belonged to what became a social phenomenon of female activism and philanthropy born out of the *Réveil* and this dire socioeconomic situation. In the first half of the nineteenth century, a specifically female expression of philanthropy developed in France—*le patronage*—that funded the education and sponsorship of children.[21] To describe a role that had become common at that time, a new term emerged in French vocabulary—*dame patronnesse* [lady patron or philanthropist]. There was no masculine equivalent.[22] Mallet and Albertine de Broglie were among the leading *dames patronnesses* at that time.

DUCHESS ALBERTINE DE BROGLIE: A RARE FRIENDSHIP

Among Mallet's many friendships, one seems to have struck the perfect combination of relational harmony and unified vision for the role of women in the work of mission. With Mallet, de Broglie was a leader in the women's auxiliary of the Protestant Bible Society and the Paris Mission women's committee, and she also provided crucial support in other works

births led to a large number of abandoned children—an average of 5,327 per year between 1830 and 1836 in Paris and its immediate surroundings, making a total of 37,291 in those seven years. In the whole country, the approximate number of abandoned children being cared for in the hospices was 40,000 in 1784 (estimate by Minister Necker); 67,966 in 1815; 99,349 in 1819; and 129,699 in 1834—a 91 percent increase between 1814 and 1834 (Duprat, *Usage et pratiques de la philanthropie*, 1:6, 9, 25, 38, 87; 2:592, 594).

21. Duprat described "*le patronage*" [translated patronage, sponsorship, support] as "the only institutional invention of French philanthropy in the early nineteenth century." Initially this form of patronage that developed between 1821 and 1843 as "assistance for training or learning" came to be defined as "protection, help that some associations give to the poor: 'Sponsorship of orphan children.'" She noted that the idea of *patronage* applied exclusively to work among youth (Duprat, *Usage et pratiques de la philanthropie*, 2:671–72).

22. One of the newer meanings of the masculine term *patron* at the time was "master of the establishment," which corresponds to the modern meaning, still in use today, of "boss." The feminine form *patronnesse,* on the other hand, was used in the expression "*dame patronnesse*" [patron lady] to describe a woman who organized charity balls to raise money for the poor. This idea of charitable impulse toward the poor was never an aspect of the masculine term in contemporary dictionaries: "The *patron* was never defined as one who, on a personal level or as a member of an association, exercised protective or educational tutelage over a poor child or anyone in a situation of weakness" (Duprat, *Usage et pratiques de la philanthropie*, 2:672–73).

of compassion such as Mallet's work in infant school education. At a time when it was not culturally appropriate for women to assume certain public roles—these were reserved for their husbands—Mallet and de Broglie were not afraid to be exceptions to the rule when Christian duty called. Not only that, they both passionately believed in women's inherent giftedness in missionary work. Together, de Broglie and Mallet developed a radical theology of women's leadership in mission.

Albertine de Broglie's Background

Duchess Albertine de Broglie (née de Staël-Holstein) was the daughter of Germaine de Staël and granddaughter of Suzanne Necker (née Curchod, wife of Minister Necker, 1739–1794), who were both illustrious *salonnières* of the eighteenth century.[23] De Broglie assumed leadership of her mother's famous salon after she died in 1817.[24] She and her husband played leading roles in Parisian Christianity, and both were on executive committees of numerous evangelical boards or women's auxiliary societies.[25] While it may be true that in 1818, the *Réveil* began to flourish in Paris after the arrival of the charismatic pastor Frédéric Monod, de Broglie also played a pioneering role in providing a forum for discussion of the new theological ideas in her salon.[26] As the daughter of Mme. de Staël, she was in an excellent position to influence public opinion and play an evangelistic role in the spread of the *Réveil* among highbrow Parisians. But she was also an extraordinary figure with her own merits, even if she was not as famous as her mother. A collection of de Broglie's essays published in 1840 under the title *Fragments sur divers sujets de religion et de morale* [*Fragments on various topics of religion and morality*] showcased her intellectual acumen, visionary spirituality, charismatic personality, and devout faith. All these traits made her an ideal

23. Madame de Staël (1766–1817) was an internationally known figure at the time. A *salonnière* was a woman of the nobility who hosted regular meetings in her home to discuss politics, literature, art, music, and other socially relevant topics with members of the nobility or the educated bourgeoisie.

24. An interesting detail in de Broglie's biography is her parentage. According to Renée Winegarten, de Broglie was the child of Germaine de Staël's passionate liaison with Swiss writer Benjamin Constant. After her mother's death, de Broglie destroyed any incriminating correspondence that would reveal her illegitimacy and damage her mother's reputation. De Broglie shared this precarious social status with Julie-Jeanne-Eléanore de Lespinasse, one of the leading *salonnières* of the eighteenth century, also the child of an adulterous liaison. See Winegarten, *Germaine de Staël and Benjamin Constant*, 100–101; Goodman, *Republic of Letters*, 308.

25. Thomas Erskine quoted in Wemyss, *Histoire du Réveil,* 112.

26. Wemyss, *Histoire du Réveil,* 113.

figure to lead the Protestant women of Paris with her friend Mallet in the missionary enterprise.

"Because it was [she], because it was I"

The manner in which Mallet describes her friendship with de Broglie resembles humanist writer Michel de Montaigne's portrait of perfect friendship. In his essay by the same title (*"De l'amitié"* or *"De Amicitia"*), Montaigne wrote, "In the friendship I am speaking of, [our souls] mingle and blend so completely into one another in so complete a mixture, that they efface the seam between them so it can no longer be found. Were I to be pressed to say why I loved him, I feel that it can be expressed only by replying, 'Because it was he, because it was I.'"[27]

Mallet and de Broglie shared a deep admiration for one another that was rooted in their shared values and their commitment to the work of mission. In her journal, Mallet describes her warm affection for her friend and an intimate connection somewhat akin to Montaigne's "mingling of souls":

> The first time that I met the Duchesse de Broglie I felt as if I had seen an angel; her eyes are so beautiful, and her soul betrays itself so clearly in them, that it would be impossible to find a more noble and intellectual countenance, although she is hardly possessed of actual beauty. I have often seen her at our schools, at the *Pensionnat* and *Société Biblique,* and have also visited with her among the poor. She is entirely devoted to good works; and thus I have quickly formed an intimacy with her which years of ordinary intercourse would not have brought about. I am much attached to her and believe that the feeling is mutual. These are our daily relations, but when we meet in society we hardly know what to say to one another; it seems as if we were two different people.[28]

Contrary to the classical model of friendship in which physical beauty plays a large role, Mallet is drawn to de Broglie because of her spiritual beauty—she appears to be like an angel and is devoted to "good works." In like manner to what Montaigne describes elsewhere in his essay, time is compressed in the development of their intimacy. Closeness deepens quickly and is rooted in their shared vision for mission and their heart for works of compassion. It is also their shared mission that prompts their friendship to flourish quickly. The shyness that Mallet mentions in the last sentence above

27. Montaigne and Boétie, *Selected Essays,* 79.

28. Witt-Guizot, *Christian Woman,* 38–39.

seems to indicate that in the prosaic context of a worldly social life, such as de Broglie's *salon,* they were somewhat at a loss. In that context, without the supporting vocation of mission, their relationship seems to have lost its center. Their piety and spiritual maturity, which fueled their life's work, was the intimate source of their friendship, the outgrowth of which was their work of compassion and mission.

As strong leaders, the two friends could depend upon one another and worked together in a complementary fashion. Mallet was more self-effacing and seems to have had a talent for organization and administration, being content to take a backseat to de Broglie's charismatic leadership. In 1823, Mallet organized the women's auxiliary of the Bible Society of which de Broglie was the leader (along with Sigismond Billing). Two years later, on April 29, 1825, de Broglie called a meeting in her home. She felt so deeply moved by the missionary reports she had heard at the annual General Assembly of the Paris Evangelical Missionary Society, that she invited Mallet and a handful of other women (also members of the Bible Society women's auxiliary) who had attended the assembly. This group of friends immediately began organizing the women's committee of the Paris Mission, in which both de Broglie and Mallet would serve in leadership roles. Here again, friendship led to visionary leadership.

FASHIONING A COMMON VISION FOR WOMEN IN CHRISTIAN LEADERSHIP

De Broglie and Mallet worked closely in their leadership roles for the Bible Society and the Paris Mission, collaborating on written reports and official documents. Both strongly defended what they believed was the divinely appointed role of, and, in fact, superiority of women for mission work because they believed women were ideally outfitted, spiritually and intellectually, to work among the poor. De Broglie authored the Paris Mission women's committee's first annual report of 1826, with input from Mallet and the rest of the women on the committee.[29] In the report, she first addressed

29. The report was complemented by two brief appended documents at the end of the General Assembly minutes. De Broglie was the leading author of the report, no doubt with input from the committee. The other two documents were signed as being "from the Paris Mission Women's Committee." It is probable that de Broglie worked on them, perhaps with help from Mallet. The handwriting of the minutes was faded and hard to decipher. The minutes of the women's committee meeting on April 5, 1826, specified that Mallet read the letter to the group and that de Broglie wrote "most of it." However, some of the language was directly taken from the monthly minutes that were probably written by Mallet. Because de Broglie was not the sole author, the 1826 annual

the all-male executive committee with a shrewd defense of their right, as women, to initiate the creation of their committee independently of male permission: "One might find, in our resolution [to create an auxiliary society to cooperate in the holy enterprise (of missions)] a sort of recklessness, since your consent didn't incite it; but the same goal, the same idea must, of course, produce the same efforts."[30] These words expressed a quiet but unshakeable confidence. The women's committee was clearly stating that they did not have to ask anyone's permission to start their committee because they answered to God alone to fulfill their Christian calling. They considered themselves to be coworkers with their male counterparts, equally and directly accountable to God for their actions.

The first reports and founding documents of the Paris Mission women's committee were directly inspired by an earlier text written by de Broglie. While she and Mallet belonged to the women's auxiliary of the Protestant Bible Society, de Broglie penned a seminal essay, "*Sur les Associations Bibliques de Femmes* [Regarding Women's Bible Associations]," that was published in the first pages of the leading missionary journal at the time, *les Archives du Christianisme* [*Archives of Christianity*], a placement that gave the text prominence even though it did not identify the female author by name.[31] De Broglie argued that women had natural gifts and deeper piety that made them better candidates than men for the work of missions. She explained that her thinking had developed from personal experience and empirical observations regarding the way men and women functioned in society.

Women Make Ideal Missionaries

In "Regarding Women's Bible Associations," de Broglie painted a profile of "Bible Women" (women who distributed Bibles for Bible Societies) that reads almost like a job advertisement. First, she said, women are detail oriented and better at running the household, making them therefore more adept at distributing "assistance and consolation." Second, women are resourceful because they can do a lot of good "at very little cost." Third, they know how to gain the trust of the poor and are less liable to be duped by false stories when giving out charity because they are better judges of character. They also know how to treat others with dignity regardless of their economic status

---

report was not republished in her *Fragments*.

30. DEFAP, *Procès Verbal de l'Assemblée Générale*, 59.

31. Broglie, *Archives du Christianisme*, 8. This appeared in the "Miscellanea" ("*Variétés*") section, at the beginning of the issue. Later, de Broglie published it in a book of her collected writings.

(e.g., the poor). Next, it follows that women more easily establish relationships between poor and rich that are not based on power dynamics "because they have no active role in the social order." In other words, the humble position of women is an advantage in their work among the poor.[32] Fifth, women are more adapted to the long-range work of missions because they are more patient, "more made for prayer," and more persevering and gentle. In a sideways reference to male character, de Broglie pointed out that women are not given to having their dignity wounded. Sixth, she argued that women, not men, should be the ones to reach out to other women—an insight that the Paris Mission did not grasp right away, initially requiring their missionaries to go to the field as single men. Seventh (and related to point four), women are better able to bridge the differences between social classes because "there are already more ties between women of all classes." Their calling as Bible women had the "secondary advantage of creating a true union between the different social classes." Eighth, as mothers and wives, their common experience of suffering allows women to break through all social barriers. Because women have a deeper "internal life" and are drawn together by "an eternal friendship," they can develop and maintain friendships more naturally.[33] It was quite a radical argument at that time.

De Broglie's profile of the woman as the "ideal missionary" in this document served as the foundation for the new international calling of French Protestant women to missions. This document provided the foundation for their first annual report to the Paris Mission in 1826, when de Broglie, Mallet, and the Paris Mission women's committee sought to demonstrate how their strengths as women could contribute to the missionary movement, specifically in their role as social mediators (bridge builders between social classes and regional groups), as advocates for international missions, and as agents of social renewal.

Mothers Make Ideal Missionaries

Expanding on de Broglie's writing, Mallet in turn based her argument for female superiority in missionary calling on women's biological roles as mothers, their emotional availability, and their inherent ability to gain knowledge from their experience of working among the poor. She taught these lessons in her letters to the *dames inspectrices* [lady inspectors] of infant schools:

32. Broglie, *Les Archives du Christianisme*, 8, 9, 11–12.

33. Broglie, *Les Archives du Christianisme*, 13, 16, 17. The original expression is "une sympathie éternelle." The term "sympathie" has several translations, including "friendship," "sympathy," and "empathy."

At home, in carrying out the duties required by family life, women have more time to reflect, and more ways to learn from the positive things of life than men do, if they wish to make use of it. . . . We have a thousand opportunities to know these facts and these miseries [of the indigent classes]: indeed, are we not constantly in contact with those who are witnesses or victims of these things? All one has to do is to seek to learn: and let us not think that to do this one needs to undertake long and difficult investigations: no, a kind word of interest or a question expressed with affection are enough to bring about the growth of the mother or the poor worker whose heart is burdened with worries. But through the exercise of active and practical charity we will take much greater steps in the knowledge of such hardships and we will discover the privations, suffering, poverty, too often caused by vice, the neglect of moral laws, the lack of habits, of religious ideas, and by the hardening of the conscience.[34]

Mallet's understanding of the maternal source of female wisdom informed her infant school pedagogy which was, essentially, the embodiment of Christ-like love: "Oh! Let us be mothers to the children in infant schools, and our indifference will give way to love! . . . Let us not grow tired of clothing the child who is naked, feeding the one who is hungry, visiting the one who is sick. 'Truly,' said Jesus Christ, the Savior of the world, 'just as you did it to one of the least of these who are my brothers, you did it to me.'"[35]

Mallet's contribution to a theology of women's leadership was informed by her daily work "in the trenches," physically ministering to the poor and raising funds from the wealthy for their needs.

CONCLUSION

The two friends, Mallet and de Broglie, were almost exactly the same age and both also suffered from a fragile constitution. Sadly, they did not get to share a full and lifelong friendship because de Broglie died in 1838 at the age of forty-one, almost twenty years before her friend. But while they were

34. "Lettre quatrième aux dames inspectrices" (*L'Ami de l'Enfance*, 58–59). Mallet penned numerous books and papers related to the work of the *dames patronnesses* and the pedagogy of the *salles d'asile*. She contributed regularly to the journal *L'Ami de l'Enfance*, published from 1835 on. She authored an anonymous brochure, *La direction morale des salles d'asile* [*The Moral Leadership of Infant Schools*], the first of its kind in France. The essence of her infant school pedagogy is a 120-page document simply entitled "*Appendice*," embedded in the third edition of the *Manuel des salles d'asile* by J-D. Cochin, published in 1845.

35. "Lettre troisième aux dames inspectrices" (*L'Ami de l'Enfance*, 167).

both alive, their friendship was the source of exemplary leadership in their collaborative work for mission, which in turn gave rise to a seminal vision for women's leadership in mission.

Both Mallet and de Broglie were inspirational leaders, and both were involved in numerous works of the *Réveil*. It is almost impossible to track the full extent of their pervasive influence because women's work was not systematically documented and female leaders generally did not receive public recognition for their work. Furthermore, the repercussions of the theology of female leadership in mission devised by Mallet and de Broglie on the involvement of French Protestant women in national and international mission work has yet to be explored.

As women leaders in nineteenth century France, Mallet and de Broglie may not have personally experienced dire economic challenges, but they certainly confronted obstacles related to gender and their belonging to a minority religion. But these women persevered because their heart for Jesus gave them the ability to "do all things through him who strengthen[ed]" them (Phil 4:13 NRSV). In his *Pensées*, Blaise Pascal offers insight into the importance of heart motivation in faith: "The heart has its reasons, which reason does not know. We feel it in a thousand things. It is the heart which experiences God, and not reason. This, then, is faith: God felt by the heart, not by reason."[36] In the 1800s, in a country still reeling from the rationalistic and antireligious attacks of the Revolution and the Enlightenment, Mallet and de Broglie drew energy for mission primarily from their love for their Lord Jesus. They were women of great heart—*des femmes au grand coeur*.[37] The source of their courage, against the most desperate odds, was their love for Jesus and for all humankind. Their friendship, thus woven of human and divine threads, empowered them to accomplish many great things for the work of mission both at home and abroad.

BIBLIOGRAPHY

Archives of the Paris Evangelical Missionary Society (DEFAP). *Procès Verbal de l'Assemblée Générale de la Société des Missions Évangéliques chez les Peuples non Chrétiens, établie à Paris*. Paris: Imprimerie de J. Smith, 1822–1858.

Broglie, Albertine de. *Fragments sur divers sujets de religion et de morale*. Paris: Royale, 1840.

Broglie, Albertine de, and Albert Broglie. *Lettres de la duchesse de Broglie, 1814–1838*. Paris: Bibliothèque Nationale, 1896.

36. Pascal, *Pensées*.

37. The French *coeur* [heart] comes from the Latin word *cor*, which is the root of the word "courage."

Cochin, Jean Denis Marie, and Jules Mallet. *Manuel des salles d'asile*. Paris: Hachette, 1845.

Douen, Orentin. *Histoire de la Société biblique protestante de Paris (1818 à 1868)*. Paris: Société biblique protestante, 1868.

Duprat, Catherine. *Usage et pratiques de la philanthropie. Pauvreté, action sociale et lien social, à Paris, au cours du premier XIXe siècle*. 2 vols. Paris: Association pour l'étude de l'histoire de la sécurité sociale, 1996; Comité d'histoire de la Sécurité sociale, 1997.

Goodman, Dena. *The Republic of Letters: A Cultural History of the French Enlightenment*. Ithaca, NY: Cornell University Press, 1996.

Houssaye, Jean, ed. *Femmes pédagogues*. Collection Pédagogues du monde entier. Paris: Fabert, 2008.

Juillerat, Henri-François [Juillerat-Chasseur], ed. *Archives du christianisme au dix-neuvième siècle*. Vol. 7. Paris: Société des Missions Évangéliques de Paris, 1824.

Labouchere, Alfred. *Oberkampf (1738–1815)*. Paris: Hachette, 1884.

L'Ami de l'enfance. Organe de la méthode française d'éducation maternelle, écoles maternelles, petites classes de l'école primaire, écoles enfantines. Paris: Hachette, 1895.

Luc, Jean-Noël. "La Diffusion Des Modèles de Préscolarisation En Europe Dans La Première Moitié Du XIXe Siècle." *Histoire de l'éducation* 82 (1999) 189–206.

―――. *L'invention du jeune enfant au XIXe siècle: De la salle d'asile à l'école maternelle*. Paris: Belin, 1997.

―――. "Madame Jules Mallet, Née Émilie Oberkampf (1794–1856), Ou Les Combats de La Pionnière de l'école Maternelle Française." *Bulletin de l'Histoire Du Protestantisme Français* 146 (2000) 15–46.

Mallet, Jules. *Prières chrétiennes à l'usage des familles*. Paris: J.-J. Risler, 1840.

Mayeur, Jean-Marie, et al. *Dictionnaire du monde religieux dans la France contemporaine: Les Protestants*. Paris: Editions Beauchesne, 1997.

Merlin, Roger. "Mme. Jules Mallet et le mouvement en faveur des salles d'asile." *Foi et Vie* 625.7 (1904) 95–97.

Montaigne, Michel de, and Estienne de la Boétie. *Selected Essays*. Translated by J. B Atkinson and David Sices. Indianapolis: Hackett, 2012.

Office du Tourisme, Jouy-en-Josas. "Bienvenue." Online. http://www.jouy-en-josas-tourisme.fr/en/maison_de_juliette_drouet.aspx.

Pascal, Blaise. *Pensées*. New York: Philosophical Library/Open Road, 2016.

Puaux, Frank. *Les oeuvres du protestantisme français: au XIXe siècle*. Paris: Comité protestant français, 1893.

Wemyss, Alice. *Histoire du réveil: 1790–1849*. Paris: Les Bergers et les mages, 1977.

Winegarten, Renee. *Germaine de Staël and Benjamin Constant*. New Haven, CT: Yale University Press, 2012.

Witt-Guizot, Henriette de. *A Christian Woman: Being the Life of Mme. Jules Mallet, Née Oberkampf*. London: Hurst and Blackett, 1882.

―――. *Une belle vie, Mme. Jules Mallet, née Oberkampf (1794–1856): Souvenirs et fragments, recueillis par Mme de Witt, née Guizot*. Paris: Hachette, 1881.

Friendship and Liberation

A Latin American Perspective

ANGEL SANTIAGO-VENDRELL

This is a story of the friendships that developed between teachers and students, missionaries and their disciples, in Latin American Protestantism, especially the Presbyterian Church USA, in the twentieth century. It tells of the friendships and events that shaped the lives of John A. Mackay, M. Richard Shaull, and Rubem Alves, and how those influences shaped Latin America Protestantism in the twentieth century. The story begins with the friendships and events that shaped the life of John Mackay in Latin America from 1915 to 1926. It continues by describing the influence of John Mackay on the life of Richard Shaull and the events that shaped Shaull's life in Latin America through a network of seminary and university students committed to the transformative power of the gospel. It ends by analyzing Shaull's influence in the life of Rubem Alves in the context of Latin American liberation theology.

JOHN A. MACKAY: "A SCOTSMAN WITH A LATIN SOUL"[1]

John A. Mackay was born on May 19, 1889, in Inverness, Scotland. He described his conversion experience at age fourteen in the highlands of Scotland as God becoming real to him. Mackay understood that, from that time on, his life would be dedicated to Christ's service. He subsequently graduated from the University of Aberdeen in 1912 with a concentration in

1. Sinclair, *Juan A. Mackay.*

73

philosophy, received a fellowship to attend Princeton Theological Seminary, and graduated in 1915 from that institution. Although he was awarded a study fellowship, the First World War made it impossible for him to study in Germany as he had hoped. A Princeton mentor, B. B. Warfield, suggested he consider Spain as an option because Mackay had expressed his desire to be a missionary in Latin America.[2] And so to Spain he went.

Mackay arrived in Spain in 1915 during a period of rapid liberalism under King Alfonso XIII. During his eight-month stay, he studied with Miguel de Unamuno. Mackay notes that it is "to this Spaniard [Unamuno] I owe the greatest cultural awakening that ever came into my life. To him I am indebted for a passionate love of Spain, her people, her culture, which began to be born within me in 1915, and which was destined to become one of the most decisive influences in my life."[3] The profound influence of Unamuno on Mackay is seen in Mackay's dissertation for the University of San Marcos in Lima, Perú, *Miguel de Unamuno: Su Personalidad, Obra, e Influencia.*

Unamuno introduced Mackay to the Spanish mystics, especially John of the Cross, Luís de Leon, and Santa Teresa of Avila. Mackay was captivated by what he read, most particularly their Christocentrism. In the Spanish mystics, he found an experiential Christology that was not subjugated to dogmatic interpretations. It was a fluid Christology like the one of Friar Luis de Léon, who spoke of nature and Christ as being in an intimate relationship, as "Christ living in the fields."[4] Mackay considered Miguel de Unamuno to be among the "last and the greatest of Spain's mystic heretics."[5] He explained how Unamuno identified the Christ of popular Catholicism as the Christ of Tangiers, the capital of Morocco, "a Christ known in life as an infant and in death as a corpse, over whose helpless childhood and tragic fate the Virgin Mother presides."[6] This was a Christ that only appeared in two dramatic roles: "the role of an infant in his mother's arms, and the role of a suffering and bleeding victim on the cross. [As such, this was] a Christ who was born and died, but who never lived."[7] Contrary to this Christ of popular Catholicism, Unamuno offered another Christ, the One "who drove the merchants from the temple, who anathematized hypocritical religious leaders, who

2. Metzger, *Hand and Road,* 59.

3. Mackay, "Miguel de Unamuno," 45.

4. Léon quoted in Mackay, *Meaning of Life,* 161. Mackay was no stranger to "feeling God in the fields"; his conversion narrative depicts him in the highlands of Dornoch becoming aware of the divine calling in his life. See Mackay's conversion account in Gillette, "John A. Mackay."

5. Mackay, *Other Spanish Christ,* 147.

6. Mackay, *Other Spanish Christ,* 102.

7. Mackay, *Other Spanish Christ,* 110.

bitterly wept over Jerusalem and anguished later in the olive garden and on the cross, the Christ who rose later from the dead to renew the redemptive struggle in the lives of His followers."[8] This Christ of the Spanish mystics became a counter-balance to the Christ domesticated and subjugated by the Roman Catholic Church in Latin America. Even though he remained in constant dialogue with the Spanish-European intellectual tradition, Mackay reinterpreted it in Perú during his first missionary appointment.

MISSIONARY TO PERÚ AND FRIENDSHIP WITH VÍCTOR HAYA DE LA TORRE AND JOSÉ CARLOS MARIÁTEGUI

When Mackay arrived in Perú in 1916, new laws guaranteeing religious freedom gave Protestants leeway to work freely. Mackay assumed the responsibility of directing a failing school with thirty students supported by the Overseas Missionary Society. He changed its name, to Colegio Anglo-Perúano, and its structure. Although the previous administration had thought teaching classes in English would attract more students from among the nation's elites, Mackay implemented a new and quite different strategy by making Spanish the official language of the school.

Mackay was convinced that by refocusing on Spanish as a language of instruction at the Colegio Anglo-Perúano, students would benefit from their own cultural and linguistic wealth.[9] The incarnational model was contrary to the missionary strategy of those days, which taught that the best way to proclaim the Gospel was if people were first civilized into Western cultures.[10] Meanwhile, perceiving that the best way to fulfill his mission was to influence university students, Mackay applied and was admitted to the University of San Marcos on November 6, 1917.[11] Now at the intellectual hub of Perú, Mackay expanded his connections and befriended members of a group nicknamed *la Proteorvia* that met to discuss the affairs of the

8. Mackay, *Other Spanish Christ*, 147. Rivera Pagán points out, "Mackay's view of the Latin American Roman Catholic Church is one-sided. He is swift to perceive the fossilized view of the baroque agonizing Christ and its proclivity to foster authoritarian and superstitious attitudes . . . but he seems unable to decipher the hidden strength of popular Catholicism" (Rivera Pagán, "Myth, Utopia, and Faith," 144).

9. Sinclair, *Juan A. Mackay*, 87.

10. Hutchison, "Moral Equivalent for Imperialism." Hutchison argues that in the period from 1880 to 1910, North American missionary efforts were directed by a post-millennial theology that saw civilization as a primary element in mission practice.

11. Metzger, *Hand and Road*, 101.

nation.[12] It was through this group and university contacts that Mackay befriended Manuel Beltroy, Rául Porras, and Victor Haya de la Torre and invited them to teach at the Colegio Anglo-Perúano. Of all the intellectuals who worked at the Colegio Anglo-Perúano, Mackay took a special interest in Haya de la Torre.

When Mackay met him, Haya was not a religious person but a law student at the University of San Marcos and the president of the Student Federation of Perú. Indeed, Haya confessed to Mackay that it was very hard for him even to mention the name of God at that time because it represented everything that he opposed, particularly how people used religion to thwart intellectual, political, and social change.[13] From this initial position of opposition to what he perceived as the tyranny of religion, Haya became a follower of Christ, and "In February 1923 Mackay had the unspeakable joy of listening to his profession of faith in Christ."[14] How did such a great change occur? Haya became very interested in the work of the YMCA and attended with Mackay an Easter week retreat in 1923, in which the two shared the same tent for the duration of the event.[15] According to Mackay, he showed Haya that "in the writings of the Old Testament prophets and in the teachings of Jesus there were more incandescent denunciations of oppression and wrong than he and his companions had ever made."[16]

At that time, politics in Latin America were dominated by alliances between politicians and the Roman Catholic Church. In May 23, 1923, the regime of dictator Augusto B. Leguía allied itself with the Roman Catholic Church to dedicate the country to a big bronze image of the Sacred Heart of Jesus—with the purpose of controlling the masses and the political future of the nation.[17] The Roman Catholic Church wanted to reassert its authority in the face of an increasing wave of secularization and modernism, and Leguía attempted to turn Catholic voters out in mass for an unconstitutional second term.[18]

The Sacred Heart of Jesus was part of what Mackay identified as the creole Christ. Creoles were those white Spaniards born in Latin America. Mackay was alluding to the fetishization of a symbol, as the sacred heart

---

12. Sinclair, *John A. Mackay*, 92.

13. Mackay, *Other Spanish Christ*, 194.

14. Metzger, *Hand and Road*, 121.

15. Metzger, *Hand and Road*, 122.

16. Mackay, *Other Spanish Christ*, 194.

17. Rycroft, "Ideology and Program."

18. Gracía-Bryce, *Haya de la Torre*.

imagery robbed Christ of his real humanity.[19] Even though Mackay had probably shared his interpretation of the creole sacred heart of Jesus with Haya, Haya's motives for opposing the procession were more mundane. His fear was that the dedicatory celebration would be a step backwards to medieval times when the church controlled the state and suppressed free expression of thought, and that it would void the new advances made in the constitution of 1915, which had granted the populace freedom of religion.[20] If the government legitimized the Roman Church and the Roman Church legitimized the state, both could control the masses by uniting them against free-thinkers, Protestants, and Marxists. In this context of political and religious turmoil, Haya organized a demonstration to stop the dedication from taking place.

The demonstration succeeded in stopping the ceremony from taking place, but his involvement put a target on Haya's life. With an arrest warrant out on him, Haya became a fugitive and sought refuge in the Colegio Anglo-Perúano with Mackay. There he stayed without anyone in the administration, students, and even Mackay's own children knowing that he was a guest.[21] Four months after the events of May 23, Haya was arrested and exiled to Panama. He later traveled to Cuba, the Soviet Union, and Mexico. It was in Mexico that he launched the APRA (Alianza Popular Revolucionaria Americana), which Mackay noted was, though "explicitly Marxist, and being much more radical in its social ideology than the National Revolutionary party of Mexico, it rejects Marxism as a dogma . . . and has an appreciation of the place and function of religion in human life."[22]

In an article defending the APRA and its ideology, Mackay praised his revolutionary friend and explained the ideology of the APRA as focusing on: (1) action against European, Japanese, and North American economic imperialism; (2) the political unity of Latin America; (3) the internationalization of the Panama Canal; (4) the nationalization of land and industry; and (5) the solidarity of all oppressed peoples and classes.[23] Mackay clearly did not perceive Haya's Marxism as a renunciation of their friendship.

Besides Haya, Mackay had another surprising friendship with "the most erudite and dynamic writer on social questions in the whole South American continent," José Carlos Mariátegui.[24] Mackay dedicated one

---

19. Mackay, *Other Spanish Christ*, 115.
20. Stanger, "Church and State in Peru."
21. Metzger, *Hand and Road*, 125.
22. Mackay, *That Other America*, 103.
23. Mackay, "APRA Movement."
24. Mackay, *Other Spanish Christ*, 190.

section in *The Other Spanish Christ* to the influence of Mariátegui in Perú and saw in him the qualities of an apostle. He pointed out, "He treated the religious problem with great reverence and acumen, fully aware of the significance of religious values, but convinced that revolutionary socialism was the true successor of religion in our day."[25] Mariátegui inspired multitudes of Latin Americans through his editorial work for the Peruvian Sociological Review *Amauta* and his well-known book *Siete Ensayos de Interpretación de la Realidad Peruana*. As Mackay pointed out, "To visit him at his home and listen to that mellow voice pour out in measured accents a militant philosophy of life, so dissonant from the fragile physique of its author, was indeed an inspiring experience. For Mariátegui, Communism was a religion, a religion which he professed and propagated with all the passion of his soul."[26]

Mackay spent quality time with Mariátegui and listened to him with enthusiasm and admiration. Perhaps Mackay admired the young Marxist not only for his social analysis of the Peruvian situation, but even more for his passion to propagate the ideals he thought would liberate Perú from the tyranny of the bourgeoisie who saw national cooperation with North American imperialists as their best source for financial security. As Luís Rivera-Pagán reminds us, "Not many Christian ministers or priests were willing to eulogize the main Peruvian Marxist theoretician of the first half of this century!"[27]

After nine years, Mackay resigned from serving in the Colegio Anglo-Perúano to work more closely with university students under the auspices of the YMCA. In this new evangelistic mission, Mackay lectured at many universities in Latin America and met thousands of Latin American youth who would leave an undeniable mark on the Scottish missionary. Not surprisingly, when he was appointed professor and president of Princeton Theological Seminary (1936–1959), all the things that Mackay learned from Latin Americans he would instill in his students in a course on Latin American Christianity.

One of the things students learned in Mackay's course on Latin America was the interrelationship between spirituality and praxis as a way of life. Students were captivated, as was most of the theological world, by Mackay's influential metaphor of the balcony and the road. In Spanish architectural design, houses of two floors had a balcony that typically overhung the street. The balcony was the place where family members gathered to see the religious public processions in the streets, political marches, and everything

25. Mackay, *Other Spanish Christ*, 191.
26. Mackay, *Other Spanish Christ*, 190–91.
27. Rivera Pagán, "Myth, Utopia, and Faith," 148.

that happened in daily life.[28] As spectators, people who observe life from the balcony never experience the lives of the people they observe. It is an existence from a distance, one that does not touch the actual events being observed. Mackay pointed out, "A man may live a permanent balconized existence even though the physical part of him has the ubiquity of the globe-trotter. For the balcony means an immobility of soul that may perfectly co-exist with a mobile, peripatetic body."[29] On the other hand, "the road is the place where life is tensely lived, where thought has its birth in conflict and concern, where choices are made and decisions carried out. It is the place of action, of pilgrimage, of crusade, where concern is never absent from the wayfarer's heart."[30]

Another important lesson for students was Mackay's understanding of Marxism. His friendship with two of the most prominent Latin American Marxists gave Mackay a different perspective from most of his missionary peers. Mackay interpreted Marxism as a secular religion. As a religion, Marxism offered the masses an eschatological vision of a new society, which was "only possible on the basis of passionate faith in a myth."[31] Mackay taught his students that the encounter between Christians and Marxists should not be based on a conflict of opposed ideologies, but rather, as an encounter between people who were dedicated to social justice with two different prescriptions leading to a better society.

RICHARD SHAULL'S THEOLOGY OF REVOLUTION

One of those Princeton students who became a life-long friend to Mackay wrote a note of gratitude commemorating his eightieth birthday:

> It is with real rejoicing that I join in sending you this word of greeting on the occasion of your eightieth birthday, for it provides me with an opportunity to tell you how much your life and witness have meant to me over the years. Ever since my earliest years as a student at Princeton Seminary your understanding of the Christian faith and your commitment to Christ's mission in the world have been a constant challenge to me. You have not only opened new worlds of thought for me but have also encouraged me to be constantly moving to the cutting edge of things and to be engaged in the human struggle there. In fact, I

28. Mackay, *Preface*, 29.
29. Mackay, *Preface*, 30.
30. Mackay, *Preface*, 30.
31. Mackay, *Other Spanish Christ*, 192.

can clearly say that no other single individual has played such a significant role in shaping my life and thought.[32]

The student who wrote this birthday message to Mackay was Richard Shaull. Shaull was born on November 24, 1919, in the small rural community of Felton, Pennsylvania. He enrolled in Elizabethtown College at the early age of fourteen. When Shaull graduated from the sociology department in 1938 at the age of nineteen, he decided to apply to Princeton Theological Seminary and sample ministry as a vocation. By the time Shaull enrolled, John A. Mackay had been president for six years. Mackay inspired Shaull to pursue a missionary vocation to Latin America and, after finishing seminary, Shaull was appointed as a missionary to Colombia (1942–1950) and then Brazil (1952–1962) by the Board of Foreign Missions of the Presbyterian Church USA.

Taking to heart Mackay's incarnational missiology, Shaull was a missionary who implemented his ministry in dialogue and involvement with situations of brokenness and despair. Faced by a world in revolution, Shaull wanted to be a witness to Christ in the midst of it all, and because of it, he was known as the theologian of revolution. For him, revolution involved the revolt of the disinherited, the crisis of modern industrial society based on the injustice of primitive capitalism, and the uneasy conscience of the privileged classes.[33] The world was going through a revolutionary process because the masses—immersed in poverty, exploited by absentee landlords, working under unbearable circumstances, and living in deplorable conditions—were awakening to the realization that their poverty was a direct result of the profits of the rich.[34] Combined with the revolt of the masses against capitalism was the revolt of human beings against God, religious ideas, and morality. This was the time when "God was dead" and many Latin Americans believed religion was the opium of the masses.[35]

Shaull used the term revolution to challenge the church to actually practice the teachings of Jesus. If the church was not involved in the struggle to create a better world, then Marxism was contributing more to solve the problems of society with a philosophy of life that gave purpose to humans based on a utopic dream for a better future.[36] In that case, "Communism

---

32. Shaull, letter to Mackay, May 12, 1969 [SP].

33. Shaull, *Encounter with Revolution*, 3–17.

34. Shaull, *Encounter with Revolution*, 4–8.

35. Lenkersdorf, "Concepto y Critica de Religión"; Dumas and Hromadka, "Dos Contribuciones."

36. Shaull, *O Cristianismo e a Revoluçao Social*. I am using the Spanish translation, *El Cristianismo y la Revolución Social*, 20.

has beaten us at our own game of evangelizing the world. It has done so, not primarily by arms but by a keener awareness of the human situation, a clear message and a more dynamic commitment to its cause."[37] Christianity had to be an alternative to Marxism, an invitation to look at the world through the eyes of faith, to see the history of the world through the redemptive work of Jesus Christ because "the God who broke into history in Jesus Christ is still active in the world, leading all things toward their final fulfilment."[38] Shaull interpreted history in light of God's sovereignty over the whole creation. He stated, "For Christians the revolution is like a small historical apocalypse, a sign that history is under the judgement of God."[39] Here, the eschatological motif of looking at the present in light of the future motivated Christians to strive to create better conditions for human beings who were struggling to survive in a political and economic system that worked against their humanity.

In a context of human disintegration, Shaull called Christians to participate with revolutionaries to establish a new order that would have as its core the humanization of individuals and the complete transformation of the means of production.[40] If the God who acts and transforms history was in the midst of the revolution, then Christians had the responsibility to immerse themselves in the problems affecting society while seeking to change the dehumanizing structures of society that perpetuate poverty. Shaull wanted Christians to be agents of reconciliation and transformation with those revolutionaries fighting at the center of the revolution. Shaull sought a dialogical ministry between Christians and Marxists that would not be based on conflict, but rather, would be an encounter between people who were both dedicated to social justice, only differing on how to accomplish it.[41]

This is illustrated by a correspondence between Shaull and Jeff Goff, a Presbyterian missionary in Colombia. Their friendship went back to the 1940s, when they were missionaries in the city of Barranquilla, Colombia. Goff wanted advice from Shaull about a situation in the Protestant Church in Cuba after Fidel Castro's revolutionary victory in 1959. Goff admitted he engaged in a "first-class brawl with Rafael Cepeda and the CCPAL" (Cuban

---

37. Shaull, "Communism Faces the Same World," An Address at the Conference of the Division of Foreign Missions, Toronto, Canada, January 1952 [SP].

38. Shaull, *Encounter with Revolution*, 60.

39. Shaull, "Hacia una Perspectiva Cristiana."

40. Shaull, "Cambio Revolucionario."

41. Shaull, "Iglesia y Teológia."

Council of Churches) because Protestantism in Cuba was taking a passive position regarding the revolution.[42] He told Shaull:

> The continued silence of the Cuban Protestant Churches vis-à-vis the communist government should be a matter of concern to Protestants throughout Latin America. Unless some representative body speaks out soon we will be called soft on communism. This is a label we cannot afford to carry. We cannot wait for the Cuban Presbyterians to make the break they should make with the Revolutionary government. Their hesitancy endangers us all.[43]

Shaull's response to Goff was a blunt critique. He considered Christians in the USA to be "naïve" on the issue, lacking a serious understanding of the social and theological implications of the Cuban revolution. He told Goff, "I think that it is extremely important for us to see that Protestant responsibility in the present situation cannot mean primarily, nor in the first place, an anti-communist position, no matter how great the threat of communist penetration is at this time."[44] For Shaull, drafting any type of statement from the Presbyterian Church or CCPAL was a grave mistake. An official statement against communism would backfire because people in Latin America recognized that Cuba and its people had been subject to the economic interest of the United States. For this reason, it would be better for the church in Cuba to be perceived as soft on communism than identified with the economic imperial machine of the United States.

Instead of condemning Marxists, Shaull strove to build bridges to them. He even adopted their emphasis on praxis, insisting, "Our starting point should be situated in *praxis,* but a *praxis* of a very special nature: one rooted in the theologian's own experience of *Exodus* and *exile* by rejecting the present social order that victimizes us and advancing in hope to a new social and political order."[45] Christians who opted to participate in the revolutionary process would construct a new theological language based on their own experiences in that struggle to transform the structures of society. In his perspective, Christians were free to participate in God's action in history through political revolutionary movements that wanted to humanize

---

42. Cepeda was a Presbyterian pastor and president of CCPAL who was committed to overthrowing the dictatorship of Fulgencio Batista and for years travelled throughout the island persuading people to engage in revolution. Tschuy, "Protestantism in Cuba." 258.

43. Goff, letter to Shaull, October 22, 1960 [SP].

44. Shaull, letter to Goff, November 19, 1960 [SP].

45. Shaull, "Iglesia y Teología," 34.

the dehumanizing conditions of life. Even when all the horizons were closing in and life seemed dark, Christians had hope that God was in the midst
of it all, directing them to a better today. Shaull pointed out, "He can hope
because he knows that the present crisis is a manifestation of God's mercy
as well as of his judgement, and he is sure that God is active in it all."[46] His
theology of revolution was born out of a critical engagement between the
Brazilian historical realities and the nature and goal of human existence in
light of God's actions in history through the redemptive work of Jesus of
Nazareth.[47]

RUBEM ALVES: "FROM LIBERATION
THEOLOGIAN TO POET"[48]

To really understand what was happening in Brazil, Shaull developed close
relationships with his students. But he saw them as more than informants
or even collaborators in the work of God; they were his friends. In 2003, the
journal *Religião & Sociedade* published a special edition honoring Shaull
in which many of them testified to his influence on them. Áureo Bispo dos
Santos remembered Shaull as a "teólogo-profeta" who changed his life by
inviting him to journey in the uncharted waters of revolution.[49] Frei Carlos
Josaphat, a Dominican in the Order of Preachers, praised Shaull as a friend
and as the first Protestant missionary to seek ecumenical relations with
Roman Catholics in a time in which such actions were not sanctioned by
the Presbyterian Church of Brazil.[50] Claude Emmanuel Labrunie owed to
Shaull his "faith in Jesus and pastoral vocation" by showing him the social
responsibility of Christians.[51] Jovelino Ramos remembered walking with
Shaull to do evangelistic work in the industrial neighborhood of Vila Anas-
tácio and how Shaull intertwined spirituality and praxis.[52]

One of Shaull's most fruitful friendships was with a young theology
student named Rubem Alves. Alves was born on September 15, 1933, in
Boa Esperança, Minas Gerais, Brazil. He was raised in a staunchly Calvinistic tradition of "Right-Doctrine-Protestantism," which stressed "agreement
with a series of doctrinal affirmations regarded as expressions of the truth

---

46. Shaull, *Encounter with Revolution*, 69.
47. Shaull, "Cambio Revolucionario," 50.
48. Alves, "From Liberation Theologian to Poet."
49. Santos, "Shaull Modou," 56.
50. Josaphat, "Uma Figura," 61.
51. Labrunie, "Richard Shaull," 62.
52. Ramos, "Caminhando com Richard Shaull."

that must be affirmed without any shadow of doubt, as a precondition for participation in the ecclesiastical community."[53] Alves's Christian upbringing taught him that his real enemies were Roman Catholics, theological liberalism, and worldliness.[54] When he was nineteen years old, he enrolled at Campinas Theological Seminary to consolidate his thought regarding a ministerial vocation. It was there that Alves's world was turned upside down by a young theologian named Richard Shaull. Shaull's influence on Alves cannot be overestimated. Alves described his life in two moments: "Before and after Shaull because Shaull taught me how to think for myself."[55]

According to Alves, Shaull was the first missionary to address the social responsibility of Christians in all shares of life, including the political realm in Brazil. It was the first time in the history of the seminary that a professor had become a companion in the struggle to develop a better world, alongside his students.[56] The incarnational principle that Shaull learned from Mackay, Alves advanced in Brazil. Alves pointed out, "God appeared as a man in a context in which real human life was lived, this is the meaning of the incarnation."[57]

This was clearly seen in the first article that Alves co-authored with Shaull on "The Devotional Life of Brazilian Protestantism." Alves and Shaull perceived a certain vitality in the devotional life of Brazilian Protestantism, rooted in the pietistic movement, the study of the Bible, and the vision of the church as a missionary community. However, the pietistic movement also had one major weakness: its inability to connect the believer's experience of Christ to the problems of society. In an attempt to bridge this divide, Alves and Shaull proposed an engaged spirituality rooted in the church's missionary mandate to propagate the gospel through student movements in the universities.[58] Christians who opted to participate in the revolutionary process would construct a new theological language based on their own experiences of struggling to transform the structures of society.

Christians at the center of the revolutionary process were not there to compete against Marxists, as if both groups were antithetical to each other. Alves pointed out, "The fact that the center of the Christian faith is not an ideology, instead the incarnation of God, means that Christians were never

---

53. Alves, *Protestantism and Repression*, 8.

54. Alves, *Protestantism and Repression*, 173–93.

55. Alves, "Su Cadáver," 92.

56. Santiago-Vendrell, *Contextual Theology*, 50–51.

57. Alves, "O Deus do Furacão," 19–24.

58. Alves and Shaull, "Devotional Life," 366.

in competition with any ideology, but in complete freedom to face it."[59] The revolution presupposes a complete breakdown of the current structures of society and the implementation of a new world order "pregnant with the possibilities of God's action in history."[60] God has always been working to redeemed God's creation, and God's activity in the revolutionary process could be the most radical answer to the human condition of alienation.

After four years of study at Princeton Seminary, in 1968, the academic institution granted Alves the degree of Doctor of Philosophy for his dissertation: *Towards a Theology of Liberation: An Exploration of the Encounter between the Language of Humanistic Messianism and Messianic Humanism.* Abbey Press published it a year later with a new title: *A Theology of Human Hope.* Alves expressed his appreciation and love to Shaull in the acknowledgement: "I have a special word of gratitude to Dr. Richard Shaull, a close friend for more than fifteen years, whose thought and words have always been the expression of his permanent personal and intellectual commitment to the creation of a new future for man."[61]

In his dissertation, Alves followed Shaull's advice to create a new language that would go beyond metaphysics and dogmatism to address the historical existence of human beings. He criticized Karl Barth, Rudolf Bultmann, and Jürgen Moltmann as formulating ahistorical postulates of a God beyond history. According to Alves, the biggest problem with these theologians was their positions on transcendence. He called them theologians of "messianic humanism" because they only offered metaphysical answers to historical problems, leaving human beings in a closed world where God was radically beyond history as Wholly Other. In contrast to "messianic humanism," Alves introduced "humanistic messianism."[62] In humanistic messianism, humans take charge of the historical moment. Alves pointed out, "Man's transcendence is thus the power that brings one day to its end and gives birth to the new one. The transcended man lives thus between the times. Nay, the times are divided between the untruth which is left behind and the truth toward which one moves because man is in history."[63]

After 1968, Alves became a leading voice in Latin American liberation theology. The irony is that his dissertation committee complained that

59. Alves, "Injusticia y Rebelión," 52.

60. Alves, "Injusticia y Rebelión," 47.

61. Alves, "Towards a Theology of Liberation"; Alves, *Theology of Human Hope,* xv. Because the term "liberation" was not in common use, the editor of Abbey Press thought the book would be more marketable as *A Theology of Human Hope* given how influential Jürgen Moltmann's *Theology of Hope* was in theological circles of the time.

62. Alves, *Theology of Human Hope,* 34–68.

63. Alves, *Theology of Human Hope,* 28.

Alves's new theological language was non-academic, and consequently he barely passed his dissertation. It also chastised Shaull, accusing him of incompetence in directing doctoral students.[64] The pressure of dealing with the doctoral committee was so intense that Alves had wanted to quit his studies and return to Brazil. It was Shaull who convinced him to play the academic game and write exclusively with his dissertation committee members in mind. Eighteen years later *The Theology of Human Hope* was finally translated into Portuguese as *Da Esperança*. In the new preface, Alves apologized to his Brazilian readers for writing such a dull text and complained about those years at Princeton Seminary where "he was forced to write in such a style in the name of academic rigor."[65] He sent a copy of the new preface to Shaull, whose response was priceless:

> This preface should be included if the book is re-published in English partly in order to call attention to the blindness of academic theologians unable to perceive where the Creative Spirit about which they wrote and lectured might be present. I am quite fascinated by what you are doing to expose the sterility and myopia of so much that happens in "intellectual" circles, to point to another world of experience, language and reflection and to call attention to other possibilities on other horizons of metaphor and poetry.[66]

Shaull affirmed the revolutionary trajectory of Alves's liberation theology. Alves's commitment to speak authentically from and to the historical moment forced him to create a new language with which to talk about God, including through poetry. In a letter to Shaull, Alves wrote that he was trying to recover the affirmation that "the Word became flesh" in a literal sense. "Theology, in my view, with its scientific pretense, can only subsist by becoming fundamentalist: turning the Bible into a peeping-hole that inhabits the metaphysical world. For is this not what the fundamentalists and all the scientists of the Bible do? It is necessary for theologians to stop being envious of scientists and to join the poets," Alves wrote.[67] Such insistence on an incarnational theology led him eventually to reject Western academic argumentations about God and embrace poetry as a way to describe a love relationship between God and humans.[68] He suggested, "I want to make a

64. Seward Hiltner, letter to Shaull, May 12, 1969 [SP].

65. Alves, *Do Esperança*. I became aware of the changes in the preface of the Portuguese edition from Barreto, "Rubem Alves and the Kaki Tree," 48.

66. Shaull, letter to Alves, January 30, 1988 [SP].

67. Alves, letter to Shaull, August 2, 1988 [SP].

68. Alves pointed out, "I am a university professor, and what I see every day is the

crazy proposal: that the church make the decision of moving from ethics to aesthetics, from doing to beauty. Because it is only by the power of beauty that we are able to resurrect the dead."[69] Thus, Alves continued to be a theological pioneer, creating a new pathway by which his disciples and friends can now speak about the excitement, beauty, and wonder of a new world.

CONCLUSION

According to Dana Robert, "friendship is a foundational practice in Christian mission," which incorporates spiritual formation, personal and social transformation, and incarnational ministry.[70] Western missionaries such as John Mackay and Richard Shaull forged friendships in Latin America despite class and religious differences and the power differentials between teachers and students and between the missionary and the missionized. As missionaries, they strove to present a spirituality of action that touched all aspects of human life, as demonstrated through their encounter with others, especially those closest to them. Their friendship with Latin Americans casts doubts about the assumption that all Western missionaries were collaborators with colonial power in subjugating their converts to an implanted religion. First and foremost, they were imitators of Christ by pitching their tent among the people they served. They understood the challenge that Jesus gave his disciples by calling them friends in John 15:15 (ESV): "No longer do I call you servants, for the servant does not know what his master is doing; but I have called you friends, for all that I have heard from my Father I have made known to you."

The lives of John Mackay, Richard Shaull, and Rubem Alves reveal that interpersonal relationships are as important or even more so than theoretical books for theological students, missionaries, and professors. The influence of Unamuno, Haya de la Torre, and Mariátegui among many other university students in the life of Mackay was so decisive that Mackay was known as the Scotsman with a Latin American soul. Shaull's many associations with university and seminary students plus all those who were part of his life in Latin America contributed to the changes Shaull experienced in those missionary years, and because of them Shaull was known as the theologian of revolution. The friendship between Shaull and Alves reveals the

power of the university to destroy the dreams of people. It converts us into specialists in critical analytical thinking, but disconnects us from the ability to dream, of creating utopias" ("Cultura de la Vida," 28).

69. Alves, "From Liberation Theologian to Poet," 24.

70. Robert, "Global Friendship," 180.

work of two kindred spirits united by the love of Christ for the salvation of individuals and the transformation of the world. Shaull's insistence to find a new theological language to talk about God in the midst of dehumanization led Alves to a place no one anticipated, from liberation theologian to poet.

BIBLIOGRAPHY

Alves, Rubem. "Cultura de la Vida." In *Hacia una Cultura de la Paz*, edited by Carlos Contreras, 15–28. Caracas: Editorial Nueva Sociedad, 1989.

———. "From Liberation Theologian to Poet: A Plea That the Church Moves from Ethics to Aesthetics, from Doing to Beauty." *Church and Society* 83.5 (1993) 20–23.

———. "Injusticia y Rebelión." *Cristianismo y Sociedad* 6.2 (1964) 40–53.

———. "Marxism as the Guarantee of Faith." *Worldview* 16 (1973) 13–17.

———. "O Deus do Furacão." In *De Dentro do Furacão: Richard Shaull e os Primórdios da Teologia da Libertação*, edited by Rubem Alves, 19–24. Rio de Janeiro: CEDI, 1985.

———. *Protestantism and Repression: A Brazilian Case Study*. Maryknoll, NY: Orbis, 1985.

———. "Su Cadáver Estava Lleno de Mundo." *Religião & Sociedade* 23 (2003) 91–94.

———. *A Theology of Human Hope*. St. Meinrad, IN: Abbey, 1971.

———. "Towards a Theology of Liberation: An Exploration of the Encounter between the Language of Humanistic Messianism and Messianic Humanism." PhD diss., Princeton Theological Seminary, 1968.

Alves, Rubem, and Richard Shaull. "The Devotional Life of Brazilian Protestantism." *Student World* 49.4 (1956) 360–66.

Barreto, Raimundo César. "Rubem Alves and the Kaki Tree: The Trajectory of an Exile Thinker." *Perspectivas* 13 (2016) 47–64. Online. https://perspectivasonline.com/downloads/rubem-alves-and-the-kaki-tree-the-trajectory-of-an-exile-thinker.

Dumas, Andre, and Josef Hromadka. "Dos Contribuciones sobre el Significado del Ateísmo Marxista." *Cristianismo y Sociedad* 3.8 (1965) 53–69.

Gillette, Gerald W., and John A. Mackay. "John A. Mackay: Influences on My Life." *Journal of Presbyterian History* 56.1 (1978) 20–34.

Gracía-Bryce, Iñigo. *Haya de la Torre and the Pursuit of Power in Twentieth Century Perú and Latin America*. Chapel Hill: University of North Carolina Press, 2018.

Hutchison, William. "A Moral Equivalent for Imperialism: Americans and the Promotion of Christian Civilization." In *Missionary Ideologies in the Imperialist Era: 1880–1920*, edited by Torben Christensen and William R. Hutchison, 167–77. Aarhus, Denmark: Aros, 1982.

Josaphat, Frei Carlos. "Uma Figura Humana e Evangelica." *Religião & Sociedade* 23 (2003) 60–61.

Labrunie, Claude Emmanuel. "Richard Shaull: Mestre, Profeta e Amigo." *Religião & Sociedade* 23 (2003) 62.

Lenkersdorf, Carlos. "El Concepto y la Critica de la Religión en Algunos Escritos de Carlos Marx." *Cristianismo y Sociedad* 3.8 (1965) 5–29.

Mackay, John A. "The APRA Movement." In *The Meaning of Life: Christian Truth and Social Change in Latin America*, edited by John M. Metzger, 177–86. Eugene, OR: Wipf & Stock, 2014.

————. "Miguel de Unamuno." In *Christianity and the Existentialists*, edited by Carl Michalson, 43–58. New York: Scribner's, 1956.

————. *Miguel de Unamuno: Su Personalidad, Obra, e Influencia*. Lima: Casa Editoria Ernesto Villarán, 1919.

————. *The Other Spanish Christ: A Study in the Spiritual History of Spain and South America*. London: Student Christian Movement, 1932.

————. *A Preface to Christian Theology*. New York: Macmillan, 1946.

————. *That Other America*. New York: Friendship, 1935.

Mariategui, Jose Carlos. *Siete Ensayos sobre la Realidad Peruana*. Lima, Peru: Biblioteca Amauta, 1928.

Metzger, John. *The Hand and the Road: The Life and Times of John A. Mackay*. Louisville: Westminster/John Knox, 2010.

Ramos, Jovelino. "Caminhando com Richard Shaull." *Religião & Sociedade* 23 (2003) 71–74.

Rivera Pagán, Luis N. "Myth, Utopia, and Faith: Theology and Culture in Latin America." *The Princeton Seminary Bulletin* 21.2 (2000) 142–60.

Robert, Dana L. "Global Friendship as Incarnational Mission Practice." *International Bulletin of Missionary Research* 39.4 (2015) 180–84.

Rycroft, Stanley. "The Ideology and Program of the Peruvian Aprista Movement." *International Review of Missions* 43.170 (1954) 220–23.

Santiago-Vendrell, Angel Daniel. *Contextual Theology and Revolutionary Transformation in Latin America: The Missiology of M. Richard Shaull*. Eugene, OR: Pickwick, 2010.

Santos, Áureo Bispo dos. "Shaull Modou o Projeto de Vida de um Jovem Seminarista." *Religião & Sociedade* 23 (2003) 56–59.

Shaull, Richard. "El Cambio Revolucionario en una Perspectiva Teológica." *Cristianismo y Sociedad* 4.12 (1966) 49–69.

————. *El Cristianismo y la Revolución Social*. Mexico: Editorial La Aurora, 1955.

————. *Encounter with Revolution*. New York: Associated, 1955.

————. "Hacia una Perspectiva Cristiana de la Revolución Social." *Cristianismo y Sociedad* 3.7 (1965) 6–15.

————. "Iglesia y Teológia en la Voragine de la Revolución." In *De la Iglesia y la Sociedad*, edited by Luis Odell, 23–48. Montevideo: Biblioteca Mayor, 1968.

————. *O Cristianismo e a Revoluçao Social*. Sao Paulo: União Cristã de Estudantes do Brasil, 1953.

Shaull, Richard, et al. Richard Shaull Papers [SP]. Special Collection, Speer Library, Princeton Theological Seminary, Princeton, NJ.

Sinclair, John H. *Juan A. Mackay: Un Escocés con Alma Latina*. Mexico: CUPSA, 1990.

Stanger, Francis Merriman. "Church and State in Peru During the First Century of Independence." In *The Conflict Between Church and State in Latin America*, edited by Fredrick B. Pike, 143–53. New York: Alfred A. Knopf, 1964.

Tschuy, Theo. "Protestantism in Cuba, 1868–1968." In *Christianity in the Caribbean: Essays on Church History*, edited by Armando Lampe, 229–68. Barbados: University of the West Indies Press, 2001.

Boundary-Crossing Friendship and Urban Mission

TYLER LENOCKER

The Emmanuel Gospel Center (EGC), an evangelical urban mission founded in Boston's South End, stands at the heart of a networked, multi-ethnic evangelical and pentecostal coalition forged in the city in the latter decades of the twentieth century. In 1964, the arrival of Douglas and Judy Hall, a young seminary couple from the Midwest, changed the organization from a fundamentalist preaching station into a multi-service evangelical parachurch organization rooted increasingly in the city's poorer, migrant Christian communities. While EGC's robust ties with these communities garnered attention in the 1980s and 1990s, early work of boundary-crossing friendships in the 1960s and 1970s forms the heart of the organization's later multiethnic bonds.

Three friendships of EGC's former president Douglas Hall shaped the organization's early ministry endeavors: friendships with Episcopalian priest William Dwyer, black Baptist pastor George Bullock, and Puerto Rican pentecostal minister and theologian Eldin Villafañe. The friendships emerged in a postwar urban environment marked by multiple levels of fracture related to space, race, and class. Each friendship took shape in response to such divisions, but within distinct yet interconnected mission practices in a common locale: Dwyer in social activism, Bullock in outdoor evangelism, and Villafañe in Christian education. Sustained shared ministry endeavors in shared neighborhoods caught in the tumult of urban crisis created the enduring relationships between the inner-city ministers. The multiplicity of boundary-crossing relationships was also encouraged by the

Halls' pioneering missionary situation. White middle-class absence in the inner city drove the Halls into novel ministry partnerships. The vulnerabilities of pioneering mission endeavors, and the ensuing boundary-crossing friendships, helped create Boston's multiethnic evangelical coalition of later decades.

CHRISTIAN FRIENDSHIP IN A FRACTURED CITY

Douglas and Judy Hall met in 1957 at Moody Bible Institute in Chicago. Both were raised in Mainline Protestant congregations but had evangelical conversions in their late teens, drawing them into fundamentalist churches and then to Moody. The Halls quickly absorbed the fundamentalist zeal for overseas missions, with Douglas sensing an early call to India. Judy likewise saw a future in cross-cultural ministry but found herself especially drawn to the city. The future relationship of Judy and Douglas was one marked by abiding friendship and common calling, a ministry in marital partnership that combined Douglas's passion for overseas missionary work with Judy's heart for urban ministry. While not the center of this study, their relationship formed the foundation upon which the remaining friendships were built.

After Moody, the Halls completed their undergraduate education at Michigan State University and then moved to the North Shore of Boston, where Douglas began a Master of Divinity program at Gordon Divinity School.[1] The Halls chafed at the cultural homogeneity of Boston's suburbs and soon took an open position at a small storefront mission in the city's impoverished South End neighborhood called the Emmanuel Gospel Center. With Douglas as superintendent, the Halls were given the apartment over the chapel and paid two hundred dollars per month. The Halls' responsibilities included upkeep of the aging facilities and organizing preaching services seven nights a week, or as then-board president Jacob Mark told them, "Get people saved and into a good church."[2] Boston in the 1960s, however, did not prove amenable to such a task.

1. Gordon Divinity School in Wenham, MA, and Conwell School of Theology in Philadelphia, PA, merged in 1969, becoming Gordon-Conwell Theological Seminary in nearby South Hamilton, MA.

2. Hall, "Judy's Story," 7.

Urban Crisis and Severing the "Bridges of God"

The Halls' move from the suburbs to Boston's inner city thrust them into an environment caught in the throes of "urban crisis."[3] Rapid deindustrialization and disinvestment in cities and the inverse mass investment in moving businesses and people into the suburbs drove the crisis. What ensued was a spatial and demographic reconfiguration of America's metropolitan regions. The country's white middle class moved, with their homes and often their businesses, into the burgeoning suburbs. Migrating black families from the American South, along with a smaller contingent of Puerto Ricans, moved into the abandoned urban neighborhoods. Metropolitan areas like Greater Boston were simultaneously expanding and dividing, sifting the booming white middle class into the suburbs and funneling migrating, poor minorities into the inner city.

Boston's South End embodied the urban crisis, with its population declining by over half between 1950 and 1970, from 57,000 to 22,000.[4] A 1967 *Boston Globe* article called the South End, "the most elegant slum in the world."[5] The neighborhood had long been home to the nation's largest rooming house district, in the past serving primarily as a transition point for aspiring migrants, both domestic and foreign.[6] By the 1960s, however, the rooming house district became a "last resort" for many of the city's most impoverished residents, mixing a poor elderly with a growing addict population.[7] These were the people attending the nightly services at the Emmanuel Gospel Center. And they became the Halls' first friends and companions in Boston, the relationships through which Judy and Douglas began to understand the city.

In 1966, two years after their arrival in the South End, Douglas Hall and his friend and ministry partner, Chester Young—a graduate of fundamentalist Bob Jones University and superintendent of a nearby rescue mission—wrote a seventy-page document to distribute to evangelical leaders in Boston, called "An Evangelical Approach to a Total Inner-City Ministry."[8] The document contained neighborhood studies, critiques of evangelical attitudes toward the inner city, appropriation of Mainline Protestant writings on urban ministry, and most conspicuously, the application of Protestant

---

3. For the classic work on the mid-century era of urban crisis in the United States, see Sugrue, *Origins of the Urban Crisis*.

4. For the population decline, see Small, *Villa Victoria*, 27.

5. Quoted in Lopez, *Boston's South End*, 119.

6. See Green, *South End*, 3.

7. Lopez, *Boston's South End*, 118.

8. Hall and Young, "Evangelical Approach."

mission theories forged in non-Western contexts caught in the throes of decolonization. Hall and Young borrowed most heavily from the early work of Disciples of Christ missionary and later famed developer of "Church Growth Theory," Donald McGavran. McGavran's 1955 book, *Bridges of God*, proved most fruitful, especially the author's critique of the colonial "Mission Station Approach" to ministry.[9] According to McGavran, mission stations drew individuals out of their indigenous contexts and converted them to Western expressions of Christianity and enmeshed them in Western institutions. The process both perpetuated an expression of Christianity that was foreign to non-Western cultures and removed local converts from their cultures and thus from any possibility of propagating their faith among their own people. Mission stations, and the Western civilization to which they were attached, effectively destroyed the "Bridges of God," or the natural relational bridges within and between cultures through which the gospel flowed.

Hall and Young read McGavran's critique into the American urban environment. The young ministers contrasted two approaches to urban ministry: "the mission on the hill" strategy versus "the indigenous community approach."[10] McGavran's schema helped make sense of patterns Hall and Young witnessed not only in ministry settings, but also in the broader urban environment. Along with evangelical urban missions, they noted how groups like "the Welfare Dept., the Board of Health, the City Hospital, etc." perpetuated relationships marked by institutional distance, thus promoting the fracture of relational ties.[11] Here, Hall and Young developed their distinction between "primary" and "secondary" relationships.[12] The distinction was not their invention and can be found as early as 1938 in the work of urban sociologist Louis Wirth. According to Wirth, "primary contacts" were those of extended kinship groups common to rural and tribal cultures. Modern urbanization severed such extended, basic familial and communal ties. In their place, the modern urban environment encouraged the proliferation of secondary, more "institutionalized" relationships, marked by distance and functionality.[13] Hall and Young's notion of the terms lacked such precision, but the sense was the same. They noted resistance among the lower classes to the "secondary" relationships perpetuated by government agencies.[14] Evangelism in such a context was ineffective as well. They wrote:

9. McGavran, *Bridges of God*, 68–69.

10. Hall and Young, "Evangelical Approach," 15–20.

11. Hall and Young, "Evangelical Approach," 18.

12. Hall and Young, "Evangelical Approach," 16–18.

13. See Wirth, "Urbanism as a Way of Life," 12, 21.

14. Hall and Young, "Evangelical Approach," 18.

> When the Gospel is communicated to the people in the South
> End through the medium of a secondary relationship, often
> the listener is not able to take it in. The present cultural trend
> of people in the South End, because of this rising bureaucratic
> "welfarism," because of the disintegration of family ties and
> resulting aloneness, has created a desperate need for personal
> relationships. It is in this context that a person can listen to the
> Gospel.[15]

Like a foreign mission station, the structures of modern urban life—whether municipal or ministerial—severed communal ties, creating a world of "secondary" relationships. In such a fractured environment, new relational "bridges" would need to be established, or found.

William Dwyer and Community Organizing in the City

The threat of the "slum clearance" of the Emmanuel Gospel Center's facilities drove Douglas Hall into his friendship with Episcopalian priest William Dwyer. The common postwar government practice of slum clearance sought to rid cities of their least productive spaces, dividing the cleared land into distinct business, commercial, and residential zones. Perhaps no single practice embodied the power of government leaders' ability to destroy social and communal ties than postwar municipal efforts to raze entire neighborhoods in countless cities across the United States. In 1964, Boston officials released a plan for the South End called "The Concept"—the largest, most extensive urban renewal plan in the nation at the time—which included razing five thousand housing units, displacing thirty-five hundred households, and in total clearing over six hundred acres.[16] As the Halls soon discovered, EGC's facilities, which included their home, stood within one district to be cleared, labeled "Parcel 19." The Center's board tasked Douglas Hall and Chester Young to research ways to work with government officials to procure new facilities in the South End. The best option they found cost sixty thousand dollars, an impossible sum for a storefront mission like EGC. At the same time Hall and Young were meeting with government officials, they quietly explored alternative means to staying in the neighborhood. In 1967, Young learned of a meeting of Puerto Rican tenants discussing organizing against government plans for their neighborhood. Young went to the meeting, convincing Judy Hall to accompany him.

---

15. Hall and Young, "Evangelical Approach," 18.
16. See Vrabel, *People's History of the New Boston*, 104.

The meetings were held around the corner from EGC in the basement of St. Stephen's Episcopal Church and were led by their young priest, William Dwyer. Dwyer took over as rector at St. Stephen's in 1963. He was educated at General Theological Seminary and absorbed the liberal Mainline emphasis on robust social engagement. Sometime after seminary, however, Dwyer had a charismatic experience, due in part to his sister's own recent evangelical conversion.[17] Under Dwyer's leadership, St. Stephen's maintained a curious mix of Anglo-Catholic worship and robust social engagement, along with commitments to principles found in the evangelical and charismatic movements.

Hall and Dwyer became fast friends in 1967 as both were swept up in organizing with their Puerto Rican tenant neighbors against municipal plans to raze Parcel 19. The relationship deepened when Dwyer invited Episcopal Divinity School seminarian and budding activist Richard Lampert to complete his field work at St. Stephen's. Lampert introduced the tenant group to more confrontational organizing tactics developed by Saul Alinsky. In the fall of 1967, Lampert, Dwyer, the Halls, and their tenant neighbors took to the streets of the South End. With strong financial backing from the Episcopal Church and other Mainline organizations, the movement grew, and in 1968 they incorporated and took the name "Emergency Tenants Council" (ETC) with the motto, "No nos mudaremos de la Parcela 19!" [We shall not be moved from Parcel 19!].[18] ETC ramped up their protests throughout 1968, and in a surprising turn, the city granted ETC ownership over redevelopment of their neighborhood. In what became a nationally celebrated instance of grassroots organizing, instead of building a neighborhood to attract white middle- and upper-class residents, ETC designed and constructed a neighborhood meant to create an urban environment more fit to the extant culture of its current residents. In what became known as "Villa Victoria," the new Parcel 19 was laid out like the center of a Puerto Rican town, with a plaza and new multi-family townhomes that mixed Boston red brick and Puerto Rican plaster facades, painted bright blues, yellows, and pinks. The work of ETC also led to larger and newer facilities for the Emmanuel Gospel Center, for which they paid only six thousand dollars, one-tenth the sum originally offered by the municipal government.

At the same time Dwyer and Hall forged their friendship on the streets of the South End, Dwyer joined Hall on broader efforts to promote united evangelical ministry in Boston. In January of 1968, Dwyer rode with Hall to Gordon Divinity School for a meeting of the fledgling Evangelical

17. Borgman, interview with the author, April 16, 2019, Rockport, MA.
18. "Historia Breve de ETC," 1.

Committee for Urban Ministries in Boston (ECUMB) pioneered by Hall and Chester Young the year prior. Dwyer soon became one of ECUMB's first members.[19] By 1970, Hall and Dwyer had grown so close that Dwyer asked EGC to move into facilities next to St. Stephen's with the church functioning as a center of worship and EGC as a center of service to the broader urban community.[20] Richard Lampert, the seminarian leading St. Stephen's community organizing efforts in the late-sixties described the relationship between St. Stephen's and EGC: "The Dwyers and Emmanuel Gospel Center were good friends (really Soul Mates). . . . Because SS [St. Stephen's] and EGC were so close in heart & mind & location . . . everything really meshed together. . . . Bill Dwyer and Doug Hall were best friends."[21]

Hall's friendship with Dwyer was forged in vulnerability. In moving to the South End in the 1960s, the Halls exposed themselves to the vicissitudes of postwar urban life, which linked the displacement of their tenant neighbors through urban renewal to the destruction of the Halls' own home and ministry. In St. Stephen's and friendship with William Dwyer, the Halls found a tradition, along with robust institutional support, that promoted a form of socially engaged Christianity which their own fundamentalism did not provide. Crossing the Mainline-fundamentalist divide came from a place of need. The saving of "Villa Victoria" did not require Hall and Dwyer's friendship, but for EGC, the organization's stability in the neighborhood did not emerge apart from the relationship. Moreover, the co-labor of Hall and Dwyer—indivisible from that of their Puerto Rican neighbors and many others—generated a community and built environment more suited to the type of "primary" bonds the Halls saw lacking in the modern city. This early work of boundary-crossing friendship contributed to the creation of an urban spatial environment more suited to the types of relationships EGC encouraged in the ensuing decades. Spatial and relational repair became intertwined.

George Bullock and Evangelizing the City

Douglas Hall's friendship with black Baptist minister George Bullock was also a product of the institutional marginality of the white evangelical community in inner city Boston, combined with Hall's missionary commitments to cross-cultural partnerships. The friendship was driven by ecumenical vision and ministerial need. The two ministers met in 1968, the same year Hall

19. For Dwyer's participation, see "Introduction of ECUMB."
20. Hall, "Philosophy of EGC," 5.
21. Lampert, email message to the author, August 4, 2019.

and William Dwyer marched the streets of the South End. George Bullock was the youngest of thirty children born to Walter Bullock, a sharecropper from North Carolina.[22] George Bullock worked the family farm as a child but migrated with his father and mother to Boston's Roxbury neighborhood in 1947. In 1950, George Bullock and six of his siblings formed "The Bullock Brothers," a gospel team that sang in black Baptist networks throughout the urban Northeast. In the 1960s, with his own family of ten children, George Bullock moved to 29 Rutland Street, only a few blocks from EGC. There, he rented a small apartment from Parnell Baxter. In 1966, Baxter took over as pastor of Mt. Calvary Baptist Church, which at the time had only seven active members. George Bullock and his family followed Baxter to Mt. Calvary.

Douglas Hall met Bullock in the neighborhood two years later and invited him to come to the Emmanuel Gospel Center to lead one of their nightly evangelistic services. Bullock agreed, and instead of bringing one or two people to lead the gathering, as was typical for white suburban congregations who frequented the Center, Bullock brought most of the fledgling Mt. Calvary congregation, including their robed choir. More than an evangelistic message, Mt. Calvary immersed the small group meeting nightly at EGC in a black worship service permeated with the rhythms of gospel music. Hall remembered that meeting as a revelation, as a discovery of "indigenous vitality" in the urban church.[23] Importantly, the service was not led by middle-class whites from outside of the neighborhood, as was the norm at EGC, but rather by fellow working- and lower-class residents from the South End. The meeting led to a decades-long relationship of "fellowshipping" between Mt. Calvary Baptist Church and the worshipping community that met at the Emmanuel Gospel Center.[24] Sometimes multiple times each month, the congregations gathered in their respective storefront meeting rooms, sharing music, teaching, and relationship.

In 1969, one year after first meeting Bullock and his Mt. Calvary congregation, Douglas Hall and the Evangelical Committee for Urban Ministries in Boston—the budding coalition of urban evangelical ministers—pioneered what became over a decade of outdoor evangelistic outreach in the city. St. Stephen's Episcopal Church hosted the opening rally in June of 1969, gathering Christian leaders from the city's white, black, Puerto Rican, and Chinese communities. Five nights a week throughout the summer,

22. The following biographical sketch of George Bullock comes from two oral history interviews: Edmund Bullock, interview with the author, April 29, 2019, Boston, MA; George Bullock, interview with the author, May 21, 2019, Boston, MA.

23. Hall et al., *Cat & the Toaster*, 36–37.

24. Edmond Bullock, interview with the author, April 29, 2019, Boston, MA.

EGC staff towed a portable stage and media system constructed by Hall and his father to Boston's parks, playgrounds, and projects, most in the city's poorest neighborhoods. There, they partnered with local church leaders to hold small outreach services. Many services included music performances, and no group performed more often than the Bullock Brothers. Edmond Bullock remembered tagging along with his father and uncles to the summer services: "They [EGC] started the ministry with our music. For us, it very much became an extension of the Bullock Brothers' ministry."[25] The Bullocks called it "going up on the truck," and the meetings took them into neighborhoods throughout the city and exposed them to communities well beyond Boston's black Baptist networks.[26]

The bond between Bullock and Hall took shape at the peak of racial conflict in Boston. The Busing Crisis of the 1970s exposed the nation to the entrenched segregation and racism in northern cities like Boston, long after the legislative Civil Rights victories of the 1960s. At a time when blacks and whites avoided each other's neighborhoods, Hall and Bullock publicly partnered in evangelistic outreach throughout the city's poor and working-class communities. As Edmond Bullock recalled, "right in the middle of the Civil Rights chaos . . . those two never acted like a black man and a white man."[27] Edmund Bullock, who was bused to a white neighborhood for school, remembered the virulent racism of many of its residents, but he also remembered the paternalism latent in the kindness of the "white liberal": "there were white teachers at school who were very nice to me, but I knew I was the black kid and they were being nice to me particularly for that reason." Rather, "in his [Hall's] presence, you never felt like you were a black person . . . there was never any idea of 'hey, let's send a message.' . . . We were just people . . . [not] a project. . . . Doug Hall always felt like a friend . . . like my Dad's friend."[28]

Intercultural friendship, then, stood as an alternative to either the exclusion or paternalism that typified relationships between white and black communities in Boston. Hall and Bullock's relationship was not one based primarily on white empowerment of the black community. There was no disinterested, invulnerable benevolence on the part of Hall, whose meager salary meant his family lived on welfare throughout the 1960s and 1970s. Nor did Hall befriend Bullock first to make a statement about interracial unity. Rather, the relationship marked by friendship and mutuality was

25. Edmond Bullock, interview with the author, April 29, 2019, Boston, MA.

26. Edmond Bullock, interview with the author, April 29, 2019, Boston, MA.

27. Edmond Bullock, interview with the author, April 29, 2019, Boston, MA.

28. Edmond Bullock, interview with the author, April 29, 2019, Boston, MA.

forged in shared mission in the heat of summer revivals in the city's parks, playgrounds, and projects. The Bullock Brothers brought an "indigenous" music ministry to EGC's vision of local communities reaching their own neighborhoods. For the Bullock Brothers, the city-wide evangelistic outreach expanded their growing music ministry, drawing them into communities well beyond Boston's black neighborhoods. Boundary-crossing friendship grew within the boundary-crossing practice of evangelism, as Hall and Bullock together transgressed the boundaries of Boston's fractured urban landscape. Their relationship is a reminder that mission from the powerful to the vulnerable does not require boundary-crossing friendship. However, such friendship is required when mission draws communities together in shared ministry from diverse yet intersecting places of need.

Eldin Villafañe and Theological Education in the City

Douglas Hall's friendship with Puerto Rican minister and theologian Eldin Villafañe took shape within the Emmanuel Gospel Center's endeavors to bring stability to its neighborhood's Puerto Rican community and Douglas Hall's unfulfilled longings for an evangelical seminary in the heart of Boston's inner city. At an outdoor evangelistic gathering in 1969, Judy Hall overheard a group of Puerto Rican pastors discussing the need to make the five-hour journey to New York City the following day to buy more Spanish Bibles.[29] The Halls' ministry partner, Chester Young, for at least the past year, had already suggested opening a Spanish-English Christian resource center in the South End. Spurred by Young's idea and the conversation between Puerto Rican pastors, in the spring of 1970, the Emmanuel Gospel Center hired a young seminarian at Gordon-Conwell Theological Seminary, Webster Brower, to run the store. Brower had spent five stints in Latin America and had plans to work there as a missionary. Under Brower's leadership, the bookstore soon became a hub for the city's growing Puerto Rican pentecostal community, providing not only much-needed Christian resources in Spanish, but also acting as a liaison between the Puerto Rican community and the many service agencies in the city. Importantly, the store emerged in tandem with the building of "Villa Victoria," thus forming a part of what was becoming the heart of Boston's Puerto Rican community.

When new patrons came to the store, Brower took their business card and then tried to network them with other leaders in the Puerto Rican pentecostal community or in Boston's broader Christian community. Early in 1975, Eldin Villafañe, a pentecostal minister and new PhD student at

29. Judy Hall, interview with the author, May 29, 2019, Boston, MA.

Boston University stopped by the store. Brower took Villafañe's card and immediately connected him with Douglas Hall. Villafañe had recently arrived from New York City, where he worked as the director of Christian education for Iglesia Juan 3:16 in the Bronx. Iglesia Juan 3:16, founded in 1938, was likely the largest Spanish-speaking pentecostal congregation in the country at the time.[30]

The year Villafañe arrived in Boston, Gordon-Conwell Theological Seminary was laboring to start an inner-city program. The institution was founded by Baptist A. J. Gordon nearly a century prior in 1889 in the South End. First called the Boston Missionary Training School, early classes were held at Gordon's Clarendon Street Baptist Church, only a few blocks from Emmanuel Gospel Center. In the ensuing decades, the school made its slow march out of the inner city, and in 1951 settled in bucolic Wenham, Massachusetts. With seminary leadership rooted in a white, suburban context, their vision to open an urban campus proved challenging to realize, as institutional support waxed and waned throughout the early 1970s. The seminary's vision was caught in the fractured metropolitan environment, an environment that had channeled the city's white middle-class, including white evangelicals and their money, through the newly constructed freeways, dispersing them into the burgeoning suburbs. Such a context made bonds between white suburban evangelical leadership and leaders in the city's minority Christian communities thin at best, but most often, nonexistent. Douglas Hall was an exception, as he maintained connections with Christian leaders in both suburban and inner-city contexts.

When Hall received Villafañe's contact information, he called him immediately. The Villafañe family invited the Halls over for dinner, and with children of the same age, as Judy Hall recalled, "we all hit it off."[31] The bond between the families remained strong over the years, especially when the Villafañes moved from Boston University family housing to the newly-built Villa Victoria neighborhood, to an apartment on San Juan St. across the street from the Emmanuel Gospel Center. The Halls' son Kenneth and the Villafañes' sons, Dwight and Eldin Jr., were a year apart and played at each other's houses on a weekly basis. The sons played on the same baseball team, and the Villafañes and Halls vacationed together outside of the city. The shared physical presence of EGC and the Halls in the South End made the intercultural friendship a possibility.

Villafañe provided Gordon-Conwell what the white evangelical community could not: a PhD-trained theological educator with cultural ties to

---

30. See Cruz, *Masked Africanisms*, 30.

31. Judy Hall, interview with the author, May 29, 2019, Boston, MA.

the many communities increasingly populating the inner city. Soon after Douglas Hall and Eldin Villafañe's relationship began to take shape, Hall hired Villafañe as the new director of their Inner-City Curriculum Project (ICCP), an effort EGC pioneered in 1973 to develop more appropriate Christian education materials for urban communities. At the same time, Hall circulated Villafañe's name among seminary leadership and in May of 1976, Gordon-Conwell's president Harold John Ockenga invited Villafañe to a meeting to discuss the seminary's ideas for an urban campus. Also at the meeting were Douglas Hall, William Dwyer, and black Baptist minister and Massachusetts state representative Michael Haynes, among others. Two months later, the seminary hired Villafañe as director for its new Center for Urban Ministerial Education (CUME).

Villafañe's pioneering efforts to found CUME brought institutional coherence to Boston's emerging multiethnic evangelical coalition. Hired in July of 1976, Villafañe had two months to plan courses, find faculty, and arrange for locations in the city to hold classes. The fall semester began with thirty students, seventeen black, eleven Spanish-speaking, and two white.[32] Less than two years later, enrollment grew to over one hundred. Courses in English were held at Michael Haynes's Twelfth Baptist Church in Roxbury and Spanish courses at the Emmanuel Gospel Center. Unlike primarily residential seminaries, CUME catered to bi-vocational pastors who resided in Boston and its surrounding communities, thus promoting enduring local ministerial relationships. By the mid-1980s, the program became a national model for urban theological education, offering classes in English, Spanish, Portuguese, and French-Creole.[33] The languages represented the multiethnic African-American, Puerto Rican, Brazilian, and Haitian evangelical network fostered through the partnership of CUME and EGC.

Douglas Hall and EGC were a constant resource for CUME, functioning as CUME's early bookstore (through EGC's Spanish-English Bookstore) and CUME's research arm for analyzing urban trends and demographic changes. Likewise, CUME was a resource for EGC, drawing them further into the city's growing migrant and minority population and educating much of EGC's future staff. Living only blocks from one another, Hall and Villafañe continued working closely, guest teaching in one another's seminary courses and partnering on writing projects. Throughout the 1980s, EGC and CUME emerged together as a nexus of Boston's growing evangelical and pentecostal communities. The organizational ties between EGC and CUME—and the intercultural friendship of Hall and Villafañe undergirding

---

32. See Jackson, "Toward a Contextualized Urban Theological Education," 148.

33. Jackson, "Toward a Contextualized Urban Theological Education," 12.

the institutional relationship—emerged as a product of the white evangelical abandonment of the inner city decades prior when Gordon College and Divinity School left the city in 1951. The evangelical institutional exodus cleared space for pioneering mission endeavors, including pioneering endeavors in theological education based on novel intercultural partnerships. Like with Dwyer and Bullock, Hall's friendship with Villafañe was forged through hours spent in shared ministry practices. Also like Dwyer and Bullock, Hall and Villafañe lived in the same neighborhood, a neighborhood EGC helped save in the late 1960s. All of Hall's boundary-crossing friendships were products of the residential proximity made possible through the activism that created the new Villa Victoria neighborhood of the 1970s. The sustained sharing of place—complemented by shared ministerial visions—generated the multiple boundary-crossing friendships of Douglas Hall.

FRIENDSHIP AND BUILDING "PRIMARY" TIES IN A FRAGMENTED CITY

The Halls' early experiences with boundary-crossing friendships shaped their missiology. The couple noticed, through participation, that churches built on the "primary" relationships common to cultures with extensive communal ties grew faster than among other communities in the urban environment.[34] Yet, through practices such as urban renewal and slum clearance, the inner city context proliferated institutionalized and individuated "secondary" relationships, often unwittingly destroying the very cultural ties that promoted the healthiest expressions of Christianity in the city. Thus, constructing communities more conducive to the city's most impoverished residents, communities often with strong "primary" relationships, led to a more vital Christianity. In a short newsletter piece titled "Beyond Contextualization," the Halls began to identify such a connection:

> Contextualization means that we study the more relational aspects of culture . . . [then] we design a method of communicating the Gospel which utilizes these natural relational bridges of the culture. . . . But what if [as had happened in urban contexts] aspects of culture have deteriorated and the natural, relational bridges have fallen in? To what then do we contextualize our ministry? . . . We have seen that the way an urban ministry relates to the community that surrounds it can determine that ministry's life or death. . . . We discovered that when

34. They first identified this trend in 1971 among Boston's growing Puerto Rican pentecostal community. See Hall and Hall, "There Is a Problem."

community-building was in process, we would be able to plant churches that were contextualized to that reviving community.[35]

The intertwined spatial and relational repair of their neighborhood promoted the health and growth of Christian communities within such an environment. Thus, according to the Halls, spatial, relational, and spiritual renewal coalesced to reconstruct the "primary ties," or the "bridges of God" through which the church grew.

Hall eventually recognized through his experience with boundary-crossing friendship that Christianity not only required strong bonds within discrete cultural communities, but that such "primary" ties could extend across such communities through friendship. In an undated paper titled "Understanding Defensive Sub-Cultures in the American City with Implications for Church Growth," Hall described the propensity of the urban environment to generate fractured, "defensive sub-cultures."[36] In such a context, the ministry leader "plays a key role in establishing a trusting primary type relationship" between such groups.[37] Then, "When a pastor or urban missionary has enough of these primary contacts, he has literally created a network that transcends the various groups."[38] Such relational work was "a necessary part of the church's ministry of producing wholeness in a fragmented world."[39] Modern urban environments, marked by fracture, hindered Christianity growing through naturally occurring "primary ties" within cultural sub-groups. Such ties had to be supplemented with the additional "primary" bonds of trusting, intimate friendships between such cultures. For the Halls, the forging of such relationships occupied the core of ministry in a postindustrial urban West.[40]

35. Hall and Hall, "Beyond Contextualization."
36. Hall and Hall, "Understanding Defensive Sub-Cultures."
37. Hall and Hall, "Understanding Defensive Sub-Cultures," 5.
38. Hall and Hall, "Understanding Defensive Sub-Cultures," 5.
39. Hall and Hall, "Understanding Defensive Sub-Cultures," 5.
40. The Halls' emphasis on maintenance of "primary" relationships shows many parallels with a body of missiological thought the Halls did not read: the German *Volk* mission theorists of the late nineteenth and early twentieth centuries. Similar to the Halls, German missiologists like Bruno Gutmann and Christian Keysser emphasized the preservation of "primordial ties" of *blut und boden* (blood and soil) and "age-set" derived from the missionaries' respective experiences in East Africa and Papua New Guinea and Protestant notions of natural theology emphasizing maintenance of the "orders of creation." Buttressing the arguments of the *Volk* missiologists was a critique of the individualism promoted by modernity—and by many Western missionaries—a critique of individualism that the Halls likewise shared. The Halls' priority of "primary" relationships, then, emerged within a longer missiological critique of the acids of modernity that eroded communal relationships. The couple's eventual emphasis on the

CONCLUSION

In his recent book, *The New Urban Crisis,* urban studies professor Richard Florida describes how North American cities are increasingly characterized by a segregated diversity, a "Patchwork Metropolis" spatially divided along mutually reinforcing lines of race and class.[41] The Emmanuel Gospel Center, and the friendships which constituted its emergence, worked against this trend. By the late 1980s, the organization identified a coherent "Emerging Church" in Boston centered in the city's poor and working-class migrant and minority communities and occupying the leading edge of Christian renewal in New England.[42] The Emmanuel Gospel Center and Gordon-Conwell's CUME program were organizational hubs of this growing multiethnic evangelical and pentecostal network. The network had its roots in the boundary-crossing friendships forged through the pioneering missionary visions and vulnerabilities of Douglas and Judy Hall. As the Halls later theorized, the trust and intimacy of cross-cultural friendships in ministry stood as a counter to a modern urban environment and social structure that worked to divide communities from one another. The dense and diverse city could promote fragmentation, but it also generated novel intercultural relationships that encouraged placing the work of boundary-crossing friendship at the heart of urban mission.

BIBLIOGRAPHY

Bullock, Edmund V., Sr. *Lessons of My Father.* Bloomington, IN: WestBow, 2015.

Cruz, Samuel. *Masked Africanisms: Puerto Rican Pentecostalism.* Dubuque, IA: Kendall/ Hunt, 2005.

Florida, Richard. *The New Urban Crisis: How Our Cities Are Increasing Inequality, Deepening Segregation, and Failing the Middle Class—and What We Can Do About It.* New York: Basic, 2017.

Green, James R. *The South End.* Boston: Boston 200, 1975.

Hall, Douglas, et al. *The Cat & the Toaster: Living System Ministry in a Technological Age.* Eugene, OR: Wipf & Stock, 2010.

Hall, Douglas, and Judy Hall. "Beyond Contextualization." 1984. Emmanuel Gospel Center Archives, Boston, MA.

———. "Case Study on the Emmanuel Gospel Center." 1980. Emmanuel Gospel Center Archives, Boston, MA.

---

promotion of "primary" relationships across cultures subverted, however, tendencies within *Volk* missiology to baptize inherited cultural divisions. For a discussion of the *Volk* theorists and subsequent critiques, including their links to Nazism, see Yates, *Christian Mission in the Twentieth Century,* 34–53.

41. Florida, *New Urban Crisis,* 121–24.

42. Hall and Hall, "EGC and the Emerging Church."

———. "EGC and the Emerging Church." 1990. Emmanuel Gospel Center Archives, Boston, MA.

———. "Philosophy of EGC." 1970. Personal papers of Douglas and Judy Hall.

———. "There Is a Problem." 1971. Emmanuel Gospel Center Archives, Boston, MA.

———. "Understanding Defensive Sub-Cultures in the American City with Implications for Church Growth." n.d. Emmanuel Gospel Center Archives, Boston, MA.

Hall, Douglas, and Chester Young. "An Evangelical Approach to a Total Inner City Ministry." 1966. Emmanuel Gospel Center Archives, Boston, MA.

Hall, Judy. "Judy's Story." 1994. Personal papers of Judy Hall.

"Historia Breve de ETC." 1970. Northeastern University Archives, Inquilinos Boricuas en Acción Collection, Boston, MA.

"Introduction of ECUMB," 1968. Emmanuel Gospel Center Archives, Boston, MA.

Jackson, Bruce W. "Toward a Contextualized Urban Theological Education: The Center for Urban Ministerial Education: An Historical and Analytical Case Study." EdD diss., Boston University, 1995.

Lopez, Russ. Boston's South End: The Clash of Ideas in a Historic Neighborhood. Boston: Shawmut Penninsula, 2015.

McGavran, Donald Anderson. The Bridges of God: A Study in the Strategy of Missions. London: World Dominion, 1955.

Small, Mario Luis. Villa Victoria: The Transformation of Social Capital in a Boston Barrio. Chicago: University of Chicago Press, 2004.

Sugrue, Thomas J. The Origins of the Urban Crisis: Race and Inequality in Postwar Detroit. Princeton, NJ: Princeton University Press, 2005.

Vrabel, Jim. A People's History of the New Boston. Amherst: University of Massachusetts Press, 2014.

Wirth, Louis. "Urbanism as a Way of Life." American Journal of Sociology 44.1 (1938) 1–24.

Yates, T. E. Christian Mission in the Twentieth Century. Cambridge: Cambridge University Press, 1994.

SECTION II

The Problems with Friendship

"Utmost Harmony?"

The Ambiguities of Friendship in the Early Serampore Mission

BRIAN STANLEY

The evangelical Protestant missionary movement originated in small clusters of like-minded individuals who became convinced that their own experience of the saving grace of God in Christ constituted a compulsion to share the knowledge of that grace with all humanity. The first evangelical mission agencies were founded in the eighteenth and early nineteenth centuries by those who were distant from the structures of power in church or state—they were either dissenters from established churches or, if members of such churches, they were marginal men who stood little chance of ecclesiastical preferment. As such, they found their support and encouragement in one another. The missionary societies that they established were close-knit communities of Christian friends. Friendship, rather than formal structures of authority and obedience, was the cement that bound them together. The intimacy of these ties of spiritual community supplied much of the strength needed to sustain missionary enterprise overseas when converts were few and discouragements were many.

However, this informal basis of missionary organization came under increasing strain with the passing of time. The intensification of competition for the funds of the Christian public favored those societies that worked hard to broaden and regularize the basis of philanthropic support. The thousands of miles that separated missionaries from their home base appeared to increase in number as sea-born news eventually reached Asia or Africa that erstwhile friends and faithful supporters had passed away.

The ravages of tropical disease also decimated the missionary force, creating gaps in the communities of friendship that were not always filled by those who shared the values of the founding generation. Perhaps most important of all, as the trickle of indigenous converts began to flow, the question arose of how—if at all—those converts were to be admitted to the tight communities of Christian friends that formed the nuclei of many of the first Protestant mission stations.

This study analyzes the ambiguities and quite widely varying meanings of friendship in the early years of the Bengal mission established by the first of the evangelical foreign missionary societies, the "Particular-Baptist Society for propagating the Gospel among the heathen"—or Baptist Missionary Society (BMS), as it soon became known.

THE SERAMPORE MISSION OF THE BAPTIST MISSIONARY SOCIETY

The Society, founded in Kettering, Northamptonshire, on October 2, 1792, drew much of its original support from the network of some twenty village and small-town churches belonging to the Northamptonshire Baptist Association. The Association, founded in 1765, was a body that extended well beyond the county boundaries of Northamptonshire to much of the East Midlands of England.[1] The primary instigator and pioneer missionary of the BMS, William Carey, was, before his departure for India in 1793, the pastor, first of the village church at Moulton near Kettering and then of Harvey Lane Baptist Church in Leicester. Its first secretary and theologian was Carey's close friend, Andrew Fuller, pastor of the Baptist church in Kettering. All three congregations were members of the Northamptonshire Baptist Association. The Association was instrumental in disseminating Fuller's missionary-minded brand of evangelical Calvinism, rooted in the theology of Jonathan Edwards, among both Particular (Calvinistic) Baptists and Independents (Congregationalists) in England. Without it, there would have been no Baptist Missionary Society.

When the Association issued its annual circular letter to its member churches in 1807, it reflected with amazement on how much had been accomplished by such a small band of Christian friends since the first meeting of the Association in 1765:

> Among the pastors who first met nearly all are gone to give account of their stewardships and many who have since been

---

1. Elwyn, *Northamptonshire Baptist Association*, 15.

burning and shining lights amongst us are removed to other stations. This, however, tho' a loss to us, we have no cause upon the whole to regret, seeing it is for the general good of the Redeemer's kingdom. On the contrary, there is reason for thankfulness. From this stock brethren a bough has been planted among the heathen, the branches of which have already begun to "run over the wall." This little band of men, whose hearts God hath touched, have in the name of the Holy child Jesus, wrought wonders; and shewn us in a measure what may be done under a divine blessing by faith & love and a united heart.[2]

"This little band of men, whose hearts God hath touched" found its replica in miniature in Bengal in the Baptist missionary community established in January 1800 sixteen miles north of Calcutta (now Kolkata) in the Danish colony of Serampore. The core of that mission community was made up by what later became known as the Serampore Trio, comprising William Carey, Joshua Marshman, and William Ward. Before settling at Serampore, Carey and his first missionary colleague, John Thomas, previously a surgeon with the East India Company, had resided in Company territory in Dinajpur district, in the north of modern Bangladesh. There they managed indigo factories on behalf of George Udney, a sympathetic Commercial Resident of the Company. All Europeans intending to reside in Company territory, whether they were missionaries or not, were required to apply for a license. The BMS missionaries knew that any such application would be promptly refused to any Nonconformist missionary at a time when religious dissent was widely associated with political subversion. One of their number, John Fountain, was a source of continual anxiety to Andrew Fuller on account of his intemperate pronouncements against "despotism." Temporary covenants with the Company and the cover of employment in the indigo business provided Carey and Thomas with a short-term expedient, but nothing more.[3] Danish colonial rule—which had provided a sheltering umbrella for the first Protestant mission in India at Tranquebar from 1706—offered a more secure basis for missionary operations.

Neither of the other two members of the Trio came from churches then in membership with the Northamptonshire Association. They had contrasting backgrounds. Joshua Marshman was an elementary schoolmaster, born in Wiltshire, who had studied at Bristol Baptist Academy (now Bristol Baptist College) under John Ryland, formerly pastor of College Street Baptist Church in Northampton and one of the founders of the BMS. William Ward

2. "To the Ministers & Messengers Assembling at Spalding on May 19, 20, 21, 1807" [BMSA B/Ho 3/6].

3. Carson, *East India Company and Religion*, 53–58.

was a printer and newspaper editor who had connections with the "corre-sponding" or political reform societies of the 1790s. As editor of the *Derby Mercury* from 1789 to 1791 he had expressed public support for the early stages of the French Revolution. In 1794 he moved to Stafford to become assistant editor of a new paper, the *Staffordshire Advertiser*. At the end of 1795 he moved to Hull, where for nine months in 1796 he became the editor of the *Hull Advertiser and Exchange Gazette*. Although he had been associated with the Particular Baptist cause during his later years in Derby, it was only in Hull that he was baptized and became a member of a Baptist church.[4]

FRIENDSHIP IN THE SERAMPORE MISSION

Although Carey knew neither Marshman nor Ward before their arrival in Bengal, he soon forged close friendships with both men and wrote enthusiastically to Andrew Fuller of the qualities of the new recruits. In February 1800, Carey lauded William Ward as "the very man we wanted, he enters into the Work with his whole soul."[5] In a later letter he described Ward as "one of the best men in the world, and a most valuable treasure to the Mission."[6] Carey's letter of February 1800 also referred to Joshua Marshman as "a prodigy of diligence and prudence," who had demonstrated exceptional speed in learning Bengali.[7] In the same letter, he singled out for praise Marshman's wife, Hannah, who was to play a pivotal role as a female educationalist, in addition to serving as "mother" of the entire Serampore mission family. Hannah was "mother" of the mission in both a symbolic and a more personal sense: as death periodically removed members of the mission, their orphaned children came under Hannah's care. By 1812, she had thirteen children, six of her own and seven adopted.[8]

The Serampore community of Christian friends was thus not restricted to the male gender. "I have very great pleasure in all my brethren and sisters here," wrote Carey to his friend, John Sutcliff, pastor at Olney in Buckinghamshire, in February 1801. "They are of the right sort; and perhaps as striking a proof as ever was exhibited of the possibility of persons of

4. The fullest source on Ward's early career is Smith, "William Ward," 218–44. See also the article on Ward in *Oxford Dictionary of National Biography*; Fearn, "Derbyshire Reform Societies," 49, 52; Stennett, *Memoirs of William Ward,* 11.

5. Carey, letter to Fuller, February 5, 1800 [BMSA IN/13].

6. Carey, letter to Fuller, February 27, 1804 [BMSA IN/13].

7. Carey, letter to Fuller, February 5, 1800 [BMSA IN/13]. On Hannah Marshman, see Chatterjee, *Hannah Marshman.*

8. Brooke, "We May Have Read," 77.

different tempers and abilities being able to live in one family in the exercise of Christian love. . . . We really love one another."[9]

What Carey did not say was that two key members of the mission family were either regularly or intermittently separated from its table fellowship by the onset of severe mental illness. One was his own wife, Dorothy, who had traveled to India with great reluctance and from the early months of 1795 began to exhibit symptoms of paranoia. She became obsessed with the notion that Carey was unfaithful to her, uttered repeated obscenities, and on at least one occasion attempted to murder her husband.[10] Ward's journal entry for May 16, 1800, painted a tragic picture: "Mrs Carey is stark mad. We keep her from table. She has got an unfounded idea that I beat the boys [i.e., the Careys' sons]; & she calls me all the vile names she can think of."[11] On the medical advice of John Thomas, Carey had agreed to keep his wife in a strict confinement occasionally interrupted with episodes of sound mind and liberty. The dining table at the mission was the hub of the community. In the absence of Dorothy Carey, it fell to Hannah Marshman to take responsibility for feeding the large numbers who frequently gathered for meals. Dorothy eventually died of fever on December 8, 1807.

The other member of the Serampore family who became mentally ill was, ironically, John Thomas himself, although his affliction was less continuous and violent than Dorothy's. On June 22, 1800, only a month after Ward confided to his journal the report of Dorothy being "stark mad," he made a similar entry in relation to John Thomas: "This day at Noon, Bro. Thos. who had been going off several days, became quite mad. He is now tied on his bed, cursing, swearing, singing, & talking all manner of profanity & filthiness."[12] Despite being Carey's first missionary companion on the voyage to India in 1793, Thomas becomes noticeably less visible in missionary correspondence from Serampore from mid-1800. He died in October 1801.

Life within the mission family was thus far from untroubled. In addition to the trauma of marital disharmony and mental illness, there were the inevitable rows between discordant personalities. Ward's journal for January 18, 1800, recorded, "This has been an awful week to us as a family on account of a quarrel" between two of the missionaries, Daniel Brunsdon (who had accompanied the Marshmans and Wards on their voyage to Bengal in 1799) and John Fountain. As it happened, neither of the warring parties survived long enough to poison the atmosphere indefinitely. Fountain died

9. *Periodical Accounts*, 2:150.

10. Beck, *Dorothy Carey*, 108–16.

11. William Ward's Journal [hereafter WJ], vol. 1, May 16, 1800 [BMSA IN/16].

12. WJ, vol. 1, June 22, 1800 [BMSA IN/16].

of dysentery on August 20, 1800. Brunsdon followed him to the grave on July 3, 1801.

The mission family at Serampore was consciously modeled on apostolic precedent. Although the account of the first Jerusalem church contained in the second chapter of the Acts of the Apostles was the ultimate inspiration, the immediate model of mission organization was that set by the pioneers of Protestant missions, the Moravian Brethren. In his famous pamphlet, *An Enquiry into the Obligations of Christians to Use Means for the Conversion of the Heathens* (1792), Carey had outlined the Moravian ideal of the missionary community as an economically self-supporting colony of married couples.[13] At the founding meeting of the BMS in Kettering on October 2, 1792, Carey produced a copy of the first issue of the *Periodical Accounts* of the Moravian missions, published in 1790.[14] Both Joshua Marshman and William Ward wrote of their indebtedness to the Moravians. "Thank you, ye Moravians," Ward wrote in his journal, "you have done me good. If I am ever a missionary worth a straw, I shall owe it to you under our Saviour."[15] Furthermore, August Gottlieb Spangenberg, Zinzendorf's successor and the chief strategist of the Moravian missionary enterprise, had written a set of *Instructions for the Members of the Unitas Fratrum, Who Minister in the Gospel among the Heathen*, which appeared in English translation in 1784. It was this brief (fifty-five-page) pamphlet that supplied the Serampore Trio with a blueprint for the idea of several missionary couples forming one mission family, united by "brotherly love" and sharing a common purse.[16]

Even before the mission found its home at Serampore, Carey wrote to Fuller setting out his vision for a Moravian-style self-supporting mission made up of seven or eight families living in community and practicing community of goods. The community would be managed by elected stewards and would observe "fixed Rules" for meals, agricultural work, study, worship, and preaching assignments. When they were forthcoming, indigenous converts would be admitted to the community, and "all should be considered equal, and all come under the same regulations."[17] Although there were never sufficient missionary recruits for this primitive apostolic vision to be implemented on the scale Carey envisaged, the Serampore mission adopted

13. Carey, *Enquiry*, 73–74.

14. Mason, *Moravian Church*, 88.

15. WJ, vol. 1, June 21, 1799 [BMSA IN/16], cited in Mason, *Moravian Church*, 169.

16. Moravian Church, *Instructions for the Members*, 11, 13; see also Carey, *William Carey*, 90, 186; Mason, *Moravian Church*, 67.

17. Carey, letter to Fuller, November 16, 1796 [BMSA IN/13].

the essence of Carey's plan from its inception. Thus, William Ward recorded in his journal for January 18, 1800:

> This week we have adopted a set of rules for the government of the family. All are equal, all preach & pray in turn, one superintends the family for a month & then another; Bro. C is treasurer & has the regulation of the Medicine Chest; Brother Fountain is his librarian. The Saturday evening is devoted to the adjusting of differences, & pledging ourselves to love each other.[18]

The monthly rotation of leadership of the mission family marked a significant departure from Moravian precedent. Spangenberg's *Instructions* required each Moravian "house-congregation" to set one person in paternal authority "over the rest" as a general or provincial "helper."[19] The Serampore mission community, on the other hand, practiced a rotating system of governance that reflected the more radical Baptist interpretation of the priesthood of all believers, and, perhaps also, something of the democratic political sentiments that Fountain and, at least originally, Ward had publicly espoused.[20]

The rules that governed communal life at Serampore underwent several revisions. In his journal for Christmas Day 1800, Ward recorded that he had submitted to each of the Brethren a "Form of Agreement" that set out their missionary principles and, in addition, a new set of rules for the mission family. He also referred to Joshua Marshman having produced an accompanying Plan of Union.[21] The "Form of Agreement" in its final form was not adopted till October 1805. It was concerned with missionary strategy rather than the details of community living at Serampore and is noteworthy chiefly for its unambiguous declaration that the European role in evangelizing India would necessarily be a minor one—"It is only by means of native preachers that we can hope for the universal spread of the Gospel throughout this immense continent."[22] Ward's rules appear to have reaffirmed the maxim that all members of the mission should pool their income in a common fund, a principle that was (perhaps *had to be*) restated in 1805. Carey subsequently recalled that, within a year from 1805,

---

18. WJ, vol. 1, January 18, 1800 [BMSA IN/16].

19. Moravian Church, *Instructions*, 40–41; Carey, *William Carey*, 186.

20. Smith believes that Ward had "washed his hands of politics and social reform by the time he threw in his lot with the BMS," but this is probably an overstatement ("William Ward," 239).

21. WJ, vol. 1, December 25, 1800 [BMSA IN/16].

22. *Periodical Accounts*, 3:205.

this financial arrangement was found impracticable and "consigned to oblivion."[23] Once Serampore had planted outstations some distance away, the attempt to pool finances aroused resentment among the outstation missionaries and had to be abandoned; those missionaries not resident at Serampore were instead made directly dependent on funds supplied from BMS in England, although Andrew Fuller still regarded them as being subject to the authority of the Serampore Trio.[24] Here lay the seeds of future conflict.

THE BREADTH OF THE SERAMPORE COMMUNITY OF CHRISTIAN FRIENDS

The increasing geographical dispersal of the Serampore Mission personnel imposed some modification of the ideal of a covenanted mission community of Christian friends, rendering ultimately impossible the replication of the model of the first Jerusalem church as recorded in Acts 2:44. Nevertheless, in principle the circles of evangelical friendship extended much more widely than Serampore itself.

One of Carey's few converts from his pre-Serampore days in the Dinajpur district was Ignatius Fernandez, a former Catholic priest of Portuguese descent, originally from the Portuguese colony of Macao. Carey left Fernandez in charge of the work in this district after he moved down to Serampore, and Fernandez paid periodic visits to Serampore thereafter to maintain the bonds of fellowship. William Ward's journal entry for October 5, 1805, suggests that Fernandez had been fully accepted as a member of the family of friends:

> This afternoon Bro. Fernandez left us. Is it that we may set a proper value on friendship, that we are so frequently called to part with friends, in some such way as this, that we love spring better because we have passed through a hard winter? I love Bro. Fernandez more than ever, & I parted from him more reluctantly than ever. He was much affected.[25]

Despite the separation imposed by distance, the ties of friendship were maintained by assiduous letter writing. The Trio maintained frequent correspondence with their erstwhile colleagues in the Northamptonshire Baptist Association, but also more widely. From 1800, members of the Trio became regular correspondents with two leading Baptist ministers in the

23. Carey and Marshman, *Letters from the Rev. Dr Carey*, 56.

24. Potts, *British Baptist Missionaries in India*, 23–24.

25. WJ, vol. 2, October 5, 1805 [BMSA IN/16].

United States—Dr. William Rogers of Philadelphia and John Williams of New York. Both men took a leading role in encouraging the development of missionary initiatives within and from the United States. In the early 1770s, Rogers had served as pastor of the First Baptist Church in Philadelphia, but by the turn of the century was a professor of oratory and English language at the University of Pennsylvania.[26] Williams was a Welsh-speaking emigrant to New York City who only learned English when he got there. He was a director of the interdenominational New York Missionary Society, formed in 1796, which worked mainly among the Chickasaw nation. Williams wrote to Carey informing him of the Society's work and inviting him to enter into correspondence. The result of these two chains of international correspondence was the growth of "a warm friendship between the brethren on both sides of the sea," even though they had never met.[27] For this generation of evangelicals, "friendship" was an elastic concept of spiritual brotherhood that did not even require personal acquaintance.

Neither were the bonds of friendship that extended from Serampore confined to the Baptist denomination. The inaugural services of the Baptist church at Serampore, held in April 1800 after the arrival of the Marshmans, the Brunsdons, and William Ward, included prayer offered by "Bror. Forsyth," that is, Nathaniel Forsyth, the solitary missionary of the London Missionary Society in Calcutta.[28] When the Serampore Mission Press was devastated by fire in March 1812, with losses of manuscripts and print fonts amounting to some £12,000 in value, the support demonstrated by the evangelical Anglican Company chaplains, David Brown and Thomas Thomason, and by John H. Harington, Anglican president of the Calcutta Bible Society, was heartfelt and practically generous. Joshua Marshman was moved to observe, "The christian [sic] sympathy of our friends almost overwhelms me."[29] However, the correspondence of Henry Martyn, the most famous of the evangelical Company chaplains, reveals that relations between the Serampore missionaries and the Company chaplains oscillated between fulsome protestations of loving brotherhood in Christ and a fair measure of mutual sniping.[30]

26. UARC, "William Rogers 1751–1824."

27. Williams and Williams, *Serampore Letters*, iii, 56–60.

28. Williams and Williams, *Serampore Letters*, 50.

29. Marshman, "Letter to John Ryland, March 12, 1812." For the generous response of the Calcutta Bible Society to the Serampore fire, see Canton, *History of the Bible Society*, 1:284–85.

30. Ayler, *Letters of Henry Martyn*, 178, 180, 182, 215, 223, 243, 264, 272, 274, 278, 316, 364, 503, 524.

The eighteenth-century evangelical revival movements created networks of friendship and missionary information that spanned the continents and, within certain limits, transcended denominational allegiance. But perhaps the stiffest challenge to the ideal of a Christian community that transcended the divisions of culture and ethnicity was posed by the conversion of the Serampore mission's first Hindu, Krishna Pal, in December 1800. A month previously, Pal, a carpenter, had dislocated his shoulder in a fall and had the shoulder reset by John Thomas. That act of healing opened Pal's mind to receive instruction in the Christian gospel from both Ward and Carey's eldest son, Felix. On December 22, when Thomas asked Pal whether he had understood what Ward and Felix had taught him, he replied that he, together with his friend, Gokul, now believed that "the Lord Jesus Christ had given his life up for the salvation of sinners." Ward records Thomas's response: "Dr T. said, Then I can call you brother; come and let us eat together in love. At this time the table was set for luncheon, and all the Missionaries and their wives, and I and Gokool, sat down and ate together."[31] This act of eating at a common table caused a sensation among the town's population. By eating with Europeans, Krishna Pal and Gokul had committed an act of ritual pollution and had broken caste. "It was reported all over the town that Krishna and Gokool had eaten with the Sahebs, and become Europeans."[32] Parents promptly withdrew their children from the Baptists' schools, out of fear that they were about to become Christians.[33] Although Gokul soon had second thoughts and for a time held back, Pal was baptized in the sacred waters of the Ganges on December 28, with an astonished crowd watching the spectacle. He went on to become a missionary in the employ of the Serampore Mission, serving in Sylhet in the north of Bengal. Ward published his biography in 1822. By June 1802, nine former Hindus had followed Pal through the waters of baptism and broken their caste by eating at the missionaries' table.[34]

Indians had been admitted to the common table at Serampore and hence to the circle of Christian brotherhood and friendship, but at a high cost. In the minds of both the missionaries and the surrounding Hindu population, conversion to Christianity was thereby equated with the renunciation of caste rules and identity. For Hindu observers, though not for the BMS missionaries themselves, the step that Krishna Pal and his successors had taken necessarily also implied their adoption of a European

31. Ward, *Brief Memoir*, 14.
32. Ward, *Brief Memoir*, 14.
33. Potts, *British Baptist Missionaries*, 116.
34. Potts, *British Baptist Missionaries*, 35.

identity—they had "become Europeans." There were plausible theological reasons for the stance that the Serampore missionaries took. To confess the lordship of Christ was to be admitted to a brotherhood and sisterhood that transcended all affiliations of ethnicity or caste. There was a strong argument that such spiritual unity should be given visible expression in a common table and indeed in eating together at the Lord's Table, as Krishna Pal soon did. Nevertheless, it is hard to resist the conclusion that for many years to come the Baptist mission in North India would pay a high price for the resulting marginalization of Christianity from the higher ranks of Indian society. Although it might appear to a modern observer that the Serampore missionaries had not grasped the centrality of caste to Indian social structure, there is evidence that, on the contrary, they understood it only too well. The issue was that, in contrast to their Lutheran predecessors in the Tranquebar mission, they felt that no compromise with caste scruples could be tolerated without infringing the radically inclusive basis of Christian fellowship.[35]

Ironically, over a century later, in June 1910, V. S. Azariah, a young Anglican clergyman from South India, would berate the missionary community, as represented at the World Missionary Conference in Edinburgh, precisely for their shameful reluctance to demonstrate Christian friendship by inviting Indian Christians into their homes to eat with them. The contrast points to the shift in the social composition of the Indian Christian community that had taken place by 1910 and also to the much greater prominence of "untouchables" (Dalits) in South India than in Bengal (they are hardly ever mentioned in the Serampore correspondence). Azariah was himself a "semi-untouchable" from the Nadar community. He spoke for the growing proportion of Indian Christians who had little or no caste status to lose and would be only too glad to have been welcomed to a missionary's table.[36]

STRAINS ON CHRISTIAN FRIENDSHIP IN THE SERAMPORE MISSION

Carey regularly informed a variety of correspondents that the Serampore community was a model of Christian friendship. Thus, he wrote to John Williams in New York City in 1801 that the missionaries, their wives, and children formed a "common Family, and live in the utmost harmony."[37] In

35. Forrester, *Caste and Christianity*, 25–28, 197–98.

36. Harper, *In the Shadow of the Mahatma*, 12–13, 147–48; Stanley, *World Missionary Conference*, 124–25.

37. Carey quoted in Brooke, "We May Have Read," 78–79.

March 1806, Carey similarly reported to Fuller that "We are, through divine mercy, all well, and living in the utmost harmony."[38] In August 1811, Carey again reassured Fuller that "we, viz. Bror M., Ward, and myself live in the utmost harmony."[39] The repeated phrase "utmost harmony" attempted to draw a veil over Carey's own domestic tragedy before Dorothy's death in 1807, not to speak of other episodes of disturbance and disagreement. Nevertheless, it would be unduly skeptical of the modern historian to dismiss such language as entirely delusional. For the first fifteen years or so of the Serampore mission, the claims of a harmonious mission community are, to an extent at least, supported by the evidence.

In the final section of this article, it is necessary to explain why, from 1815 onwards, the dominant note of the Serampore mission in its relationships, both with the BMS committee at home and with a younger generation of Baptist missionaries who had come out to Bengal, was one of disharmony. There were complex issues of property and finance involved that I have explored elsewhere.[40] But three main reasons may be adduced for the increasing strain that was now imposed on the ethos of Christian friendship that had marked the Serampore Mission before 1815.

First, operational realities made sustaining the ethos problematic. The working assumption of Carey, Marshman, and Ward was that the human agency through which God would in time transform the structures of Bengali Hindu society was their local mission community in which the rhythms of corporate prayer, the availability of the Scriptures in vernacular translation, and the witness of Christian family life and industrious labor, would together point Hindus to the truths of the gospel. The BMS Committee, meeting thousands of miles away in Northamptonshire, was not, and could not be, the seat of authority, even though it was the source of both funds and missionary recruits. The Trio accordingly expected to make the necessary decisions about where new recruits from Britain were to be stationed and therefore about which ones it was feasible to admit to the covenanted union that was the Serampore mission family. In 1813, the Charter of the East India Company was renewed, with the crucial addition that, for the first time, the Company grudgingly acknowledged a responsibility to allow persons to apply for licenses to enter its territories for the purposes of disseminating "useful knowledge, and of religious and moral improvement."[41] This circumlocution for the admission of "missionaries" represented the

---

38. Carey, letter to Fuller, March 14, 1806 [BMSA IN/13].
39. Carey, letter to Fuller, August 2, 1811 [BMSA IN/13].
40. Stanley, *History*, 57–67.
41. Carson, *East India Company and Religion*, 151–52, 250.

modest extent of the achievement won by the mass evangelical petition-
ing campaign for modification of the Charter, which William Wilberforce
had orchestrated. Missionaries still had to apply for a Company license,
but from 1813, for the first time, evangelical Nonconformists felt confident
enough to do so. Though initially rebuffed by an unsympathetic Court of
Directors, the BMS appealed to the Board of Control and gained its desired
licenses.[42] As a result, BMS missionaries could now reside in Calcutta and
other parts of the Company's territories without fear of expulsion. A mode
of mission suited for an operation restricted to a small Danish colony would
prove decreasingly appropriate in the new and more dispersed context of
Baptist missionary work.

A second and related problem was that the widening disjunction between the older generation of missionaries in Serampore and the "younger
brethren" now stationed in Calcutta brought to the surface existing resentment among the latter at the central role played in the affairs of Serampore
by Joshua Marshman. Even before 1813, the younger missionaries had
begun to criticize Marshman as ambitious for himself and his family and
suspected him of seeking to amass his own private fortune.[43] Carey was
not blind to "Br. M's 'imperfections.'"[44] As he admitted to Andrew Fuller in
1811, Marshman was "excessively tenacious of any idea which strikes him as
right or important," and "his regard for the feelings of others very [sic] little,
when the cause of God is in question."[45] Carey and Ward had always seen
another, more attractive side to Marshman, but for the more recent arrivals,
his obstinacy and fondness for power were major obstacles to the unity of
the now expanded mission force. After the opening of Marshman's pet, and
extraordinarily grandiose, project, Serampore College, in 1817, his critics
found more plentiful ammunition for their attacks on Marshman, and increasingly Carey was caught in the crossfire, to his great personal distress.[46]

A third, and perhaps decisive reason for the change of tone in the Mission after 1815 was the passing of the founding fathers of the Society in
England. One of Carey's closest associates in the Northamptonshire Baptist
Association, John Sutcliff, died in June 1814. Andrew Fuller, the Society's
first secretary and Carey's personal friend, died in the following May. He
was replaced as BMS secretary by another of the original Northamptonshire
circle, Dr. John Ryland. Ryland was not, however, Fuller's or Carey's first

42. Carson, *East India Company and Religion*, 151–52.

43. Stanley, *History*, 60.

44. Carey, letter to John Ryland, June 14, 1821 [BMSA IN/13].

45. Carey, letter to Fuller, August 2, 1811 [BMSA IN/13].

46. Stanley, *History*, 65.

choice. Fuller had hoped that the Committee would appoint as his successor, to both the Kettering pastorate and the BMS secretaryship, Christopher Anderson, pastor of the Baptist congregation meeting at Richmond Court in Edinburgh, which in 1818 would move to the former Episcopalian building of Charlotte Chapel. Anderson had been Fuller's companion on his fund-raising tours in Scotland and remained the lynchpin of Scottish support for the society. However, Anderson declined to consider the position, pleading the weight of his pastoral duties in Edinburgh and aware that some members of the Committee would oppose his nomination.[47] Ryland was a stop-gap appointment and was himself declining in health. Although he remained as nominal secretary until his death in 1825, from 1818 the reins of power passed increasingly to a full-time paid secretary, John Dyer. Dyer, formerly a pastor in Reading, was "a Pharaoh who knew not Joseph." Carey complained to Ryland in 1821 that "I cannot write to Mr Dyer, all his communications are like those of a Secretary of State, and not, as was formerly the case, with dear Br. Fuller, those of a Christian Friend."[48] At length, in 1823, Carey bared his soul to Dyer in reply to the latter's sincere attempt to narrow the gap of understanding that had opened up with Serampore:

> I formerly had friends whose hearts beat in unison with my own. All the letters of Fuller, Pearce,[49] Ryland, Sutcliffe, and others were dictated by the most sincere affection: But except my very highly esteemed friends Ryland and Burls,[50] no person belonging to the Mission Society, or more properly to the Committee, has, since the death of Dear Fuller, written me a single letter of friendship, till that sent by yourself, to which this is a reply.[51]

The era of a mission that was held together by ties of friendship, rather than by more formal lines of responsibility between home committee and missionaries on the field, was drawing to an end. The claims of "utmost harmony" were heard no more. By 1827, the Serampore Mission and the BMS had severed their formal relationship. Although the divorce was eventually healed in 1837, none of the Trio lived to see the healing of the breach. Ward died of cholera in March 1823. Carey died in June 1834. Marshman lived long enough to participate from India in the written negotiations of reunion but died in December 1837 before the news of a settlement reached India.

47. Meek, *Mind for Mission*, 25–26.

48. Carey, letter to Ryland, June 14, 1821 [BMSA IN/13].

49. Samuel Pearce of Birmingham was a founding member of the Society and close friend of Carey who had died in 1799.

50. William Burls, treasurer of the BMS.

51. Carey, letter to John Dyer, January 23, 1823 [BMSA IN/13].

CONCLUSION

Evangelical approaches to Christian mission are often criticized, not without reason, as unduly individualistic. However, perhaps the most important conclusion to draw from this study of the Serampore Mission is the extent to which Carey and his colleagues adhered to a corporate vision of Christian witness. It drew from their own baptistic understanding of Christian churches as covenanted fellowships of baptized believers, but also was deeply influenced by the Moravian model of missions, with its emphasis on self-supporting communities governed by a rule of life that encompassed work, worship, study, and proclamation. The result was a Protestant form of missionary monasticism. In principle the missionary community was one that originally transcended the categories of missionary and indigenous convert, but in the context of a Hindu caste society, the irony was that the admission of indigenous converts to the table fellowship of the mission community severed them so absolutely from their own society that Christian communities developed in North India which were unhealthily dependent on European protection and financial support. Cross-cultural friendship could all too often mean cross-cultural dependency. The other irony was that the bonds of friendship that united the Serampore missionaries with the founding fathers of the mission at home proved over time sources of tension and exclusion. Serampore's insistence on maintaining the intimacies of friendship constrained the ability of the mission to adapt to the passing of the generations.

BIBLIOGRAPHY

Primary Sources

Ayler, Scott D., ed. *The Letters of Henry Martyn: East India Company Chaplain*. Woodbridge, Suffolk, UK: Boydell, 2019.

Baptist Missionary Society Archives [BMSA]. Boxes B/Ho 3/6, IN/13, IN/16. Regents Park College, Oxford, UK.

Carey, William. *An Enquiry into the Obligations of Christians to Use Means for the Conversion of the Heathens*. 1792. Edited by E. A. Payne. Reprint, London: Carey Kingsgate, 1961.

Carey, William, and Joshua Marshman. *Letters from the Rev. Dr Carey: Relative to Certain Statements Contained in Three Pamphlets Lately Published by the Rev. John Dyer, Secretary to the Baptist Missionary Society: W. Johns, MD, and the Rev. E. Carey and W. Yates*. 3rd ed. London: Parbury, Allen & Co., 1828.

Marshman, Joshua. "Letter to John Ryland, March 12, 1812, printed in 'Printed Circular Letter from Andrew Fuller addressed to the Friends of Christianity and Oriental

Literature.'" n.d. [ca. 1812]. Reeves Collection, MCR, R4/1. Regents Park College, Oxford, UK.

Moravian Church. *Instructions for the Members of the Unitas Fratrum, Who Minister in the Gospel among the Heathen*. London: Brethren's Society for the Furtherance of the Gospel among the Heathen, n.d. [ca. 1784].

Periodical Accounts Relative to the Baptist Missionary Society. Vols. 2–3. Clipstone; London: J. W. Morris, 1799–1809.

Stennett, Samuel. *Memoirs of the Life of the Rev. William Ward, Late Baptist Missionary in India*. London: J. Haddon, 1825.

Ward, William. *Brief Memoir of Krishna-Pal, the First Hindoo, in Bengal, who Broke the Chain of the Cast, by Embracing the Gospel*. 2nd ed. Serampore: John Offor, 1823.

Williams, Leighton, and Mornay Williams, eds. *Serampore Letters: Being the Unpublished Correspondence of William Carey and Others with John Williams 1800–1816*. New York: Putnam's Sons, 1892.

Secondary Sources

Beck, James R. *Dorothy Carey: The Tragic and Untold Story of Mrs. William Carey*. Grand Rapids, MI: Baker, 1992.

Brooke, Jonathan. "'We May Have Read—but the Reality!': Narrating Baptist Missions in Bengal, 1800–1855." PhD diss., School of Oriental and African Studies, University of London, 2010.

Canton, William. *A History of the British and Foreign Bible Society*. 2 vols. London: John Murray, 1904.

Carey, S. Pearce. *William Carey, DD, Fellow of Linnaean Society*. 7th ed. London: Hodder & Stoughton, 1926.

Carson, Penelope. *The East India Company and Religion, 1698–1858*. Woodbridge, Suffolk, UK: Boydell & Brewer, 2013.

Chatterjee, Sunil Kumar. *Hannah Marshman: The First Woman Missionary in India*. Calcutta: Sri Sunil Chaterjee, 1987.

Elwyn, T. S. H. *The Northamptonshire Baptist Association: A Short History 1764–1964*. London: Carey Kingsgate, 1964.

Fearn, E. "The Derbyshire Reform Societies 1791–1793." *Derbyshire Archaeological Journal* 88 (1968) 47–59.

Forrester, Duncan B. *Caste and Christianity: Attitudes and Policies on Caste of Anglo-Saxon Protestant Missions in India*. London: Curzon, 1980.

Harper, Susan Billington. *In the Shadow of the Mahatma: Bishop Azariah and the Travails of Christianity in British India*. Grand Rapids, MI: Eerdmans, 2000.

Mason, J. C. S. *The Moravian Church and the Missionary Awakening in England, 1760–1800*. Woodbridge, Suffolk, UK: Boydell, 2001.

Meek, Donald E., ed. *A Mind for Mission: Essays in Appreciation of the Rev. Christopher Anderson (1782–1852)*. Edinburgh: Scottish Baptist History Project, 1992.

Oxford Dictionary of National Biography. Oxford: Oxford University Press, 2014.

Payne, E. A. "Review of *William Carey, Especially His Missionary Principles*, by A. H. Oussoren." *Baptist Quarterly* 12 (1948) 165–67.

University Archives and Records Center [UARC], University of Pennsylvania. "William Rogers 1751–1824." Online. https://archives.upenn.edu/exhibits/penn-people/biography/william-rogers.

Potts, E. Daniel. *British Baptist Missionaries in India 1793–1837: The Story of Serampore and its Missions*. Cambridge: Cambridge University Press, 1967.

Smith, A. Christopher. "William Ward, Radical Reform, and Missions in the 1790s." *American Baptist Quarterly* 10 (1991) 218–44.

Stanley, Brian. *The History of the Baptist Missionary Society 1792–1992*. Edinburgh: T&T Clark, 1992.

———. *The World Missionary Conference, Edinburgh 1910*. Grand Rapids, MI: Eerdmans, 2009.

Interracial Friendship in the Era of Jim Crow

KENDAL P. MOBLEY

In 1922, Charlotte Hawkins Brown (1883–1961), founder of Palmer Memorial Institute,[1] published a brief essay entitled "Cooperation Between White and Colored Women" in the *Missionary Review of the World*. She expressed appreciation for white women who wished to engage in interracial cooperation but stressed that genuine cooperation would not be possible until white women accepted black women as their equals in human dignity. "There can be no cooperation between white and colored women," she declared, "unless we approach it by way of the teachings of the Lord Jesus Christ: 'Thou shalt love thy neighbor as thyself.'"[2]

At thirty-nine years old, Brown had two decades of experience working with whites who supported her school in Sedalia, North Carolina, and for ten years she had been a leader in "interracial cooperation." She was one of four black women invited to address the Memphis Conference, a gathering

---

1. Palmer Memorial Institute, in Sedalia, North Carolina, became a leading black preparatory school in the era of segregation. It closed in 1971. Brown also organized the Sedalia Home Ownership Association, helping blacks in Sedalia to purchase property and escape the sharecropping system. She was a state-wide and national leader in women's clubs and teachers' organizations, and she was active in the YMCA, YWCA, the Federal Council of Churches, and the National Urban League. See Wadelington and Knapp, *Charlotte Hawkins Brown*. See also Marteena, *Lengthening Shadow*, which highlights the accomplishments of many Palmer graduates.

2. Brown, "Cooperation," 486. Her essay was one of several in that issue of the *Missionary Review* intended to prepare the way for Haynes, *Trend of the Races*, the 1922 united mission study.

of white Protestant churchwomen sponsored by the Women's Committee of the Commission on Interracial Cooperation (CIC) in 1920, and she served subsequently on the North Carolina CIC's Women's Committee.[3]

Brown's personal experience with white women fell far short of the equality and reciprocity implied in Jesus' love ethic. She cited as examples two of her white friends, one from the South and the other from the North. Her Southern friend showed a casual disrespect by using Brown's first name and blithely assuming a special knowledge of black people. "Charlotte," she said, "the Northern white people do not understand the Negro as we do. We Southern women understand you perfectly. We have been reared with you, nursed by you. Your folks have been everything in our homes and we know you through and through." Brown recalled, "I was struggling not to resent her calling me by my first name, because I knew it was from force of habit in dealing with Negroes as servants . . . and not as a term of endearment." Her Northern friend, a longtime supporter of Palmer Institute, insisted that using Brown's first name was indeed a term of endearment, but when Brown addressed the woman's fourteen-year-old daughter by her first name, her friend said, "You must not call my children by their first names; you are not their social equal."[4]

For Brown, *friendship* described a range of relationships with whites. She often spoke of fundraising as "making friends" for Palmer, and she counted anyone who supported her work as a friend of the school. But in a few cases, her friendships with longstanding supporters transcended shared interest and grew into relationships of mutual caring and emotional intimacy, even though they were still infected by the inequality and ethical double-standard of white supremacy. This essay will focus on her friendships with several key supporters: Mary Grinnell, Galen and Lucy Stone, and Lula McIver. Analysis of Brown's interracial friendships reveals key principles for the anti-racist practice of missional friendship today.

Friendship is "a distinctively personal relationship that is grounded in a concern on the part of each friend for the welfare of the other, for the other's sake, and that involves some degree of intimacy."[5] The jarring incongruities in Brown's relationships with whites forced her to question the very meaning of friendship, and she concluded that white supremacy created an ethical double-standard in interracial friendships. They could be real, but they were fraught with irony and contradiction. Of the two white

3. On the Memphis Conference and Brown's involvement, see Gilmore, *Gender and Jim Crow*, 199–202; Commission on Interracial Cooperation, "Southern Women," 5–6; Knotts, "Race Relations," 201–2; Hall, *Revolt against Chivalry*, 87–95.

4. Brown, "Cooperation," 485.

5. Helm, "Friendship."

friends who had demeaned her, she wrote, "I must speak of them as friends for they have met the test, although we are taught that there can be no real friendship except upon a basis of mutual respect. Do these women respect me? Of course they do. They recognize two codes of ethics—one for white women and another for colored."[6] The friendships were genuine, yet they were afflicted with the ethical dualism of white supremacy.

LOTTIE HAWKINS BECOMES CHARLOTTE HAWKINS BROWN

Lottie Hawkins was born in Henderson, North Carolina, near the plantation where her grandparents were enslaved. Her grandmother, Rebecca Hawkins, daughter and half-sister to the people who enslaved her, was used for breeding slaves, yet Brown claimed that the white Hawkins family favored Rebecca. By 1870, Rebecca's family lived on a forty-acre farm, a "splendid economic start" that Brown attributed to the white Hawkins's care. Yet there was also pain associated with that relationship. Brown described the experience visiting the crumbling remains of the plantation when she was about forty years old and feeling "the commingling emotions of pride and humiliation."[7]

Brown's mother, Caroline Hawkins (1865–1938), the youngest of Rebecca's twenty-one children, was raised among the "financial giants" of Raleigh in the home of Rebecca's white half-sister, Jane A. Hawkins (1827–98), who never married and asked to raise the child. When Caroline began socializing with young men, "Miss Jane" told her, "Caroline, if there be anything like a colored lady, I want you to be one." The ambiguity in that statement—the expression of doubt—shaped not only Caroline's consciousness but Brown's. Years later, Brown remarked, "What a challenge to Negro

6. Brown, "Cooperation," 485.

7. Brown's biographers described Rebecca as part of the class of enslaved persons "whose covertly positive relations with their masters caused them to internalize the values of well-to-do whites" (Wadelington and Knapp, *Charlotte Hawkins Brown,* 14). For the quotations from Brown, see "Some Incidents" (Charlotte Hawkins Brown Papers [CHBP] 2.1–3). Items are identified by folder (f.) and sequence (seq.) numbers. Typescript documents in CHBP often contain typographical errors, which I have corrected for the sake of easier reading. Manuscripts and typescripts contain inconsistent capitalization, grammar, word divisions, etc. I have left them as they appear in the documents. In "Some Incidents," Brown noted that white tenant farmers, whom she called "Po' white folks," rented land on Rebecca's farm. With these whites, though there was no blood kinship, she claimed an enduring and almost familial affection. Note Gilmore's claim that Brown's account of her family history was a myth calculated to play on white sympathies (*Gender and Jim Crow,* 179–82).

womanhood! That story—that challenge burnt its way into my very soul, and I now suspect my first real knowledge of difference in races was born when I heard it." When Caroline became pregnant out of wedlock, she was sent back to Rebecca, but she remembered the social and cultural sensibilities she learned from Raleigh's white elite and passed them on to Lottie.[8]

When Lottie was six years old, her family moved to Cambridge, Massachusetts, where she attended public schools. Her mother ran a laundry from the basement of their home, a short distance from Harvard University. Brown claimed that she was never made to feel racial difference at school and only became aware of segregation in high school,[9] but she was aware of differences in status. She often referred to the symbols of middle-class respectability ("a well-furnished parlor, a piano, a well-lighted dining room and pretty bedrooms . . . the growing vines and flowers around the front door and the windows")[10] that her grandmother and mother were careful to incorporate into the décor of their homes. Although she was named "Lottie" at birth, as a senior at the Cambridge English High School preparing for graduation, she adopted the name "Charlotte Eugenia" for her diploma because she thought it was as dignified as the "long beautiful names" of her classmates.[11]

That year, Brown met Alice Freeman Palmer (1855–1902), the second president of Wellesley College, who made it possible for her to attend the Salem Normal School in Salem, Massachusetts, at no cost.[12] After her first year of college, a second unlikely encounter changed her life again. As she boarded a train with several white students one day in 1901, a woman introduced herself as the field secretary of the Woman's Department of the American Missionary Association (AMA). She was looking for qualified black teachers for AMA schools in the South. Brown regarded the encounter as a sign from God. She left Salem Normal School after only one year to take charge of Bethany Institute, a small AMA school in McLeansville—later known as Sedalia, North Carolina.[13]

8. Brown, "Some Incidents" (CHBP 2.3); "Biography" (CHBP 1.5); Wadelington and Knapp, *Charlotte Hawkins Brown*, 16–18.

9. Brown, "Biography" (CHBP 1.4); "Some Incidents" (CHBP 2.3–4).

10. Brown, "Biography" (CHBP 1.5–6).

11. Jenkins, "Twig Bender" (CHBP 7.29).

12. Brown, "Biography" (CHBP 1.7–10); Wadelington and Knapp, *Charlotte Hawkins Brown*, 31–34.

13. Jenkins, "Twig Bender" (CHBP 7.39–40); Wadelington and Knapp, *Charlotte Hawkins Brown*, 28, 34–35. The AMA was organized in 1846 by abolitionists, led by Arthur Tappan, who wanted an alternative to the American Home Missionary Society and the American Board of Commissioners for Foreign Missions. See Beard, *Crusade of*

Although born in North Carolina, Brown presented herself as a well-educated New Englander whose early life experience was free of segregation. She regarded good manners and refined culture as ways to resist and subvert white supremacy, and she incorporated them into the curriculum of Palmer. She tried to create a perception of herself and her students as members of a black elite. She became famous on the radio and through her best-selling etiquette manual as an authority on the social graces, and she protested when whites who were not intimate friends refused to address her as "Miss Hawkins" before her marriage, "Mrs. Brown" after she was married, or "Dr. Brown" after she was awarded an honorary doctorate. As one scholar argued, Brown always endeavored "to claim the status of a lady in the eyes of white people."[14]

THE ORIGINS OF THE PALMER MEMORIAL INSTITUTE

The AMA's support for Bethany Institute was inadequate, so Brown solicited financial assistance from Northern friends. She traveled to Massachusetts in the summer, visiting friends, churches, and resort hotels, to make her appeal. The AMA abruptly withdrew support from Bethany Institute after her first year, closing all their one- and two-room schools. They offered her a position elsewhere, but Brown, only nineteen years old, decided to stay and open her own school, which meant that she had to raise all the funds. Once again, she turned to supporters in the North.

Brown appealed to Alice Freeman Palmer, but their relationship was cut short by Palmer's sudden death in 1902. Brown asked Harvard University professor George Herbert Palmer (1842–1933), Alice's husband, for permission to name the school after her. He agreed and supported the school for decades. Palmer's name gave Brown's school instant credibility among Palmer's friends and admirers, and Brown's story of her first encounter with Palmer added a sense of divine destiny.

Brown's fundraising work depended upon the support of upper-class whites, who had the resources she needed. She was devoted to the strategy

---

Brotherhood; Richardson, *Christian Reconstruction*; Hollyday, *On the Heels of Freedom*. The AMA took control of Palmer Memorial Institute in 1926, as the Palmer board of trustees sought a permanent and reliable source of revenue, but Brown's rigid leadership of the institution led to the AMA's withdrawal in 1934. See Wadelington and Knapp, *Charlotte Hawkins Brown*, 124, 132–55.

14. Chirhart, "Charlotte Hawkins Brown." For an example of Brown's protest, see Brown, letter to Lowe, May 9, 1921 (CHBP 43.72). See also Brown, *Correct Thing*. Brown's first marriage to Edward Sumner Brown ended in divorce (1911–1916), and another to John William Moses was annulled (1923).

of racial uplift, believing that with enough time and resources, blacks would achieve a level of social and cultural development that demanded recognition of their right to full social and political equality. Whites, having benefitted from generations of slavery and oppression, owed a debt to blacks that could be discharged in part by supporting the work of racial uplift. She tried to subvert white supremacy incrementally without alienating white supporters who were willing to help with what she called "the problem of adjustment."[15] It was a difficult balancing act that required great subtlety and skill. One of her main strategies was to appeal to white notions of honor, fairness, propriety, and respectability, and she accommodated her message to whites in ways that sometimes drew criticism from those who chose a more radical approach.[16]

BROWN'S INTERRACIAL FRIENDSHIPS

Paradoxically, Brown discovered that curiosity about racial difference sometimes facilitated friendships with upper-class white people that would not have been available to a white woman of her economic status. She wrote that her racial status conferred—if not advantages—at least unique opportunities:

> Being a negro with an ideal and a message has opened doors to which white people of financial standing and broader backgrounds of education and culture would covet entrance. Friendship through common interest, association and ideals have been made purely on curiosity of the other person . . . to plumb the depth of Negro thinking, which friendship I could not have had as a white woman in my place.[17]

Initial curiosity on the part of high-status whites about the black "other" could develop into friendship based on shared interests and values. It was a rare sort of friendship—imperfect, to be sure. It was an oddity of segregated society—generally prohibited and improbable (yet, as Brown noted, uniquely possible) because of the separation and inequality enforced under white supremacy.

Brown deftly leveraged friendships with elite whites to build financial support and social capital for Palmer Institute. She could rarely afford to be completely forthright with her white friends. As she indicated in her

15. Brown, "Cooperation," 487.

16. See Gilmore, *Gender and Jim Crow,* 178–86; Denard, "Introduction," xv–xxxv.

17. Brown, "Some Incidents" (CHBP 2.11).

Missionary Review essay, she sometimes had to endure racist slights and insults quietly as the cost of friendship. As one scholar observed, Brown developed a "covert style" of relating to whites that helped her to "circumvent the obstacles she knew she faced."[18] Whites were more disposed to help her if she presented herself in ways that seemed to affirm white values and expectations. It was an effective but costly strategy that sustained her school for more than fifty years.

Brown and Mary Grinnell

Mary Russell Grinnell (1877–1968) of New Bedford, Massachusetts, wealthy and unmarried, was a frequent, generous, and long-term supporter. She inherited part of an insurance fortune through her father, Richard W. Grinnell, and her grandfather, Lawrence Grinnell, who was the senior partner in Lawrence Grinnell & Co. She also inherited part of the Howland whaling fortune through the estate of Silvia Ann Howland in 1916.[19] In the early years, she gave a minimum of $200 annually, served on the Palmer board of trustees, and contributed so substantially to the building of the domestic science cottage that it was named in her honor.[20] Like many white supporters, Grinnell was very much in favor of teaching agricultural, domestic, and industrial subjects, but she was less enthusiastic about the liberal arts because she regarded blacks as intellectually inferior. She queried Brown regarding the alleged correlation between race and intelligence, not for herself, she claimed, but on behalf of those who

> think that the true full blooded negro has not brains enough to learn any thing outside of manual labor. There are those who think if a colored person cares for books it is because they have white blood in their veins somewhere which gives them that taste for learning. A lady once . . . asked if I ever knew of an educated colored person who had no white blood. . . . I said yes, I thought I did know of such a person, and I was thinking of you. . . . I began to think that I might possibl[y] be mistaken after all. But I see now your own parents were colored. But do you know anything about the generations back of them? . . . I am expressing the views of some of my race more plainly than those who hold them would dare to but I have always been frank with

18. Gilmore, *Gender and Jim Crow,* 179.

19. Howland, "Gideon Howland's 439 Heirs," 112; Pease and Hough, *New Bedford,* 279; Emery, *Howland Heirs,* 263, 429.

20. Wadelington and Knapp, *Charlotte Hawkins Brown,* 63–64, 74.

you and I trust that I always can be. I should like to know your opinion on this subject as I should regard it as more authentic than anything my white friends might tell me.[21]

Grinnell's questions must have been disheartening to Brown, especially since they came from a generous woman who often addressed her letters to "My dear Charlotte" and ended them with "Sincerely your friend."

Grinnell enjoyed Brown's friendship and looked forward to her letters, as when she wrote, "The other day I was feeling depressed and then your letter came to me like a sunbeam out of a cloudy sky. I thought how foolish to feel lonely when such a friend as you are, were thinking of me in such a warmhearted way." On another occasion, she wrote: "I want to thank you for all the loving thoughts expressed in your letter. No one has ever given me the compliments that you do and when I realize their sincerity I feel almost overpowered. It is beautiful to have such a friend and your depth of feeling would make it impossible for me to ever forget you." Grinnell invited expressions of intimacy from Brown: "I hope you always will continue to come to me with everything, I do not mean hesitatingly but with the assurance you should feel in turning to a friend, who is ever ready to sympathize and advise whenever it is desired that I should do so."[22]

Brown did turn to her for advice about very personal matters, including marriage, and Grinnell responded with warmth and comfort.[23] Yet Grinnell balked at having Brown stay overnight in her home. She wrote:

> I want you and yet it is with some hesitation that I ask you. If I put you in one of my guest rooms my colored cook won't know what to think of me and if I put you in the room next to her you will think I am not treating you according to your station in life. I think you will understand if I do not care to create any back-door gossip or to be criticized by my friends. . . . If you do not want to come here for the night I might inquire of a respectable colored family I know if they would take you in. . . .
>
> I mean to be cordial and I am sure if you do decide to come and stay with me that you will be comfortable wherever I put you. . . . I shall pay for your car fare from Boston and return.[24]

21. Grinnell, letter to Brown, May 29, 1909 (CHBP 32.87–89).

22. Grinnell, letters to Brown, January 28, 1910 (CHBP 33.2); July 15, 1911 (CHBP 33.84); October 11, 1909 (CHBP 32.105).

23. For example, Grinnell, letter to Brown, July 28, 1909 (CHBP 32.99–103).

24. Grinnell, letter to Brown, January 25, 1910 (CHBP 33.4–11); March 4, 1910 (CHBP 33.18–21).

For Grinnell, insulting her black friend was better than being criticized by her white friends, and she was unabashed by the contradiction. She could begin a paragraph by seeming to affirm equality, writing, "it seems to me that hereafter the same life is intended for all regardless of race or color," only to end with a racist backhanded compliment that combined an ethical double-standard with religious legitimation: "with your education you are able to fill the position you hold without seeming too free with the white people. And if you understand your own position never mind what the rest of the world think. 'God is in his Heavens, and all's right with the World!'"[25]

Brown and the Stones

Brown's most important Northern friends, in many respects, were Galen Luther Stone (1862–1926) and Carrie Morton Stone (1866–1945). Galen Stone was a Massachusetts native who became a wealthy financier in Boston and New York. He began supporting the school in 1913 and became its largest benefactor. Brown developed tremendous affection for Stone, thinking of him as a father-figure, and she often praised his commitment to equal education and opportunity for black people.

Stone refused to serve on Palmer's board until 1921, when Brown appealed to him for help in resisting "some men who occupy high places," who treated her with disrespect. He had long encouraged Brown to seek Southern support, and Brown told him of the racist insults she endured from Southern whites for the sake of Palmer: "I have succeeded in getting a good strong southern backing. It has taken years to do it, I've had to close my eyes sometimes to many things that hurt my heart to make this friendship."[26] Brown wanted Stone's support in case she had to take a stand against further indignities.

> I have already gained the interest of some people who will give me money for the school, but absolutely have no regard for the rights of [a] negro woman in terms of courtesy. . . . The question in my heart and mind, and God only knows how it hurts, is just what are they going to ask me to submit to as a negro woman to get their interest [?] . . . in my efforts to get money now I don't want my friends in the North to tie my hands so I can't speak out when I am being crushed.[27]

25. Grinnell, letter to Brown, December 21, 1910 (CHBP 33.35–36).
26. Fragment (CHBP 44.74).
27. Fragment (CHBP 44.74).

She needed a friend like Galen Stone, "a big man from the North,"[28] to help her resist others, also called friends, who might humiliate her. She used Stone's friendship as a buffer against the racist paternalism of powerful Southern white men.

Brown was also close to Carrie Stone, Galen's wife, whose correspondence was often marked by signs of intimate friendship. In a note thanking Brown for a gift, she addressed Brown as "Dear generous, thoughtful Charlotte,"[29] and she frequently closed with expressions of affection. Stone invited Brown to her home, shared family news, chatted about the weather and recent social events, and shared spiritual counsel.[30]

In a letter dated only with "Oct. 24," Stone expressed consolation for the pain Brown had experienced because of "indignities" inflicted by Southern racists, and she congratulated Brown for overcoming anger and bitterness through prayer. The indignities followed the distribution of a fraudulent letter from a nonexistent organization called the "Colored Women's Rights Association of Colored Women," allegedly distributed to black women in several counties, encouraging them to register and vote for Republican candidates and take control of state government in North Carolina.[31] The *Greensboro Patriot,* an explicitly white supremacist paper, reported that Brown wrote the letter, setting off a firestorm that forced Brown to issue a denial through the *Greensboro Daily News* three weeks later. She believed the fraudulent letter was written by "some white person to cause trouble," while she had worked all her life to promote "accord and good feeling between the races." She named several white leaders who supported her work and could attest that she had "rigorously respected and acted in accordance with the best of southern traditions governing the relations of the two races." The Palmer board purchased an advertisement that appeared on the previous page, offering a $100 reward for proof of the true authorship of the letter.[32]

28. Fragment (CHBP 44.74).

29. Stone, letter to Brown, undated (CHBP 54.34). Carrie Stone was very generous to Palmer and to Brown. She once paid for a European vacation for Brown, and in her will she left $5,000 to Palmer and $5,000 to Brown, who used her money to construct a faculty cottage named in Stone's memory. See Wadelington and Knapp, *Charlotte Hawkins Brown,* 132, 178.

30. Stone, letter to Brown, undated (CHBP 54.17–49).

31. In August 1920, Tennessee became the thirty-sixth state to ratify the Nineteenth Amendment, giving women the right to vote under the United States Constitution. The fraudulent letter was a voter suppression tactic aimed at black women. See Gilmore, *Gender and Jim Crow,* 214–15.

32. "Challenge," *Greensboro Patriot,* September 27, 1920; "Explanation," *Greensboro Patriot,* October 19, 1920; "Knows Nothing of Source; $100 Reward; Reward Offered for Information," *Greensboro Daily News,* October 14, 1920.

Apparently, Brown told Stone that she had turned to prayer to overcome her bitterness over the situation. With friendly intimacy, Stone offered spiritual counsel from a Christian Science perspective:

> The way Christian Science helps any situation is to know the truth about it, and deny the lie. While error seemed to be rampant, you knew in your prayer, that Love was greater than any sense of bitterness and resentment, and that gave you strength to do your duty.
>
> I am proud of you, for this overcoming of evil with good, and know that your path will grow brighter every day, for your larger understanding that 'Ominpotent love reigneth supreme.'[33]

Worried that Brown's anger was not completely abated, Stone encouraged Brown to avoid situations that could lead to racial conflict with Southern whites. She wrote, "It was truly a very hard experience to go through, but would it not be wiser, as long as the feeling is so strong in the south, not to subject yourself to any indignities?"[34] From Stone's perspective of white privilege, Brown was responsible for staying out of trouble, but Brown understood all too well that avoiding racial trouble was impossible for black people. The trouble caused by white supremacy was the responsibility of white people. Just three weeks before, she had declared to the white women at the Memphis Conference, "The negro women of the South lay everything that happens to the members of her race at the door of the Southern white woman. Just why I don't know but we all feel that you can control your men."[35] She did not express these sentiments to Carrie Stone. Instead, she complained of the lingering nervous anxiety she felt over the controversy and told her friend that she could not accept Christian Science beliefs. Stone replied with more expressions of sympathy and spiritual counsel.[36]

But the Stones had much more to offer than sympathy. The *Greensboro Daily News* reported that Galen Stone visited Palmer Institute on October 23, about a month after the fraudulent letter was published, to inspect a new building that he had largely financed. He met with several local leaders while in Greensboro, including E. P. Wharton (1859–1932), president of Greensboro National Bank, who hosted a luncheon in Stone's honor. At the luncheon, Stone gave a speech commending education as the best way to address "racial questions." After Stone's address, Brown spoke about her work at the Palmer Institute, stating that "it was her one aim in life to assist

33. Stone, letter to Brown, undated (CHBP 54.20–21).
34. Stone, letter to Brown, undated (CHBP 54.20).
35. "Speaking Up for the Race," 470.
36. Stone, letter to Brown, undated (CHBP 54.25–27).

in solving the racial problem in a Christian-like manner." In the wake of the controversy over the fraudulent letter, Galen Stone used his influence to calm the waters, lend credibility to Brown, and get her a platform before the most powerful men in the white community.[37]

After attending Galen Stone's funeral in 1926, Brown held a special memorial service for him at Palmer, in which she described him as "the best friend we had in the world" and "the most unprejudiced man I ever knew." Brown expressed her grief in paternal terms:

> I feel as though I have come to you from the funeral of my own father, for he has been to me what my father could not be. His keen interest and insight into the dream I held for you, his tender interest for your welfare, his loyalty to the ideals we have [tried] to uphold, . . . was unlike that of any friend we had in all the years. I can think of no one white man in all of America of whom I could speak so tenderly, so lovingly unless it could be . . . Professor George Herbert Palmer.[38]

Brown and Lula Martin McIver

Before Brown left Cambridge in 1901, her mother advised, "Try and make friends of those southern white people, for they can make you or break you." One of Brown's best Southern friends was Lula Martin McIver (1864–1944), who was then "the state's foremost white female educational advocate." Her husband, Charles Duncan McIver (1860–1906), was the first president of the State Normal and Industrial School for Girls, president of the segregationist Southern Education Association, a trustee of the University of North Carolina, and secretary and district director of the Rockefeller-funded Southern Educational Board. Despite several requests from Brown, Charles McIver wrote only one letter of support for Brown in his lifetime—at his wife's urging—and there is no evidence they ever met in person. Yet Brown was able to build a friendship of almost forty years with Lula McIver, who served many years on Palmer's board and remained a faithful supporter until her death.[39]

In a fundraising letter written in 1941, McIver described her first impression of Brown, who showed up on McIver's doorstep in 1905: "Her

---

37. "Mr. Stone Is Pleased," 16.

38. "On the Passing of Mr. Galen L. Stone" (CHBP 18.10–11).

39. Brown, "Some Incidents" (CHBP 2.5); Gilmore, *Gender and Jim Crow*, 187–88; McIver, "To Whom It May Concern," June 5, 1905 (CHBP 30.8).

daring, her enthusiasm, her faith intrigued me and I kept her for more than an hour, offering advice as to the best way to win friends." McIver recruited prominent white supporters for Brown, including E. P. Wharton. She promoted Palmer to white clubwomen throughout North Carolina and helped Brown raise thousands of dollars. The two traveled together, and when Northern white women visited Palmer, they stayed with McIver.[40]

Brown dedicated her 1919 novella, *Mammy: An Appeal to the Heart of the South,* to McIver, writing, "It is with gratitude that I acknowledge her personal interest in the colored members of her household and trust that many others may follow her example."[41] *Mammy* is a sentimental story couched in the unvarnished language and symbolism of Southern white paternalism, and several of Brown's Northern supporters questioned why Brown had written it. The story juxtaposes the faithfulness and devotion of formerly enslaved Mammy and Pappy with the thoughtless indifference to their suffering shown by their former enslavers, the Brethertons, whom they still served. It was Brown's way of saying, in language that she knew white Southerners would understand, that they owed an unpaid debt to blacks.

After reading the proofs, McIver wrote appreciatively to Brown, addressing her as "My dear Charlotte" and thanking her for the dedication. While she was polite and affirming, she implied that white Southerners did not bear the whole burden of responsibility for creating racial harmony, and blacks should accept social inequality and respect the limits of segregation. She hoped for "understanding and sympathy" between the races "as there was in the days of our parents," but that would require "knowledge of each other's problems and an active interest in solving them," with "each maintaining its racial integrity." As if to acknowledge Brown's underlying point while defending herself, she reflected on her "treasured memories" of the faithfulness of her family's black servants: "Their children and their children's children have an acknowledged claim to any help I can render them." Then she defended Southern paternalism and white Southern womanhood by claiming that just as "the white Southern woman was entrusted the task of training the uncivilized African" in antebellum America, once again it was left to "the intelligent southern white women" to guide "our 'ship of state' off the rocks of racial antagonism." She closed with "Your friend."[42]

On the surface, McIver and Brown seemed to agree that white women were the key to ending racial conflict, but McIver meant that white women

40. "Worthy Cause Seeks Assistance" (CHBP 61.15); Gilmore, *Gender and Jim Crow,* 187–89.

41. Brown, *Mammy,* v.

42. McIver, letter to Brown, April 6, 1920 (CHBP 41.45–46).

must offer paternalistic benevolence in a context of continuing social in-equality and segregation, while Brown meant that white women should use their influence to end the violence of white men and recognize black women as equals in the work of social reform and racial uplift.

Brown's novella and discourse with McIver are examples of her willing-ness to speak the language of racist paternalism to underscore the human dignity of black people. Her message struck home, for some white people found Brown's implicit criticisms in *Mammy* too harsh. Mrs. W. T. Bost, a reviewer in the *Greensboro Daily News,* claimed that Brown had overstated her case. In her view, any real-life "mammy" could expect her final years to be filled with "loving care and protection and loyalty" from the whites whom she had served. During the "Colored Women's Rights" controversy, several newspapers, including the *Fayetteville Observer,* ran an item call-ing *Mammy* "a crude attempt to foment racial differences." On the other hand, some black leaders found Brown too willing to voice white values and expectations. In 1926, W. E. B. Du Bois wrote that "Mrs. Charlotte Hawkins-Brown [sic] represents the white South."[43]

INTERRACIAL FRIENDSHIP, ANTI-RACISM, AND CHRISTIAN MISSION

Brown's interracial friendships, imperfect as they were, speak to the power and possibilities of friendship as a foundational practice of Christian mis-sion in a racist social structure.[44] While Brown's case is particular to the United States in the first half of the twentieth century, it has broader impli-cations because racism is a global problem connected with the history of colonialism.

Friendship is essential to the gospel. Jesus called his disciples "friends" (John 15:13–15), gave them a "new commandment" to "love one anoth-er," and made love the distinguishing virtue of the Christian community (John 13:34–35). In the missional context, friendship is a primary channel through which the transformational power of the gospel flows. Racism is a potent counterforce resisting missional friendship. To be true to the gospel, missional friendship must adopt an anti-racist theological praxis. To the

43. Bost, "Activities of Tar Heel Women," *Greensboro Daily News,* June 27, 1920; "Author of Plea," *Fayetteville Observer,* October 22, 1920; Du Bois quoted in Ellis, *Racial Harmony and Black Progress,* 173.

44. Friendship as a "foundational practice in Christian mission" is foregrounded in Robert, "Global Friendship," 180–84.

extent that it does not, it denies the gospel and becomes an instrument of oppression.[45]

It is important for the privileged partners in an interracial friendship to critique cultural hegemony, acknowledge unjust power relations, and use privilege intentionally to establish equity. Brown managed the power dynamics of white supremacy with remarkable skill; nevertheless, her effectiveness was limited, and her suffering was often exacerbated because her white friends were either silent or complicit in the face of racial injustice. Her white friends were willing to use their influence on her behalf, but they acted out of hegemonic whiteness and *noblesse oblige* more than genuine partnership. White cultural dominance was virtuous and unproblematic; black culture was deficient and deviant to the extent that it did not conform to white norms. As Brown wrote, "The natural assumption that all black is inferior and all white is superior must be eliminated before any really cooperative spirit can be fostered."

White fragility in the face of righteous black anger inflicts harm, stands in the way of justice, and bears false witness to the gospel. Brown resented Jim Crow, but she never took the risk of calling for an immediate end to segregation. She chose her words carefully to avoid losing white friends and supporters. Yet conforming to the dehumanizing expectations of white privilege for the sake of her work was physically and emotionally costly. Among other things, she suffered frequent bouts of exhaustion and illness due to overwork, and she subjected the Palmer faculty and students to unpredictable explosions of displaced anger over trivial matters.[46]

Anti-racist missional friendships must avoid the insidious practice of shifting responsibility for solving racism to the victims. In Brown's day, it was called "the Negro problem." Today, it is often called "the race problem." But racism has always been the problem of white privilege, and whites have contrived numerous strategies to avoid responsibility for it. One of the most effective is the gradualist approach, which Brown herself embraced, and for which she faced criticism from some of her black contemporaries. Yet, despite her gradualism, Brown grew increasingly impatient for change. Realizing that some of her most faithful supporters maintained racist sentiments despite decades of friendship and seeing no evidence of progress in the Jim Crow South, Brown came to regard white racial intransigence as a betrayal of Christian and democratic virtues, and she laid the responsibility for establishing justice at the feet of whites, especially white women. "If the

45. For an anti-racist theological critique of whiteness by a US theologian, see Perkinson, *White Theology*. For an earlier South African example, see Kritzinger, "Black Theology."

46. On Brown's unpredictable anger, see Jenkins, "Twig Bender" (CHBP 7.7).

white woman could *think* black twenty-four hours, better still, *be* black for two hours, there would be no Negro problem in America," she wrote.[47]

C. S. Lewis described friendship as love that grows from the side-by-side experience of companionship. He said friendship grows, despite status differences, when companions come to "*see the same truth.*" Similarly, Aristotle argued that great inequality makes friendship unlikely or impossible, but through the giving of love, the essential virtue of friendship, virtuous people can sometimes overcome inequality.[48]

In contrast, racist social structures like the Jim Crow South are designed to prohibit the companionship, shared vision, and giving of love that is necessary for interracial friendship. The very existence of Brown's interracial friendships, despite their flaws, is a remarkable and hopeful sign of the kingdom of God. Like the seed that sprouts and grows even though the farmer sleeps (Mark 4:26–29), the gospel has a vital force of its own and can take root in ways that defy expectation. Framed by white supremacy and motivated initially by utility, many of Brown's friendships became much more than transactional relationships. They were authentic, growing, and enduring—in some cases spanning four or five decades. Although they were far from ideal, they reveal essential lessons for the practice of anti-racism in a world still wrestling with the consequences of white supremacy.[49]

BIBLIOGRAPHY

Aristotle. *The Nicomachean Ethics*. Translated with an Introduction by David Ross. Revised by J. L. Ackrill and J. O. Urmson. Oxford World Classics. 1925. Reprint, New York: Oxford University Press, 1998.

Beard, Augustus Field. *A Crusade of Brotherhood: The American Missionary Association*. New York: Pilgrim, 1909.

Brown, Charlotte Hawkins. "Cooperation Between White and Colored Women." *Missionary Review of the World* 45 (1922) 484–87.

———. *The Correct Thing to Do, to Say, to Wear*. 1941. Reprint, Raleigh, NC: Charlotte Hawkins Brown Historical Foundation, 1990.

———. *Mammy: An Appeal to the Heart of the South*. Boston: Pilgrim, 1919.

47. Brown, "Cooperation," 487; see also her uncharacteristic expression of anger to the white women at the Memphis Conference, quoted in Gilmore, *Gender and Jim Crow*, 201, and her indictment of systemic racism in "Where We Are in Race Relations" (CHBP 14.19–26).

48. Lewis, *Four Loves*, 77–79. Discussions of friendship frequently begin with Aristotle's discourse in his *Nicomachean Ethics*, Books VIII and IX.

49. This hopeful reading of Brown's interracial friendships is informed by Robert, "Cross-Cultural Friendship," 100–107.

————. "Speaking Up for the Race at Memphis, Tennessee, October 8, 1920." In *Black Women in White America: A Documentary History*, edited by Gerda Lerner, 467–71. 1972. Reprint, New York: Vintage, 1992.

Charlotte Hawkins Brown Papers (CHBP). 1900–1961. A-146. Schlesinger Library, Radcliffe Institute, Harvard University, Cambridge, MA. Online. https://id.lib.harvard.edu/ead/sch00160/catalog.

Chirhart, Ann Short. "Charlotte Hawkins Brown: Living the Correct Way." In vol. 2 of *North Carolina Women: Their Lives and Times*, edited by Michele Gillespie and Sally G. McMillen, 52–76. Athens: University of Georgia Press, 2015.

Commission on Interracial Cooperation. "Southern Women and Race Coöperation. A Story of the Memphis Conference, October Sixth and Seventh, Nineteen Hundred and Twenty." Online. https://docsouth.unc.edu/nc/racecoop/racecoop.html.

Denard, Carolyn C. "Introduction." In *Mammy: An Appeal to the Heart of the South; And, the Correct Thing to Do—To Say—To Wear*, by Charlotte Hawkins Brown, xv–xxxv. New York: G. K. Hall, 1995.

Ellis, Mark. *Racial Harmony and Black Progress: Jack Woofter and the Interracial Cooperation Movement*. Bloomington: Indiana University Press, 2013.

Emery, William M. *The Howland Heirs: Being the Story of a Family and a Fortune and the Inheritance of a Trust Established for Mrs. Hetty H. R. Green*. New Bedford, MA: E. Anthony and Sons, 1919.

Gilmore, Glenda Elizabeth. *Gender and Jim Crow: Women and the Politics of White Supremacy in North Carolina, 1896–1920*. Chapel Hill: University of North Carolina Press, 1996.

Hall, Jacquelyn Dowd. *Revolt Against Chivalry: Jessie Daniel Ames and the Women's Campaign against Lynching*. New York: Columbia University Press, 1993.

Haynes, George Edmund. *The Trend of the Races*. New York: Council of Women for Home Missions and Missionary Education Movement of the United States and Canada, 1922.

Helm, Bennett. "Friendship." *Stanford Encyclopedia of Philosophy*, May 17, 2005. Revised Aug 7, 2017. Edited by Edward N. Zalta. Online. https://plato.stanford.edu/archives/fall2017/entries/friendship.

Hollyday, Joyce. *On the Heels of Freedom: The American Missionary Association's Bold Campaign to Educate Minds, Open Hearts, and Heal the Soul of a Divided Nation*. New York: Crossroad, 2005.

Howland, Ellis L. "Gideon Howland's 439 Heirs, 2nd Installment." *The Massachusetts Magazine* 10.2–3 (1917) 3–157.

Knotts, Alice. "Race Relations in the 1920s: A Challenge to Southern Methodist Women." *Methodist History* 26.4 (1988) 199–212.

Kritzinger, J. N. J. "Black Theology: A Challenge to Mission." DTh thesis, University of South Africa, 1988.

Lewis, C. S. *The Four Loves*. New York: Harcourt, Brace, Jovanovich, 1960.

Marteena, Constance H. *The Lengthening Shadow of a Woman: A Biography of Charlotte Hawkins Brown*. Hicksville, NY: Exposition, 1977.

Pease, Zephaniah W., and George A. Hough. *New Bedford, Massachusetts: Its History, Industries, Institutions, and Attractions*. New Bedford, MA: Mercury, 1889.

Perkinson, James W. *White Theology: Outing Supremacy in Modernity*. New York: Palgrave Macmillan, 2004.

Richardson, Joe M. *Christian Reconstruction: The American Missionary Association and Southern Blacks, 1861–1890*. Athens: University of Georgia Press, 1986.

Robert, Dana L. "Cross-Cultural Friendship in the Creation of Twentieth-Century World Christianity." *International Bulletin of Missionary Research* 35.2 (2011) 100–107.

———. "Global Friendship as Incarnational Mission Practice." *International Bulletin of Missionary Research* 39.4 (2015) 180–84.

Wadelington, Charles W., and Richard F. Knapp. *Charlotte Hawkins Brown: What One Young African American Woman Could Do*. Chapel Hill: University of North Carolina Press, 1999.

Friendship, Gender, and Power

ANICKA FAST

In the Mennonite Church USA archives in Elkhart, Indiana, dozens of boxes document the work of North American missionaries of the Congo Inland Mission (CIM) in the Kasai and Kwilu regions of the Democratic Republic of Congo. More than 200 North Americans were sent to the Congo under the auspices of this mission agency—founded as a collaborative effort between two progressive Amish Mennonite conferences in the American Mid-West—between 1911 and 1998.[1] Their encounter with a growing number of believers in Congo eventually led to the formation of one of the largest Mennonite churches in the world.[2] Since primary source documents from the first few decades of this missionary encounter are extremely sparse in Congo, historians naturally turn to these boxes of archival records, carefully preserved in North America, in order to reconstruct its events and

1. See personnel roster in Bertsche, *CIM/AIMM*, 815–33. For a more in-depth study of this missionary encounter between 1911 and 1939, see Fast, "Becoming Global Mennonites."

2. Today, just over a century later, 226,000 Congolese claim membership in one of three Mennonite or Mennonite Brethren church conferences in D. R. Congo that had their origins in this missionary encounter. See Mennonite World Conference, "World Directory." The Communauté mennonite au Congo (CMCo) is most straightforwardly related to the work of the CIM; the Communauté des Frères Mennonites au Congo (CEFMC) traces its origins to the work of former CIM missionaries Aaron and Ernestina Janzen, whose independent work at Kafumba was adopted by the Mennonite Brethren Conference of North America in 1943; and the Communauté évangélique du Congo (CEM) was organized in the 1960s by Congolese Mennonites following the migration of a large number of Baluba refugees to Eastern Kasai during a time of political turmoil. Bertsche, "Communauté Évangélique Mennonite."

144

trajectory. And since these records—made up largely of official correspondence, reports, and minutes—are largely authored by the white men of the home board and of the male-dominated leadership structures on the field, it is perhaps not surprising that for many decades, historical accounts of this encounter have tended to portray the work of the CIM as, overall, deriving from the vision and actions of North American Mennonite men.[3]

However, within the collection of personnel files that document the service record of the North American CIM missionaries, two folders stick out from the rest. Instead of typewritten correspondence with board members, these folders contain handwritten personal letters, still in their original envelopes. They were likely donated to the archive by the family of Edna Kensinger, the young American missionary woman who wrote most of them while working in Congo with the CIM between 1919 and 1925. One envelope contains a photograph of Edna being carried in a traveling hammock by two young Congolese men, one of whom is identified on the back as "Kazadi Matthew . . . eventual president of the Congo Mennonite Church" (see Figure). Most of the letters are from Edna to her family members in the United States, but five letters are written by Kazadi to Edna or her mother. This correspondence, so striking within the archive, offers important evidence that despite the dominance of white male missionaries in the official decision-making roles of the CIM, the relationships of friendship and solidarity that developed on the margins of official meetings and deliberations—such as this one that developed between a young, childless white missionary woman and a Congolese household helper with whom she shared many of the tasks and challenges of daily life—had a major impact on the progress of the missionary encounter within a complex political context of inequality and oppression.

3. See, for example, Weaver and Bertsche, *Twenty-Five Years*; Weaver, *Thirty-Five Years*; Loewen, "Congo Inland Mission"; *Three Score*. Later accounts have called more attention to the role of Africans and of expatriate CIM missionary women in the growth of the Mennonite church in Congo but remain hampered in some ways by the bias inherent in these primary sources. See, for example, Bertsche, *CIM/AIMM*; Kumedisa, "Mennonite Churches," 44–94; Tshidimu, *Centenaire*; Hollinger-Janzen et al., *Jesus Tribe*.

Kazadi Matthieu (left) and unknown household helper carrying Edna Kensinger in hammock/kipoy, ca. 1919–24
Source: Series 3 (Personnel records), Box 73, Folder 6 (Edna Kensinger, 1919–1925), Africa Inter-Mennonite Mission Records, 1911–2018, X-68, Mennonite Church USA Archives, Elkhart, Indiana. Used by permission of Africa Inter-Mennonite Mission.

The friendship between Kazadi (ca. 1900–1994) and Edna (1893–1959) began in 1919, at the close of the First World War, when the nascent Mennonite church in Congo was at a crossroads. Labor exploitation in the Belgian colony was increasing dramatically. With the global demand for raw materials from the colony at an all-time high, the Belgian colonial state began to take increasingly draconian and violent measures to recruit and coerce Africans into what was still called "free wage labor."[4] After an internal conflict that had led a number of the expatriate CIM missionaries to resign in 1916 and 1917, the few who were left were traversing an unsettled period, without strong leadership.[5] Meanwhile, the demographic balance of the mission station was shifting dramatically. Even as the number of CIM missionaries dropped off, the number of Congolese church members was growing rapidly. Between 1918 and 1923, the number of baptized church

4. Seibert, "More Continuity than Change?," 383. See also Buelens, "Le tournant de 1908," 197–209; Likaka, *Naming Colonialism*, 32–38; Vansina, *Being Colonized*, 125.

5. In 1922, there were only eight CIM missionaries in Congo, compared with the twenty-one who had been present in 1916. For more on this conflict that resulted in the resignation of several European Pentecostal CIM missionaries, see Fast, "Becoming Global Mennonites," 255–332.

members more than doubled, from 60 to 146.[6] The number of young male teacher-evangelists was also steadily increasing. In mid-1923, 52 trained teachers had been placed in villages, while 24 more were in training.[7] As the expatriate CIM missionaries were in a holding pattern, the Congolese teacher-evangelists outnumbered them for the first time.

During these unsettled years, CIM missionaries and Congolese evangelists attempted to locate themselves ecclesially vis-à-vis the pervasive new reality of dramatically worsening economic exploitation. CIM missionaries were confronted with new opportunities to align with, or differentiate from, the logic that guided state and commercial interests, as they sought to work out their ecclesial relationship with Congolese church members while also attempting to benefit from and control Congolese labor on the mission stations. Meanwhile, Congolese evangelists who associated with the CIM were engaged in boundary-crossing missionary efforts as they attempted to articulate a trans-local ecclesial identity that directly challenged the narrower ethnic and territorial categories of Belgian indirect rule.[8] This ideal of catholicity—that is, this commitment to shared membership within the church as a political body capable of transcending competing claims of race, ethnicity, gender, or nation-state—co-existed uneasily with the reality of exploitative interaction between white missionaries and Congolese laborers on the station. In this context, boundary-crossing friendships became the terrain on which various Mennonites in Congo—both white and black—sought to articulate an understanding of the church that had the potential to disrupt some of the social, economic, and ecclesial boundaries that separated them.

Historians of early twentieth-century missions have documented the impact of relationships of "mutual dependence," friendship, and mentorship between North American women missionaries and indigenous men in their fields of labor.[9] The present research continues in the same vein by tracing the story of a particular friendship while paying attention to intersecting dynamics of gender and race. However, it also uses an ecclesiological lens of analysis. It was often between white women and young Congolese men, in the intimate and private domain of the household, that relationships of friendship and solidarity could and did develop. Yet the changed attitudes that developed through such relationships spilled out into major public

6. Haigh, "Close of 1918," 101–2; Loewen, "Congo Inland Mission," 399.

7. Sommer, "Lost Opportunities," 107, 111. Compare with only six placed teachers in 1916. Haigh, "Review of the Work," 154–55.

8. Maxwell, "Remaking Boundaries," 58, 73–75. See also Vansina, *Being Colonized*, 28, 159.

9. See Robert, *Gospel Bearers, Gender Barriers*, 10, 15–16, and especially essays in that volume by Bonnie Sue Lewis, Kevin Xiyi Yao, and Silas Wu.

events and intersected with the broader ongoing efforts of Congolese evangelists to reconfigure the ecclesial landscape.

"I AM NOT LONESOME": EDNA KENSINGER AND KAZADI MATTHIEU

Kazadi Matthieu was born around 1900 to a Luba sub-chief and his eighth wife, more than five hundred miles away from the CIM station of Djoko Punda.[10] Kazadi had initially received a Catholic baptism and education, but eventually traveled to Djoko Punda, where his older half-brother was employed as a manual laborer.[11] Sometime between 1915 and 1918, he had what he later described as a "conversion experience"; after this, he said, he "never turned back from following and serving the Lord."[12] Kazadi attended school at Djoko Punda and eventually became an evangelist.[13] He was ordained as a deacon in 1930 and as an assistant pastor in 1940.[14] Kazadi would become a prominent leader in the Congo Mennonite Church, serving at its first president in 1960.[15] After the political turmoil of the early 1960s, when he and many other Baluba were pushed out of the area by other ethnic groups, he was instrumental in founding another Mennonite church in Eastern Kasai, the Communauté évangélique mennonite, or CEM.[16] Throughout his long life, Kazadi would be recognized as an "outstanding" leader, a visionary, a gifted speaker, and a founder of many congregations.[17] In 1919, however, Kazadi was still a young adult. Fresh from his recent conversion experience and familiar with labor conditions on the station through his half-brother, he now began working for the first time in the home of a white missionary as a household helper.

10. "High Lights," 3, 17.

11. "High Lights," 3, 17.

12. These words are quoted from an interview with Kazadi in "High Lights," 3, 17. In this interview, he dated his conversion between 1916 and 1918. In his diary, CIM missionary Oskar Anderson mentioned the conversion of Kazadi and Tshitambatem on May 2, 1915, after he had preached a sermon "about the pouring out of the Holy Spirit." Anderson, diary. Anderson may have been referring to Kazadi Matthieu's half-brother, or, as seems more likely, offering a different interpretation of what constituted conversion.

13. "High Lights," 3, 17. See also Chimbalanga, "Matthieu Kazadi," 119–21.

14. Minutes, CIM Field Conference, Kalamba, December 17–23, 1930, 7; Minutes, CIM Annual Missionary Conference, Mukedi, December 2–6, 1940, 5.

15. Loewen, Three Score, 119.

16. Chimbalanga, "Matthieu Kazadi"; Bertsche, "Communauté Evangélique Mennonite."

17. Bertsche, CIM/AIMM, 31–32; Chimbalanga, "Matthieu Kazadi," 119–20; Loewen, Three Score, 90–91.

Far fewer details are available about Edna Kensinger. She and her husband William spent only a few years in Congo with the CIM, serving from 1919 to 1922 and again in 1924 after a furlough. They left the CIM abruptly in 1925, prior to the end of their second term of service, in conflictual circumstances.[18] During their time in Congo, William was involved in supervising the work on CIM "outstations"—where Congolese evangelists were placed— and also served as the mission's secretary and treasurer. It is unclear what Edna's official assignment with the mission was, and no information is available about the Kensingers' trajectory after ending their work with the CIM.

Newlywed Edna Kensinger and her husband William arrived at Djoko Punda for the first time in April 1919, at a time when the other CIM missionaries were desperate for reinforcements.[19] Twenty-six-year-old Edna had a cheerful, friendly disposition and was full of excitement to make her first home with her new husband. "Both of us are just as happy as can be and we are glad that we at last have found our dear little home," she wrote.[20]

Initially, Edna appeared to take for granted the rhythms of work and worship that her CIM missionary predecessors had established on the station. In many ways, the organization of time and space at the Djoko Punda station reflected the profoundly unequal colonial relationship that existed throughout the territory, through its segregation of white and black station residents and its promotion of paternalistic control by white missionaries over the labor, the bodies, and the spiritual development of Africans.[21] In Edna's second letter home, she matter-of-factly described the weekly worship schedule that sometimes brought expatriate and African believers together, but also often separated them in ways that reflected a subtly two-tiered understanding of the church:

> The Native Service will be at ten o'clock this morning. S.S. at four o'clock this afternoon and our meeting this evening. We have Native Services every Tuesday and Friday mornings at six o'clock. Prayer Meeting for the Natives at seven Wednesday evenings and ours at eight. I had to lead the Prayer meeting last Wednesday.[22]

18. Minutes, CIM Field Conference, Djoko Punda, February 16–23, 1925. William Kensinger suffered a nervous breakdown which may have been related to a protracted conflict over CIM mission strategy. For Kensinger's own account, see "Return of Missionaries," 123.

19. Haigh, "Djoko Punda, Congo Belge," 279–80.

20. Edna Kensinger, letter to relatives, April 6, 1919.

21. See Vansina, *Being Colonized*, 35–36. For more detailed analysis of labor conditions on CIM stations, see Fast, "Becoming Global Mennonites," 249–52, 341–63.

22. Edna Kensinger, letter to relatives, April 19, 1919.

Edna also expressed pleasant surprise at the comfortable standard of living, the household arrangements, and the familiar foods that she could enjoy as a white missionary in Africa. "I am so sorry we did not bring our silverware with us," she wrote; "everywhere we go they have such nice things just like at home."[23] A few weeks later, after having successfully completed a Saturday baking that included bread, oatmeal cookies, lemon pie, "nuddle soup," and baked chicken—"almost like home"—she added, "Africa is not as bad as some people think it is."[24]

Even as Edna became habituated to the lifestyle disparities that separated blacks and whites at Djoko Punda, she also immediately began to develop friendly relationships with Congolese on or near the station. The schoolgirls would come over after church on Sunday to look at her photos, and Edna found them to be "very nice girls." She also made daily visits to nearby villages and interacted with visiting village women. She longed for the day when she could speak to all these people in their own language; "they are so interesting," she wrote.[25] However, Edna's closest everyday contact developed with the three young men who worked in her home, whom she described to her parents as "Kasadi the washjack; Cimbulu the Dining Room boy and Cibangu the kitchen boy."[26] For Edna, impressed with Kazadi's efficient handling of her first "big wash," he "certainly was a washjack."[27] Even though these young men did the bulk of household tasks, Edna was far from having "nothing to do," she explained. "They get the things ready but I always help them with the cooking."[28] For example, Edna was up before 5:30 in the mornings to "help the boys get breakfast."[29]

Over the following months, Edna began to express her appreciation for her household helpers as a kind of family. Despite differences in status, all were members of the same household to an extent, and a certain intimacy naturally developed around the sharing of daily tasks. To her relatives, she described a moment when the three young men had sought companionship with her and William during a heavy rainstorm:

> This afternoon when it began to rain William and I were in the room here and all our boys came in and sat on a trunk by us. I told William it reminds me of home, when a heavy rain would

23. Edna Kensinger, letter to relatives, April 6, 1919.
24. Edna Kensinger, letter to relatives, April 19, 1919.
25. Edna Kensinger, letter to relatives, April 19, 1919.
26. Edna Kensinger, letter to relatives, April 19, 1919.
27. Edna Kensinger, letter to relatives, April 19, 1919.
28. Edna Kensinger, letter to relatives, April 19, 1919.
29. Edna Kensinger, letter to relatives, July 22, 1919.

come up we usually gathered together in one room, and so it was with us, we had our whole family with us.[30]

When the Kensingers were briefly stationed at the other CIM station of Kalamba, she was relieved that these three would be accompanying them.[31] And when William was called back to Djoko Punda in early 1920 to go over some financial records, Edna's loneliness for her husband was tempered by the presence of Kasonga—presumably a new household helper—and Cimbulu, who were to "sleep in the Dining Room so I will not be alone in the house" during her husband's three-week absence.[32]

Edna continued to get to know her household helpers as people to whom she could transfer certain skills and in whom she took a friendly interest. Rhythms of life in Edna's household included laughter and fun. "Cimbulu and Misenga are washing the dishes," she wrote in 1921, "and are having a great time. If anyone can laugh it is Misenga."[33] Edna taught Kazadi English, and by the time the Kensingers began their second term in Congo in 1924, he had become quite fluent.[34] Together with a new single American missionary woman, Alma Diller, Edna also shared her love of singing with the schoolchildren and evangelists, as well as with her household helpers. Kazadi and Bacidi sang bass and alto, respectively.[35] The two young women sang special numbers during Sunday worship—"the people sure listen when we sing"—and initiated choir rehearsals. "I wish you could be here to listen to them singing sometime," wrote Edna to her parents. "I know you would say it pays a hundred times to come and teach them the Word of God. Alma plays the organ and I lead. I put my whole strength and soul into it and the Lord blesses the efforts."[36]

FRIENDSHIP AND ECCLESIAL IDENTITY

As Edna and Kazadi shared their linguistic and musical skills with each other, their interactions moved beyond the domain of household tasks alone to include church-based and familial connections. In at least two

30. Edna Kensinger, letter to relatives, September 16, 1919.

31. To her family she wrote, "All our boys are going with us and I am glad of that" (Edna Kensinger, letter to relatives, October 14, 1919).

32. Edna Kensinger, letter to relatives, January 11, 1920.

33. Edna Kensinger, letter to relatives, June 15, 1921.

34. Matthieu, letter to Mrs. Moser [Edna's mother], May 26, 1924.

35. Edna Kensinger, letter to relatives, June 15, 1921.

36. Edna Kensinger, letter to relatives, May 8, 1921.

ways, their relationship led to new connections and changed habits, which in turn helped to subtly reshape the ecclesial self-understanding that was developing within the missionary encounter.

First, the relationship between Edna and Kazadi helped to showcase Kazadi's strong aspiration for the expansion of the church across ethnic frontiers in the Kasai region, as well as his own developing trans-local Christian identity. Within a year of the Kensingers' arrival, Kazadi and some of the other household helpers had begun a correspondence with Edna's mother in the United States, with assistance from Edna in translating the letters from Tshiluba to English. Kazadi's letters to Edna's mother offer an important window into his ecclesial imagination. In his first letter, Kazadi expressed his strong desire for more missionaries to be sent from the United States in order to share the gospel with other "tribes" in the Kasai region who did not yet have a gospel witness:

> They [Edna and William] came to help us about the affair of God, but we want other missionaries, they do not have love for us, or do they? The tribes of the people of the Kasai, they are many. We are waiting you to send us your other speakers. I want to beg you for them. The tribes are not with speakers of God. Their names: Baketo, Bataki, Bashoke and Bakafui. These tribes are not with speakers of God. Are your hearts glad to go to heaven without us? You come to help us to go to heaven to see each other at the feet of Jesus with happiness. I am your friend . . . Kazadi of the Baluba.[37]

Kazadi expressed his trans-local ecclesial identity by appealing to the image of heaven as the place where members of the universal church, to which he now claimed allegiance, would finally be united. He used the motif of heavenly citizenship to motivate the relatives of his missionary employers to demonstrate their "love" by crossing geographic boundaries in order to contribute to the expansion of this new, inter-ethnic peoplehood united in Jesus. Like the Congolese evangelists in whose footsteps he would soon follow, he did not hesitate to accuse the North American Christians of lacking in "love" if they failed to send sufficient representatives or to educate the white missionaries about the ethnic composition of the surrounding population through his list of unreached "tribes." Kazadi's choice to refer to himself with an ethnic label suggests that, like other Luba evangelists of his time, he was drawing on his Luba identity as a way to claim allegiance to a larger body that transcended the particularities of clan, nationality, and

37. Matthieu, letter to the mother of Edna (Swila) Kensinger, January 4, 1920. Translated from Tshiluba to English by Edna Kensinger. I corrected Edna's spelling of Kasadi to Kazadi (following the Tshiluba original).

race.[38] Kazadi's friendship with Edna allowed his aspirations for the church to be expressed to fellow believers on the other side of the world and to be preserved for future generations.

Second, as Edna poured her "soul" into activities that put her into friendly contact with Congolese residents of the mission station, she began to question and subvert some of the conventions—especially culinary ones—that kept white missionaries separate from Congolese in daily life. Like his wife, William developed close relationships with Congolese mission residents and "enjoyed so much" his evenings "talking to the natives."[39] The Kensingers' friendly relationships with Kazadi and other Congolese household helpers and evangelists sensitized them to the role of shared meals and food preparation in facilitating cross-cultural friendship, and gave them a greater awareness of the double standards in lifestyle and labor that pertained to black and white church members on the mission station. As a result, they increasingly supported the efforts of Congolese evangelists to alter these dynamics and so participated in a limited way in shifting structures of racial and ecclesial separation.

During her second term in Congo, Edna began to write regularly of her new appreciation for *bidia*, the porridge-like African staple prepared with manioc and/or corn flour. Edna and William enjoyed eating *bidia* when spending an extended day leading church services in a nearby village and began to eat it several times a week. "[Our] stomachs just cry out for it," said Edna, and she noted that they shared a love of *bidia* with two of the other young, single CIM missionaries, Alma Diller and Lester Bixel.[40] As the Kensingers' appreciation for *bidia* grew, they no longer relied as heavily

---

38. In recent research, David Maxwell has emphasized the agency and participation of Luba Christians in shaping the ongoing process of ethnic identity formation in Congo's Katanga region at the turn of the twentieth century. As the colonial state sought to reify, through indirect rule, a narrow ethnic identity that disrupted broader pre-colonial trade networks, they were assisted by the language standardization efforts of Protestant missionaries who were busy creating vernacular literature. However, such narrow definitions of ethnicity were contested by Luba evangelists through their active participation in the broad dissemination of literature in the regional vehicular language of Tshiluba. Maxwell traces the ways in which freed slave returnees from Angola drew on Tshiluba Christian literature, not to root themselves in "local politics," but to develop a mobile, "supra-local" identity that spread through a "web of mission stations and Christian villages across the Luba territory . . . forming a network of congregations to rival a territorial cult of old." Maxwell claims that similar dynamics were likely at play in the neighboring Kasai region as well. Maxwell, "Remaking Boundaries," 71, 75–77.

39. Edna Kensinger, letter to relatives, February 10, 1924.

40. Edna Kensinger, letter to relatives, February 25, 1924. Alma Diller and Lester Bixel married in 1924, and Kazadi later worked as a household helper for the Bixels. See "High Lights."

on imported groceries supplemented with local fruits and vegetables and could enjoy local cornmeal without having to bake it first into Western-style cornbread.[41] Yet Edna's comments about *bidia* indicate that only a minority of the white missionaries were willing to try it; by partaking of *bidia,* she and William were setting themselves apart from some of the other white station residents.

Eventually, Edna and William developed a preference for living their lives away from the ambiguities of the mission station altogether. When the Kensingers returned to Congo from furlough in 1924, William began to serve as "Permanent Itinerating Man of the Mission," which required extensive travel on foot and by hammock.[42] By October of that year, Edna and William had established themselves at a new site across the Kasai River from Djoko Punda, near a road and railway owned by the American Forminière diamond company. Life away from the mission station was clearly to Edna's liking despite the hardships. "Road life as I have found out this last month is not going to be an easy job," she admitted, "but we are hoping it will be a blessed one. And we are just anxious to get away from the stations and just live with the natives."[43] About their brief stays at Djoko Punda, Edna reported that "we cannot call this home because we do not hope to be here very much."[44] In fact, Edna seemed to enjoy being far from the other white missionaries. "I have not seen another white person for a week but I am not lonesome," she wrote.[45]

Edna's and William's separate accounts of the wedding of CIM missionaries Alma Diller and Lester Bixel in mid-1924 provide important evidence of their growing sensitivity to the details of food-sharing in effecting social and ecclesial transformation on the mission station. Edna's description demonstrates that the white missionaries maintained or reinforced separation between themselves and black mission station residents through the organization of the wedding meals, while also highlighting her own willingness to partially transgress these boundaries. The first special "wedding feast" took place inside a CIM missionary dwelling, with eleven white missionaries and seven white Forminière workers gathered around a long table.[46] For this event, Edna and Kazadi worked together to make food

41. For a description of the Kensingers' diet when they first arrived, see Edna Kensinger, letter to relatives, April 19, 1919.

42. Minutes, CIM Field Conference, Djoko Punda, August 15, 1921.

43. Edna Kensinger, letter to relatives, April 6, 1924.

44. Edna Kensinger, letter to relatives, April 6, 1924.

45. Edna Kensinger, letter to relatives, October 13, 1924.

46. Edna Kensinger, letter to relatives, May 26, 1924. As a joint enterprise since 1906 of the Belgian colonial government and a variety of American shareholders,

that would appeal to a Western palate. "Kazadi and I were the cooks," she related. "I worked in the kitchen all day, and enjoyed it so much."[47]

This "wedding feast" that was attended only by whites contrasted with the "native feast" the next day, when about five hundred Congolese partook of goat meat and *bidia* alongside the white missionaries. This was a grand and joyful occasion, with more guests than Edna had ever seen "on the Mission Station at one time."[48] Edna noted that the food and seating arrangements had been delegated to "three of the teachers" who "made [the villagers] sit down in companies" and who put the white missionaries at a "table out in the yard in the midst of them" and fed them the "goat and *bidia* also."[49] It did not escape Edna's attention that not all the white missionaries appreciated the African food: "Several of our Party did not like it very well, but the rest of us enjoyed it very much," she commented.[50] Yet by this time, even new CIM missionaries were aware that refusing to eat *bidia* would be considered offensive by Congolese.[51]

After spending years cooking alongside Kazadi, teaching him how to prepare food that was familiar to her while learning in turn to appreciate *bidia*, Edna had grasped the importance of exchanging food as a way of crossing social boundaries. As she cooked together with Kazadi for an all-white group and then saw some of those white missionaries turn up their noses at the arrangements that Congolese teachers had made for a shared feast, she must have felt the incongruity. Her and William's own involvement in Kazadi's much less ostentatious wedding to Elizabeth just a few weeks earlier—William had officiated for both weddings—would have reinforced the blatant contrast between the powerful moments of solidarity that she

Forminière had many American employees. An American journalist visiting Djoko Punda in 1921 emphasized the American flavour of this "outpost of Little America in the Belgian Congo," with its "American jitneys scooting through the jungle," its "American slang and banter on all sides," and even its "American hot cakes with real American maple syrup" (Marcosson, *African Adventure*, 225). Some friendly relationships and even friendships developed between the fellow Americans—CIM missionaries and Forminière workers—who lived just across the river from each other; see, e.g., Edna Kensinger, letter to relatives, May 8, 1921.

47. Edna Kensinger, letter to relatives, May 26, 1924.

48. Edna Kensinger, letter to relatives, May 26, 1924.

49. Edna Kensinger, letter to relatives, May 26, 1924.

50. Edna Kensinger, letter to relatives, May 26, 1924.

51. One of the new missionaries who arrived in 1923 recounted her experience of being invited, along with the other white missionaries, to a wedding feast in a village near Djoko Punda. The villagers offered *bidia* to the missionaries and this new missionary felt sufficiently pressured to "bravely" force down some of this Congolese staple, remarking that "they feel insulted if we do not eat" ("Letters from Africa," 249–51, 263).

had experienced when Congolese and expatriates ate together and the alienation that resulted from separate standards for both eating and marrying.[52]

William's description of the Bixels' wedding went further in explicitly pointing out the importance of the large wedding feast in a *rapprochement* between white missionaries and Congolese evangelists and village chiefs. His account called attention to the role of evangelist Nundeke in supervising the construction of two "small native pavilions" for the event—one for the "missionaries" and one for "the neighboring chiefs and our evangelists."[53] William emphasized that the sharing of African food by all and the choice of the evangelists to seat themselves off the ground together with the chiefs "served to bring the natives and the missionaries into closer touch than ever before." "It was felt by many," he opined, "that only as the missionaries mingle with the natives, will they be able to reach them for Christ."[54] William also noted that the evangelists and chiefs remained at table long after the white missionaries had retired, and that the teacher Ngalula used the event as a platform to try to convince the chiefs to associate more closely with the mission and to "discuss their problems" with the white missionaries.[55] Clearly, the Congolese evangelists were taking a leading role in this event as brokers or mediators of a new kind of community, centered around the mission rather than around the specific local identities of "clan or chiefdom."[56] William's friendly relationships with Congolese on the station led him, like his wife, to be sympathetic to such aspirations and to seek to transmit these ecclesial ideals to his fellow CIM missionaries.

Overall, the friendly relationships that developed among Edna and William and Congolese household helpers and evangelists contributed to a subtle shift in the segregated dynamics of the mission station by helping to amplify or give voice to the catholic aspirations of Congolese young men associated with the mission. Both the Kensingers and the Congolese with whom they developed friendly relations were transformed. Edna looked to Kazadi and her other household helpers for companionship and fun as well as help with household tasks. She spent time teaching them English, music, and bread-baking skills and learned to appreciate the foods they prepared in return. Her interaction with these young men played a role in helping her to tentatively transgress certain social—and especially culinary—boundaries

52. In her description of the Bixels' wedding, Edna commented, "Alma got married just thirteen days after Kazadi" (Edna Kensinger, letter to relatives, February 10, 1924).

53. [Kensinger], "Wedding," 202, 205. William Kensinger's authorship is clear from the contents.

54. [Kensinger], "Wedding."

55. [Kensinger], "Wedding."

56. Maxwell, "Remaking Boundaries," 60.

that kept white and black Mennonites in Congo separate in various domains of daily life. For their part, household employees gained certain advantages from their association with young missionary women like Edna. Kazadi expanded his social network to include friends in faraway countries, and through the learning of English, he developed a direct link to members of the global church half a world away. He also gained access to allies among the CIM missionaries who could help him with his schooling and wedding preparations and take a sympathetic interest in his affairs. Although the power difference between Edna and Kazadi remained significant, the sharing of household tasks and space permitted a *rapprochement* that differed from those employer-employee relations that were centered outside the home.

Kazadi maintained a lifelong desire to contribute to boundary-crossing fellowship and friendship between expatriate and Congolese Mennonites. In 1959, as CIM missionaries were grappling with the awkward and overdue challenge of integrating Congolese delegates into their annual missionary conferences, he proposed as a first step that all delegates eat together and that they all eat African food. He enlisted the help of white missionary women in making the necessary arrangements.[57] Kazadi also actively sought to respond to the poverty and suffering of his fellow Congolese. He prospered through the cultivation of coffee and vegetables, and modeled the integration of a productive livelihood with his work as a pastor and respected church leader.[58] A friendship that crossed racial and even gender boundaries helped to empower a church leader to respond to the injustice of colonial exploitation and to the ecclesiological ambiguities of a mission station economy where, even on the eve of Independence, white missionaries and Congolese still rarely ate together.[59]

57. In a report on the work of the "Integration Committee," elected in 1959 in order to spearhead "mission-church integration," CIM missionary Frank J. Enns noted that one of its first proposals was for "an integrated conference with African and missionary representation." Enns continued, "Kazadi Matthew [sic] made the suggestion that all delegates eat together. The meals would be mostly on the African level, but more variety would be introduced. Such as porridge might also be served. Some of the missionary ladies would be asked to work with the Africans to get such meals planned" (Enns, "Mission-Church Integration").

58. "High Lights," 17; Chimbalanga, "Matthieu Kazadi," 119.

59. Kikweta A. Mawa Wabala Jean-Claude, interview with the author, Mazala, D. R. Congo, September 26, 2018.

CONCLUSION

One of Dana Robert's major contributions has been to steadfastly remind scholars of the central role played by mission in bringing about a new global reality in which Christianity is truly a world religion.[60] Today, a century after the events related in this chapter, members of the global church in both North and South seek new ways to understand and to participate in the mission of the church, while trying to avoid paternalism, dependency, or unwitting collaboration with regimes of oppression.[61] In such a post-colonial context, taking the time to remember and reflect on the friendships that developed during missionary encounters in the past can shape both our identity and our missional practice as global Christians in several ways.

First, this story shows that friendship is a missional practice that shapes the very identity of the church. Moreover, by depicting the friendship that developed between Kazadi and Edna as a process of church formation, I have sought to show that the cultivation of boundary-crossing friendship is of direct relevance in responding to situations of injustice and inequality. The story of Kazadi and Edna offers evidence that within a colonial context of worsening labor exploitation, friendships and relationships of solidarity that developed on the margins of official deliberations and strategies could help to constitute the church in a new way by enfolding white and black believers into a single ecclesial imagination. In the kitchen, on the path, and outside regular church hours, white missionary women and Congolese young men developed relationships in which they ate, cooked, laughed, sang, and celebrated together. These relationships amplified the voices and catholic aspirations of Congolese evangelists and in turn transformed other expatriate missionaries. Although the overall situation was still one of grave and deepening inequality, friendships and alliances such as those that formed between Kazadi and Edna caused the ground to shift slightly; they were the terrain on which a catholic vision of the church continued to move forward in small yet noticeable ways. Here, I concur with Dana Robert, who has argued that "diverse, cross-cultural friendship" is a gospel practice that both "witnesses to" and actually "creates Christian community."[62] Telling

---

60. The most detailed analysis of the role of mission in shaping Christianity as a world religion is Robert, *Christian Mission*. Robert also calls attention to the crucial role played by missiologists in launching the discourse and discipline of World Christianity. Robert, "Locating *Relocating World Christianity*," 126–33. See also Robert, "Naming 'World Christianity,'" 12.

61. For one useful historical summary of changing discourses about mission, see Part 1.c in Robert, "Missiology and Post-Colonial Consciousness."

62. Robert, *Faithful Friendships*, 4, 7.

the story of progress in mission as a story of friendship thus invites further analysis of the role played by factors of age and gender in facilitating the intercultural boundary-crossing that is at the heart of the formation of the church as a boundary-crossing people.[63]

Second, this story reminds us that our calling as Christians today, within a global economic context that still tends to "contain" Africans and exclude them from participation in a global order, is no less simple, and no less challenging, than was Kazadi's and Edna's.[64] In a context of ongoing global inequality, small gestures of sharing meals, learning to appreciate new foods, and claiming others as "friends," can subtly but profoundly reshape the political and economic order, contributing to the formation of a global church whose members' allegiance to each other surpasses their commitment to nationalist imaginations and global systems of domination. Too often, in cross-cultural missionary encounters, subtle everyday practices and habits still lead to the separation of expatriate and local believers at the meal table, within the household, and so within the church.[65] The story of Edna and Kazadi reminds us of our own human propensity to wall off the "private" details of our lifestyle as irrelevant to "mission." Yet none of us are exempt from the missionary calling to cross boundaries of social status, race, and gender, so knitting the body of Christ together in new ways as a foretaste of God's redeemed new humanity.

BIBLIOGRAPHY

Anderson, Oskar. [Diary]. 1914–1916. Edited by Elvina Martens. Translated by Agri Nilsson. Series 7 (History, Manuscripts, and Publications), Box 195 (Research by African and Missionary Writers), Item 1 (Diary of Oskar Anderson, August 14, 1914–November 4, 1916). Africa Inter-Mennonite Mission Records, 1911–2018, X-68, Mennonite Church USA Archives, Elkhart, IN [hereafter AIMMR].

Autesserre, Séverine. *Peaceland: Conflict Resolution and the Everyday Politics of International Intervention.* Problems of International Politics. New York: Cambridge University Press, 2014.

63. Robert, "Cross-Cultural Friendship," 100–107; "Global Friendship as Incarnational Missional Practice," 180–84. See especially Robert's synthesizing claim that "women's webs of human relationships have been a chief means by which Christian ideas and values cross cultural boundaries" (*Christian Mission*, 141).

64. Maxwell, "Historical Perspectives on Christianity Worldwide," 63–64; Ferguson, *Global Shadows*, 186; "Reply to the Comments," 273.

65. Several scholars have called attention to these ongoing inequities. See, for example, Bonk, *Missions and Money*; Bessenecker, *Overturning Tables*; Tizon, "Lifestyles of the Rich and Faithful," 6–28. Séverine Autesserre argues this point with respect to development and aid workers in the global South, but it is of relevance to Christian missionaries as well. See Autesserre, *Peaceland*.

Bertsche, James E. "Communauté Évangélique Mennonite (Democratic Republic of Congo)." *Global Anabaptist Mennonite Encyclopedia Online (GAMEO)*, 1990. Online. https://gameo.org/index.php?title=Communaut%C3%A9_ Evang%C3%A9lique_Mennonite_(Democratic_Republic_of_Congo).

Bertsche, Jim. *CIM/AIMM: A Story of Vision, Commitment, and Grace*. Elkhart, IN: Fairway, 1998.

Bessenecker, Scott. *Overturning Tables: Freeing Missions from the Christian-Industrial Complex*. Downers Grove, IL: InterVarsity, 2014.

Bonk, Jonathan J. *Missions and Money: Affluence as a Missionary Problem—Revisited*. Rev. and expanded ed. American Society of Missiology Series 15. Maryknoll, NY: Orbis, 2006.

Buelens, Frans. "Le tournant de 1908: de l'État indépendant du Congo au Congo belge." *Outre-Mers. Revue d'histoire* 99.376 (2012) 197–209.

Chimbalanga, Jean Felix. "Matthieu Kazadi and the New Evangelical Mennonite Church." In *The Jesus Tribe: Grace Stories from Congo's Mennonites 1912–2012: A Project of Africa Inter-Mennonite Mission*, edited by Rod Hollinger-Janzen et al., 119–21. Elkhart, IN: Institute of Mennonite Studies, 2012.

Enns, Frank J. "Mission-Church Integration (An Explanatory Letter of the Conference Decision on the Above Subject)." [4 pages, ca. 1959]. Series 4 (Regional records), Sub-Series 1 (Congo Inland Mission), Box 103, File "Field Minutes and Correspondence, 1950s." AIMMR.

Fast, Anicka. "Becoming Global Mennonites: The Politics of Catholicity and Memory in a Missionary Encounter in Belgian Congo, 1905–1939." PhD diss., Boston University, 2020.

Ferguson, James. *Global Shadows: Africa in the Neoliberal World Order*. Durham, NC: Duke University Press, 2006.

———. "Reply to the Comments on Global Shadows." *Singapore Journal of Tropical Geography* 29.3 (2008) 270–73.

Haigh, L. B. "At the Close of 1918—Congo Mission." *Christian Evangel*, May 1919. 101–2.

———. "A Review of the Work of the Congo Mission for 1916." *Christian Evangel*, July 1917. 154–55.

Haigh, Mrs. L. B. "Djoko Punda, Congo Belge, Aug. 22, 1919." *Christian Evangel*, December 1919. 279–80.

"High Lights in the Life of Pastor Kazadi Matthew." *Congo Missionary Messenger*, July–September 1957. 3, 17.

Hollinger-Janzen, Rod, et al. *The Jesus Tribe: Grace Stories from Congo's Mennonites 1912–2012: A Project of Africa Inter-Mennonite Mission*. Elkhart, IN: Institute of Mennonite Studies, 2012.

Kazadi, Matthieu. [Correspondence]. Series 3 (Personnel records), Box 73, Folder 6 (Edna Kensinger, 1919–1925) and Folder 7 (Edna Kensinger, 1919–1950). AIMMR.

Kensinger, Edna. [Correspondence]. Series 3 (Personnel records), Box 73, Folder 6 (Edna Kensinger, 1919–1925) and Folder 7 (Edna Kensinger, 1919–1950). AIMMR.

[Kensinger, William]. "Wedding of C. Alma Diller and Lester H. Bixel at Charlesville, Congo Belge, WC Africa." *Christian Evangel*, September 1924. 202, 205.

Kumedisa, Erik. "Mennonite Churches in Central Africa." In *Anabaptist Songs in African Hearts: Global Mennonite History Series: Africa*, edited by John Allen Lapp and C. Arnold Snyder, 44–94. Global Mennonite History Series. Intercourse, PA: Good, 2006.

"Letters from Africa, Djoko Punda, July 12, 1923." *Christian Evangel*, November 1923. 249–51, 263.

Likaka, Osumaka. *Naming Colonialism: History and Collective Memory in the Congo, 1870–1960*. Madison: University of Wisconsin Press, 2009.

Loewen, Melvin. "The Congo Inland Mission: 1911–1961." PhD diss., Université Libre de Bruxelles, 1961.

———. *Three Score: The Story of an Emerging Mennonite Church in Central Africa*. Elkhart, IN: Congo Inland Mission, 1972.

Marcosson, Isaac Frederick. *An African Adventure*. New York: John Lane, 1921.

Maxwell, David. "Historical Perspectives on Christianity Worldwide: Connections, Comparisons and Consciousness." In *Relocating World Christianity: Interdisciplinary Studies in Universal and Local Expressions of Christianity*, edited by Joel Cabrita et al., 47–59. Leiden: Brill, 2017.

———. "Remaking Boundaries of Belonging: Protestant Missionaries and African Christians in Katanga, Belgian Congo." *International Journal of African Historical Studies* 22.1 (2019) 59–80.

Mennonite World Conference. "World Directory." 2015. Online. https://www.mwc-cmm.org/article/world-directory.

Minutes, CIM Field Conference and Field Committee. Series 4 (Regional records), Sub-series 1 (Congo Inland Mission), Box 101 (transcriptions, 1913–1942). AIMMR.

"Return of Missionaries." *Christian Evangel*, June 1925. 123.

Robert, Dana L. *Christian Mission: How Christianity Became a World Religion*. Malden, MA: Wiley-Blackwell, 2009.

———. "Cross-Cultural Friendship in the Creation of Twentieth-Century World Christianity." *International Bulletin of Missionary Research* 35.2 (2011) 100–107.

———. *Faithful Friendships: Embracing Diversity in Christian Community*. Grand Rapids, MI: Eerdmans, 2019.

———. "Global Friendship as Incarnational Missional Practice." *International Bulletin of Missionary Research* 39.4 (2015) 180–84.

———. *Gospel Bearers, Gender Barriers: Missionary Women in the Twentieth Century*. American Society of Missiology Series 32. Maryknoll, NY: Orbis, 2002.

———. "Locating *Relocating World Christianity: Interdisciplinary Studies in Universal and Local Expressions of the Christian Faith*." *International Bulletin of Mission Research* 43.2 (2019) 126–33.

———. "Missiology and Post-Colonial Consciousness." In *Oxford Handbook of the Reception History of Christian Theology*, edited by Sarah Coakley and Richard Cross, Part 1.c. Oxford: Oxford University Press, forthcoming.

———. "Naming 'World Christianity': Historical and Personal Perspectives on the Yale-Edinburgh Conference in World Christianity and Mission History." *International Bulletin of Mission Research* 44.2 (2020) 1–18.

Seibert, Julia. "More Continuity than Change? New Forms of Unfree Labor in the Belgian Congo, 1908–1930." In *Humanitarian Intervention and Changing Labor Relations: The Long-Term Consequences of the Abolition of the Slave Trade*, edited by Marcel van der Linden, 369–86. Leiden: Brill, 2010.

Sommer, E. A. "The Tragedy of Lost Opportunities." *Christian Evangel*, May 1923. 107, 111.

Tizon, Al. "Lifestyles of the Rich and Faithful: Confronting Classism in Christian Mission." *Missiology: An International Review* 48.1 (2020) 6–28.

Tshidimu Mukendi, François. *Le centenaire de la Mission mennonite au Congo-Kinshasa (1912–2012): cas de la 27ème Communauté Mennonite au Congo. Quelle vision?*. 2011. Online. https://anabaptistwiki.org.

Vansina, Jan. *Being Colonized: The Kuba Experience in Rural Congo, 1880–1960*. Madison: University of Wisconsin Press, 2010.

Weaver, William B. *Thirty-Five Years in the Congo: A History of the Demonstrations of Divine Power in the Congo*. Chicago: Congo Inland Mission, 1945.

Weaver, William B., and Harry E. Bertsche. *Twenty-Five Years of Mission Work in Belgian Congo*. Chicago: Congo Inland Mission, 1938.

SECTION III

The Practice of Friendship

Interfaith Friendship

BONNIE SUE LEWIS

Dana Robert claims in her excellent book, *Faithful Friendships*, "The very definition of friendship is that of joy in relationship with others."[1] A leading authority on the history and theology of transcultural friendship in mission, she points to the mutual enrichment and delight of such relationships across social, cultural, racial, and even religious boundaries. I simply want to affirm here that such joy has been my own experience in interfaith friendships. These relationships are crucial in our day of growing vitriolic exchange between those of different cultural, ideological, and religious commitments. Furthermore, interreligious friendships nurture and sustain us, open our eyes to the larger work of God in the world, and deepen our own friendship with the One in whom we as Christians have put our trust, Jesus Christ. I am a better Christian, more hospitable, generous, and joy-filled, because of my interfaith friends.

WHY INTERFAITH FRIENDSHIPS

In his masterful book, *Understanding Christian Mission* (2013), Scott Sunquist sets the conversation around interfaith engagement in the chapter on the Holy Spirit. He does so to make clear that Christians participate in God's mission of reconciling the world through Jesus Christ, but it is the work of the Holy Spirit that does all the heavy lifting. God, through the Spirit, is already hard at work in every tribe and nation, in every heart and human

1. Robert, *Faithful Friendships*, 141.

created in God's image, to bring to completion what was conceived at creation: a world in love with and loved by its Creator. Hence the calling of the baptized is to seek out the aroma of the Spirit in everyone they encounter and to fan the flames of human awareness of the God who seeks us all. He notes, "Those whom we love, and those whom God loves, deserve to become known by us. Mission is about communication, and communication involves relationship. The more intimate a relationship, such as communicating the deep love of God, the more knowledge and empathy is required."[2] Thus, our encounters with those of other religions require us to get to know them, to love them as we are loved, and to simply enjoy them. This is the gift God gives us: getting to know and be known by one another. This brings glory to God and joy to human hearts.

So, it is not surprising that Pope Francis claims, "Interreligious dialogue is not a luxury. It is not something extra or optional, but essential, something our world, wounded by conflict and division, increasingly needs."[3] The dialogue of which he speaks can take many forms. In a 1991 Vatican document entitled *Dialogue and Proclamation*, the Catholic Church delineated four categories of dialogue. Accepted among many Protestants as well as Catholics, all these modes of dialogue or engagement with those of other religions assume a posture of openness to others, a willingness to listen attentively and learn, compassion and empathy, and honesty and trust—all undergirded by a humility that sees the religious other as equal before God, in need of God's grace, and bearing the Divine image.[4] The four types of interreligious dialogue are:

- theological exchange (often, but not always, theological experts seeking understanding of another's faith)
- acts of social justice and compassion that serve the common good
- shared spiritual experience (prayers, texts, worship)
- the neighborliness of everyday life

Having participated in all four of these modes of encounter in this last decade, I find the last one the most accessible and the most satisfying. As Kosuke Koyama claims, it is the daily walking in the midst of the lives of our neighbors, or our "neighborology," that not only speaks most to the neighbor of God's love, but which also enhances our own sense of the presence

---

2. Sunquist, *Understanding*, 262.

3. Quoted in Gregory, *Go Forth*, 139.

4. Bevans and Schroeder, *Constants*, 383.

of God.[5] "Our task," said Pope Francis, "is that of praying for one another, imploring from God the gift of peace, encountering one another, engaging in dialogue, and promoting harmony in the spirit of cooperation and friendship."[6] The following is the story of some of my encounters with the "religious other," and why it is, finally, the "neighborliness of everyday life" that I believe is the most conducive to producing interfaith friendship. These relationships are what bless me the most and what bring me the most joy. From Psalm 133 it appears that God also takes joy when we come together in love and harmony. "How good and precious it is," claims the psalmist!

THEOLOGICAL EXCHANGE

I approached my first real encounters with Muslims in terms of theological exchange. When, around 2010, IBM moved into the thriving river community of Dubuque, Iowa, we began to see women in hijabs and a sign pop up on a store-front near the mall announcing the Tri-State Islamic Center. My students asked me to teach them about Islam, and I had homework to do. Fortunately, a friend introduced me to the local imam, a Syrian and a psychiatrist in town, Dr. Adib Kassas, whom I promptly invited to coffee so I could talk to him about giving a lecture in a new class I was offering on Christianity and Islam. He laughingly told me he would love to go to coffee, but it would have to be after dark. To my shame, I had been clueless that it was the holy month of Ramadan, and he was not eating or drinking from sun-up to sun-down. And then, to my surprise, he invited my friends and me to join him and the whole Tri-State Muslim community in the Eid-al-Fitr celebration marking the end of Ramadan, which happened to fall that year on September 11, 2010.

In the course of that delightful day as guests of the imam and his community, when I was able to speak with Adib Kassas about giving a lecture in my class, he offered to move up his clientele so that he could join us for forty-five minutes or so of every class session. Thus, he became a weekly conversation partner with us, brought others from his community to the classroom, and invited us into the mosque. Our stimulating conversations covered all manner of theological beliefs, spiritual practices, and cultural customs, and due to the imam's great sense of humor, frequently erupted in laughter. He was engaging and not at all intimidated by the many and diverse questions of twenty Christian theological students who had never had the opportunity to examine Islam with one so steeped in the faith. It

5. Koyama, *Water Buffalo*, 65.

6. Quoted in Gregory, *Go Forth*, 138.

was the perfect setting for my initial encounter with theological dialogue. I learned so much about Islam as a lived faith, but even more, I began to learn the skills of listening closely, asking relevant questions, and articulating my own beliefs in ways that led to greater trust and enhanced our theological exchange.

These skills were honed when, at some point that fall, several colleagues from neighboring colleges asked Adib Kassas to lead us in a study of the Qur'an. Some of these colleagues had attended the Eid dinner or met the imam in town and began to gather for coffee with the imam, including a Jewish professor at the University of Dubuque. From these early conversations and gatherings, we birthed Dubuque's Children of Abraham, a public forum for exploration of our faith traditions that has continued to meet, along with the Qur'an study, every month during the school year since 2011. Composed primarily of members of the Abrahamic faiths—Islam, Judaism, and Christianity—we seek to create "an atmosphere of civic life that builds inter-religious solidarity, cooperation, and friendship."[7] We arrange these monthly conversations around topics such as creation stories, common prophets, the after-life, difficult passages of our sacred texts, and ethics, to name a few. We meet on college campuses around town and in "sacred spaces" such as churches, the mosque, and the synagogue. Panelists speak from within their traditions but not for that tradition. There is usually a time afterward for questions and answers, table conversations, and simply fellowship. Together we have sharpened our ability to engage in theological discourse with honesty, openness, and genuine friendship.

A benefit of participating in such theological exchanges over a number of years is a growing understanding of the faith traditions of these "siblings of another mother," as well as a growing appreciation for the things we hold in common. These include a belief in the sovereignty, mercy, and compassion of God, a common ancestry traced through Abraham, and a common ethic of love of God and neighbor.[8] What has most impressed me, perhaps, has been seeing how much my Jewish and Muslim friends love God. Adib Kassas grows absolutely rhapsodic over such Qur'anic verses as Sura 57:5: "He knows . . . what comes down from the heaven and what ascends thither. He is with you wherever you are. God is aware of all you do." He is as awe-struck by God's omnipotence and omnipresence as I am. He finds comfort in knowing that God is always there and knows us completely. So do I. Moreover, this shared experience of the love of God has opened spaces for further conversations around the joy I find in a personal friendship with the

7. Children of Abraham, "Children of Abraham."
8. Volf, Allah, 110; Kateregga and Shenk, Muslim and a Christian, 205.

One we call Son of God, Jesus Christ, for whom Muslims have great respect and even love, if not the same trust as I have. It has been eye-opening for me to find ones who share my awe of God and gratitude for God's revelatory nature toward humankind.

What I did not anticipate is how these dialogues and conversations have deepened my own faith. Learning more about these other religious traditions steeped in such practices as prayer and fasting, meditation, sabbath rest, and social activism, has drawn me to explore further the same traditions found in mine. In so doing, I have experienced a quickening of my own sense of God's presence, stronger appreciation of the grace and mercy of Jesus Christ, and an increasing awareness of the power of the Holy Spirit in opening my heart toward these who orient around faith differently than I do.

SERVING THE COMMON GOOD

Over the ten years that our "beloved community," the Children of Abraham, has been meeting, we have often participated in the second mode of inter-religious engagement, acts of social justice and compassion that serve the common good. One way that we have done this is by gathering together in a show of support for one another when national tragedies have occurred. In 2015, we learned of the shooting of three Muslim college students in Chapel Hill, North Carolina, reportedly gunned down in their apartment over a parking dispute. In response, the Children of Abraham sponsored a couple of rallies in which we marched together carrying signs and placards speaking out against religious intolerance: "Jews, Christians and Muslims belong together," read one sign.[9] In October of 2018, a lone gunman killed eleven members of the Tree of Life Synagogue in Pittsburgh, Pennsylvania, while they were at prayer, the largest mass shooting of Jews in American history. The Children of Abraham, at the invitation of Temple Beth El, participated in gathering for prayer and a show of solidarity with our Jewish community. There was standing room only as the Reform synagogue leadership shared the bema with Adib Kassas of the mosque and members of local churches in a show of concern and support. In these ways, we become a visible sign to the larger community of what it means to stand up with those who are marginalized and extend friendship to those who suffer.

Religious intolerance is not the only form of marginalization people can face. Poverty, incarceration, and violence plague most cities. One of the organizations in our town that addresses these issues is the Circles Initiative

9. Children of Abraham, "Children of Abraham."

of Dubuque. Besides individual counseling, this group meets monthly with those on the edge to provide resources and friendships to build skills for moving out of the downward cycle of poverty. Along with other groups throughout the city, Children of Abraham regularly provides the meal for these gatherings at a local school. When we do so, we are applauded for bringing much more succulent dishes than hotdogs and hamburgers or macaroni and cheese casseroles. Our menu usually includes several Middle Eastern dishes that most cannot pronounce nor identify but for which they always go back for seconds.

One of the services that Children of Abraham excels in is what Eboo Patel of the Interfaith Youth Core in Chicago calls "religious literacy," educating Dubuque about our various faith traditions. We do this by welcoming invitations to speak in classrooms, libraries, churches, and other venues. This offers people for whom religious diversity consists largely of the divide between Catholics and Protestants occasions to see the greater diversity of religious belief and expression. Through these educational opportunities, we have found that audiences are impressed by the camaraderie and joy we take in being with one another. They witness our friendships and take more seriously our words when they see the authenticity of our relationships. We illuminate our differences, but it is our common humanity, humor, and pathos that most touches those who come to learn about our religions, how they shape who we are, and how we live together with our differences. In this way we avail ourselves to showing the community how to build religious cooperation for the sake of all.

SHARED SPIRITUAL EXPERIENCE

In her book, *Holy Envy*, Barbara Brown Taylor tells the story of her discovery through teaching world religions that there is much to covet in other religious traditions. She envied the rapturous dancing of Hindus' Lord Shiva, the meditative mindfulness of Buddhism, and the Jewish emphasis on both doing as well as hearing. But she warns that though we can appreciate what we find in other religions, "I may look, but I may not poach."[10] In other words, we can appreciate and in some cases even adapt some understandings or practices to our own faith, but we must be careful not to appropriate what is sacred in one tradition to decorate our own. As she puts it, "What I see in my neighbor's yard does not belong to me."[11] Her illustration echoes Roger Schroeder's image of the stranger who, on invitation to explore another's

10. Taylor, *Holy Envy*, 71.
11. Taylor, *Holy Envy*, 72.

faith, must do so reverently as though "entering someone else's garden."[12] We are welcome to admire the exotic flowers but not to pick them.

There are many ways in which the Children of Abraham invites opportunities for observing certain spiritual practices of our faiths. One of the most delightful was when we sponsored "Songs of the Soul: An Interfaith Celebration of Chant," held at the Dominican Mother House, Sinsinawa Mound, Wisconsin, in January 2016. The event brought us together to learn of and listen to the music that inspires our worship of God. While the chants and songs differed, they offered an insight into the sacred spaces that singing and chanting our Scriptures and hymns creates in each of us, and they helped us to understand a little better our common yearning for and comfort in the presence of the Divine.

This year we will celebrate the Thirty-seventh Annual Dubuque Area Congregations United (DACU) Interfaith Thanksgiving Service held at a local Catholic church. When the congregation of Temple Beth El asked to join DACU, originally called the Dubuque Area Churches United, the ecumenical organization agreed and changed the word "Churches" to "Congregations." Their mission statement reads, in part:

> We, . . . people of diverse faiths and beliefs, are united by our belief in God, our concerns for justice and our call to serve others. Through prayerful dependence on God and respectful cooperation with each other, we will make a difference in our world by fostering an awareness and understanding of human need. We will be a supportive presence in this community and beyond through the generous sharing of our time, talents, and resources.[13]

Resources available include local food banks, emergency funds through People in Need (PIN), and lists of programs and services by the member congregations of DACU. Seven or eight years ago, the Tri-State Islamic Center also joined DACU. The annual Thanksgiving Service now includes readings from the Hebrew Bible, the New Testament, and the Qur'an, as well as songs and prayers offered from these traditions in thanksgiving to God for all we have received.

The questions raised around such shared spiritual experiences often go to whether or not we can actually worship together. Do we, in fact, worship the same God? Or do we trample one another's gardens when we try to come together before God? While theologians uphold varying views on the subject, I would simply argue along with Miraslav Volf that, at least among the

---

12. Bevans and Schroeder, *Prophetic Dialogue*, 33.

13. DACU, "Mission Statement."

Abrahamic faiths (the monotheistic faiths), there is only One God, however understood. He claims, "To the extent that people love their neighbors, they worship the one true God, even if their understanding of God is inadequate and their worship is seriously lacking in other regards."[14] I agree that none of us fully comprehends God, but any attempt to give God our praise and thanksgiving is pleasing to the God who is, who was, and who is to come.

With that in mind, though, I must conclude as Taylor does, "However many other religious languages I learn, I dream in Christian. However much I learn from other spiritual teachers, it is Jesus I come home to at night."[15] I, too, realize that it is still Jesus that I come home to. In Jesus I find not only forgiveness but also "God with arms," as I like to call it. I believe that this Jesus is the answer to all of those things that hurt and destroy us here on earth and that he not only waits for but also seeks to find those who know not how much God loves them, especially in the midst of our greatest suffering. It is my privilege to be able to participate with God in bringing this message of love and forgiveness to those God puts in my path.

Jesus is also my guide in meeting the stranger and sharing the good news of God's unimaginable hospitality. Jesus loves people. He enjoys dinner parties, opportunities to feed, both literally and spiritually, those who come to him. He never tires of welcoming all who are troubled, hurting, lost, or devastated. He gently points those who seek him to the banquet table in the kingdom of God. I agree with Scott Alexander of Catholic Theological Union in Chicago who claims that "the divinely ordained diversity we see in the world—even and perhaps especially religious diversity—is designed to be a medium by which every human being deepens her or his own God-consciousness."[16] And it is the impact of that "God-consciousness," or awakening of the Holy Spirit within me, which brings me to the final mode of interfaith dialogue: neighborliness of everyday life.

NEIGHBORLINESS

In her book, *Faithful Friendships*, Dana Robert begins with the example and call of Jesus to engagement with others through relationships of love that include real relationships in space and time, the mutuality of giving and receiving hospitality, and empathetic walking with others through all the

14. Volf, *Allah*, 122.

15. Taylor, *Holy Envy*, 49.

16. Alexander, "Encountering," 49–59.

ups and downs of life.[17] Friendship is, after all, "not a noun but a verb."[18] For these reasons, I don't think that it is a mistake that Jesus is found most often at the table. As I have heard it said, it seems that Jesus ate his way through the Gospels. Not only did he bind up the broken-hearted, heal the sick, free the oppressed, and bless all with the good news of God's inbreaking kingdom, he ate with them. He demonstrated good neighborliness when, in the incarnation, Jesus literally took on "flesh and blood and moved into the neighborhood" (John 1:14, *The Message*). He lived in Jewish homes, worshipped in the local synagogues, and ate Middle Eastern food. It seems that he dined with anyone who asked him over, and he loved a good party. In fact, the Gospel of John claims, he began his ministry at a wedding feast where he even provided the best wine for the meal. He ended his ministry as the host at the table with his disciples, using the very bread and wine they were served to institute one of the church's greatest sacraments, the Eucharistic meal.

It is as the guest at another's table that one affirms the hospitability of the host and opens opportunity to deeper encounters. In the preface to a cookbook on foreign foods, a former missionary couple to the Argentine Chaco tell the story of when, new to the field, they had asked one of the older indigenous church leaders how they should begin their work. The man "paused and then responded, 'I would go and eat their food.' He began to weep . . . and his translators wept with him."[19] It is in breaking bread with others, accepting what is provided, however humble, and participating in the daily lives of neighbors that this intimate gesture of fellowship can lead to rich and enduring friendships in the way of Jesus.

Krista Tippett, in her weekly public radio broadcast, *On Being*, recently interviewed two college friends, Derek Black and Matthew Stevenson. What caught my attention was that Derek Black was the godson of white nationalist David Duke, and Matthew Stevenson was an Orthodox Jew. While at New College, Florida, the two, who could not be more different, began getting to know each other when Stevenson invited Black, an atheist who had just been "outed" as a white nationalist, to weekly Shabbat dinners he had been hosting in his dorm room. The openness and warmth of the table fellowship, which continued weekly for the two years they were in school together, enabled a friendship that so completely transformed Black that he left the group he had been groomed to lead. According to Black, "I entered it [the Shabbat meals] thinking that I was just talking to a friend, and then,

17. Robert, *Faithful Friendships*, 27–28.

18. Pipher, *Women*, 177.

19. Longacre, "Foreword," 7.

a couple years later, came out the other end, realizing that everything I believed about human nature was totally incorrect, and what do I do about this now?"

Black went on to explain that what had changed for him, was the impact of becoming part of a new community that was being hurt by the group to which he claimed allegiance. As he put it, "The reason why I was not willing to listen to the argument that sounded very straightforward—that we should work towards inclusion, not separation—was because I didn't empathize with people who weren't part of my in-group." What changed for him, was the development of friendships outside his "in-group" who cared for him—who fed him and conversed with him and with whom he began to feel great empathy. His friend, Stevenson, acknowledged that the face-to-face contact with Black is what made the difference in fostering empathy. "I think it's much harder, much harder to discount the person's humanity when he's staring you in the eyes," he told Tippett. Furthermore, Stevenson and Black both acknowledged that the basis of Black's transformation was truly a friendship—not something contrived as a means to change him—that came about through conversations begun over weekly dinners and that extended into other venues. When such conversations are only between those who share your own views, "the terrible cost . . . is that you run a very real risk of losing empathy for people who disagree with you," Stevenson concluded.

Black has not become Jewish. But he has abandoned—and now speaks out against—the white nationalist worldview he held prior to supping regularly with Stevenson and his community. Table fellowship enabled the growth of friendships that had a far-reaching impact on both Black and Stevenson and beyond. Their interview was held at the National Holocaust Museum in Washington, DC, a place that houses the memory of all that Black once discredited and despised.[20]

While not nearly as extreme a transformation as Black's, my own experience of personal transformation through encounters with religious others holds similarities to his. It was often over table fellowship that I was ushered into a new series of relationships that stretched my faith and changed my life. Around the table at the feast of Eid that sunny afternoon in September of 2010, I found I had "family" I didn't know I had. I began to get to know these other members of Abraham's house through theological discourse in classrooms, in regular meetings of the Children of Abraham, and in the weekly Qur'an studies. Our friendships deepened as we grabbed coffee together, served meals together to the marginalized of Dubuque, and sat on

20. Tippett, "Derek Black and Matthew Stevenson."

panels together to educate others about our religious traditions. And, as we prayed together for peace in the midst of bloodshed and with thanksgiving for the bounties received from God, we became family for one another.

Relationships across cultural and religious boundaries must be intentional. They take time to cultivate, and they must be mutually rewarding, according to Dana Robert. The delight that the Dalai Lama and Archbishop Desmond Tutu take in their friendship as recorded in their memoir, *The Book of Joy* (2018) makes the point that, according to His Holiness, "Genuine friendship is entirely based on trust. . . . If you really feel a sense of concern for the well-being of others, then trust will come."[21] Over the years as my Muslim, Jewish, Buddhist, and Hindu friends and I have sat at one another's tables, we have exchanged hugs and delicious ethnic foods, and we have come to respect and care for one another. There is, indeed, great joy in sharing from the heart, in celebrating together births and birthdays, accomplishments and benchmarks. And there is great gratitude in having friends you know you can count on in times of loss, disappointment, and tragedy.

My interfaith friendships are one of the wonderful means that God uses to show God's love for me. When I broke a bone in my foot last fall, Adib Kassas and his wife, now referred to as my Big Brother and Sweet Sister, were on my doorstep the next day to fix my wobbly handrail and to bring me flowers and a container of her famous lentil soup. Several months later they gave me a cat to keep me company. My Buddhist friend, who knows about cats, came over to try to trim her nails for me who has never owned one. When I was stranded due to an unexpected snowstorm and had to get to a doctor's appointment, my Jewish friends came to my rescue. Since this has happened more than once (I live in Iowa, after all!) I began to call them my Uber-friends. Amos Yong makes a radical claim that relationships with those who are not like us can not only enable us to show them God's love, but can also actually be God's "means through which the love of God is given to us."[22] Through these friends, whose big hearts have been shaped by their faith, I feel the more beloved.

It started with the nudge to learn more about a religion I had little knowledge of so that I could teach a group of students about Islam. It ended with membership in a new community that has given me love and life. You, too, can share in the joy of such relationships. Have you a neighbor or co-worker of another faith? Is there a mosque or a synagogue or, perhaps, a temple near you? Are there any organizations in your community engaged in interfaith activities that you can join? If not, be the catalyst to start one!

21. Dalai Lama and Tutu, *Book of Joy*, 74.

22. Yong, *Hospitality*, 153.

Ask God to open up to you avenues for building interfaith friendships. Begin to learn about the faith of those God brings into your life. Ask questions and give the gift of attentive listening. Seek opportunities to share a meal, enjoy a mutual hobby, get to know one another's families. As my mother always said, "It takes a friend to have a friend!"

We all know that this global world of ours no longer allows us to be isolated from events, ideas, or people who are religiously, culturally, socially, or ideologically different than us. Somehow, in God's great scheme of things, through the vast migrations of peoples worldwide, the reach of global technology, and the common threats to our globe environmentally, politically, and economically, we have become more visible and accessible to each other than at any other time in world history. And misunderstanding, distrust, and even the possibility of war looms ever larger. As Pope Francis has said, "Either we dialogue or we end up shouting at one another; there is no other way."[23] Interfaith friendships offer an opportunity to begin to tear down walls of hatred, of indifference, and of fear. In their wake, they bring awareness of the vastness and goodness of God's creation in all its diversity. Interfaith friendships allow us to love as Jesus loved and to be loved in return. As Dana Robert notes, "Friendship seeds fellowship, and fellowship points to the kingdom of God."[24] Where better to enjoy these relationships than over a delicious meal where strangers, even enemies, can become friends? For there we get a glimpse of that heavenly banquet to which all are invited, where love abounds, and where fellowship with the Divine never ends.

BIBLIOGRAPHY

Alexander, Scott C. "Encountering the Religious 'Stranger': Interreligious Pedagogy and the Future of Theological Education." *Theological Education* 51 (2018) 49–59.
Bevans, Stephen B., and Roger P. Schroeder. *Constants in Context: Theology of Mission for Today*. Maryknoll, NY: Orbis, 2004.
———. *Prophetic Dialogue: Reflections on Christian Mission Today*. Maryknoll, NY: Orbis, 2011.
Children of Abraham. "Children of Abraham." Online. http://www.cofabraham.org.
Dalai Lama, and Desmond Tutu. *The Book of Joy: Lasting Happiness in a Changing World*. New York: Avery, 2018.
Dubuque Area Congregations United (DACU). "Mission Statement." *DACU Monthly Newsletter* 41.11 (2019). Online. http://www.cgim.org/dacuonline/newsletter/2019DecemberNewsletter.pdf.

---

23. Quoted in Gregory, *Go Forth*, 126.

24. Robert, *Faithful Friendships*, 166.

Gregory, William P. *Go Forth: Toward a Community of Missionary Disciples*. American Society of Missiology Series 58. Maryknoll, NY: Orbis, 2019.

Kateregga, Badru D., and David W. Shenk. *A Muslim and a Christian in Dialogue*. Scottsdale, PA: Herald, 1997.

Koyama, Kosuke. *Water Buffalo Theology*. Maryknoll, NY: Orbis, 1999.

Longacre, Paul. "Foreword." In *Extending the Table: World Community Cookbooks*, edited by Joetta Handrich Schlabach, 7. Scottsdale, PA: Herald, 1991.

Pipher, Mary. *Women Rowing North: Navigating Life's Currents and Flourishing as We Age*. New York: Bloomsbury, 2019.

Robert, Dana L. *Faithful Friendships: Embracing Diversity in Christian Community*. Grand Rapids, MI: Eerdmans, 2019.

Sunquist, Scott W. *Understanding Christian Mission: Participation in Suffering and Glory*. Grand Rapids, MI: Baker Academic, 2013.

Taylor, Barbara Brown. *Holy Envy: Finding God in the Faith of Others*. New York: HarperOne, 2019.

Tippett, Krista. "Derek Black and Matthew Stevenson: Befriending Radical Disagreement." *On Being*, May 17, 2018. Updated October 3, 2019. Transcript. Online. https://onbeing.org/programs/derek-black-and-matthew-stevenson-befriending-radical-disagreement/#transcript.

Volf, Miroslav. *Allah: A Christian Response*. New York: HarperOne, 2011.

Yong, Amos. *Hospitality and the Other: Pentecost, Christian Practices, and the Neighbor*. Maryknoll, NY: Orbis, 2008.

Transnational Deaf Friendships

KIRK VANGILDER

In 2000, a group of seventeen Deaf[1] and hearing United Methodists from around the United States travelled to Mutare, Zimbabwe, to embark on a short-term mission visit that began a number of life-changing friendships. These friendships bridge significant national, cultural, linguistic, and socio-economic chasms to form a foundation for lasting partnerships in mission that build communities and change lives. These friendships were built around cooking *sadza*, a traditional staple dish of our Shona hosts. Teaching me to cook *sadza* was a communal effort of Deaf Zimbabwean women who argued their varied approaches among each other in trying to explain to me the proper techniques. In the midst of this conversation, my own laughably awkward attempt to make smooth *sadza* resulted in a need for them to guide me through how to fix it. This experience provided a framework for reconsidering how theological construction could be done in partnerships across cultures. As the experience of learning to make *sadza* inverted the usual power dynamics of "missionaries" and "recipients" by making Zimbabwean women the bearers of expertise, adopting this as a theological model

---

1. The capitalization of Deaf is used in Deaf Studies to denote the use of Deaf (or Deafhood) as a cultural and linguistic identity marker rather than a physical sensory deficit. The use of this capitalization was developed in North American and Western European Deaf scholarship, and there is currently debate on whether it remains helpful to make such distinctions, particularly when d/Deaf people from the global south may understand their identities in different ways. I have chosen to retain it for this essay, as much of the audience will be hearing people who may be unfamiliar with seeing Deaf community as a cultural and linguistic group.

serves to remind us that expertise is found in many places and power must be shared across our friendships.

In *Making Sadza with Deaf Zimbabwean Women*,[2] I used this experience to explore strategies that might refocus methods of practical theological construction on the interests and capacities of the people being studied. This chapter revisits the Deaf community, ministries, and missions in the Mutare District of the Zimbabwe East Annual Conference of The United Methodist Church and explores how transnational Deaf friendship enables Deaf communities to flourish and grow. I also introduce a new metaphorical model of "making salad with Deaf Zimbabweans" for understanding the complexities of these friendships and their effects on Deaf lives.[3]

DEAF-SAME AS A CONDUIT FOR TRANSNATIONAL DEAF FRIENDSHIPS

That Deaf people have traveled the globe to connect with one another and forge friendships is not a new phenomenon. Transnational relationships between Deaf people have been noted since the late nineteenth century when Deaf communities in France were planning for the gathering of two hundred Deaf people from around the globe during the 1900 Paris World Fair.[4] Many of the early transnational Deaf connections were built by Deaf people on the conduits of social connection that were being built by hearing people at the time. These included cultural and religious exchanges such as the World Fair, the Parliament of World Religions, and international mission efforts. What makes these early transnational connections notable is the degree to which Deaf people developed deep connections based on similarities of experiencing their lives as Deaf communities within larger hearing societies. Despite the differences of their signed languages, the written languages they knew, and the socio-cultural differences they embodied, Deaf people formed strong bonds with one another aimed toward common goals of equity and access. This phenomenon of deep interpersonal connection has been expressed in many signed languages as DEAF-SAME,[5] which

---

2. VanGilder, *Making Sadza*.

3. I remain indebted to Dr. Dana Robert as one of my advisors on my PhD dissertation that led to my book and her personal commitments to my interests that arise from her own work on women's agency in mission and her familiarity with Shona culture through the life and work of her husband, Dr. Inus Daneel.

4. Gulliver, "Emergence," 3–14.

5. The use of all capital letters for this term is a writing convention used in Deaf Studies to indicate a concept conveyed in a Signed Language.

communicates a sense of familiarity and similarity between people who are Deaf. In expressing this fundamental sameness, DEAF-SAME denotes something closer than simple social bondedness and signals a deeper and more complex web of connection.[6] Such bonds can be seen in very early Deaf ministry contexts such as the Chicago Mission for the Deaf, formed as a Methodist congregation in 1893,[7] and their relationship with international mission efforts for Deaf education. From 1907[8] through 1937,[9] this Deaf congregation raised and sent money to support Deaf students at a mission school run by Presbyterian missionaries in Chefoo (now Yantai), China. Even through WWI and the Great Depression, they were able to raise, on average, $100 annually for this effort. This is a significant amount for a congregation comprised of economically disadvantaged people. While their commitment to Christian mission was surely a motivator, their efforts were also built on a sense of sameness as Deaf people. The church newspaper reporting these fundraising efforts often included updates on the school and the lives of Deaf people in China.

DEAF-SAME bonds can be seen in contemporary experiences as well. In 2016, while returning from Kenya and Zimbabwe and passing through London, I arranged to meet a Deaf scholar with whom I was co-writing a piece. In addition to the differences between American Sign Language, Kenyan Sign Language, and Zimbabwean Sign Language I had been negotiating, I was now trying to converse with someone who uses British Sign Language—all of which are distinct from one another. As we sat at the hotel pub, two tourists walked in conversing in signs neither of us comprehended, but immediately recognized as signed language. Naturally, we waved them over and discovered they were from Germany, using German Sign Language. None of these language differences really mattered as we spent the next forty-five minutes introducing ourselves. This eagerness to connect is something very natural and expected among Deaf people from cultures around the world. One simply doesn't pass another Deaf person and not acknowledge it in some manner.

The closeness of DEAF-SAME creates a conduit for rapid friendship development and powerful bonds that lead to common cultural expressions across various Deaf cultures and communities. The Deaf goodbye is another

6. Kusters and Friedner, "Introduction," ix–xxix.

7. VanGilder, "Deaf America's Encounter," 243.

8. Chicago Mission, "Mission Notes [1907]," 4. This is the first of several mentions of support for the Chefoo school in a self-produced newspaper of the church's activities.

9. Chicago Mission, "Mission Notes [1937]," 2. This is the last mention of support to the Chefoo school. Presumably, the school's life was disrupted by the Japanese invasion of mainland China later that year.

example of emotive and personal connections that develop among Deaf people. Leave-taking from a gathering of Deaf people often takes much longer than hearing people of similar socio-cultural backgrounds. This is in part due to the relative isolation that Deaf people encounter in hearing worlds and thus the high valuation placed on times when Deaf people can communicate without barriers. When leaving a Deaf social gathering, it is not uncommon to plan your exit well before you actually need to leave in order to spend time letting everyone, not just the hosts, know that you'll be leaving. Such leave-taking includes conversations on when you might meet again, things for further discussion, and other sundry social items. The degree to which you are "close friends" with people in the room does not factor in the need to make rounds with them; it is expected as a part of one's DEAF-SAME bonds.

On one of my mission trips to Zimbabwe in 2004, I was there to work with a team to develop a proto-curriculum for teachers of Deaf children. This was a short trip and largely limited to working with a team of educators. But we did bring the entire curriculum team to the Nzeve Children's Centre in Mutare, where the Sanganai Deaf Club is housed. As the tour would be the only opportunity I would get to spend time with my Deaf friends, I split off to find them. They proudly showed me all the projects and programs they had been working on as we swapped stories, jokes, and news about others. When it was time to depart, a Deaf goodbye ensued against the pressures of a schedule set by hearing people. Finally extracted and in the van, I could do little but fall silent and hold back some tears. One of the hearing Zimbabweans on the tour tried to inquire what was wrong and all I could manage was, "I've not seen them in years, and I'll miss seeing them until we're together again." The impact this leave-taking had didn't seem fathomable to this hearing person. Fortunately, one of my hearing friends from the United States explained how DEAF-SAME bonds work and what this meant to us.

The bonds of friendship between Deaf Americans and Deaf Zimbabweans keep us working together even when we're apart and motivate us to be together again in person as frequently as possible either through continued visits of Americans to Zimbabwe or sponsoring Zimbabweans for travel to the United States for training, conferences, and other shared ministry opportunities. With the rise of more readily available internet technologies and access, video messages have become another way we keep our friendships connected while physically apart. What DEAF-SAME bonds reveal for missiology is the power of friendships to transcend differences in ways that cultivate mutual care and concern for one another. They offer a glimpse into the speed at which friendships can grow when built on shared experiences that link to our core identities. Our friendships, while empowering mission, also facilitate a cross-cultural exchange of ideas and technologies that transforms the differences that separate us. Such exchanges create a cultural mixing that allows Deaf people and communities to flourish but also carries risks that come with any transformative experience.

MAKING SALAD WITH DEAF ZIMBABWEANS

While *making sadza* has served well as a model for mission partnerships, I now also use *making salad* to discuss the complexities of Deaf transnational friendships and their effects. Tapiwa Mucherera observes that the younger generation in Zimbabwe, including those with whom we began our friendships in 2000, "has been nicknamed *masalala*, meaning a salad generation. They have a little of both Western and Shona cultures but can't fully embrace any one of them, meaning they have become *cultural refugees,* not rooted in any of the cultures."[10] This nickname was one I encountered while on one of my mission partnership visits in Zimbabwe, when we met with a group of young hearing Zimbabweans who were learning Zimbabwean Sign Language from Deaf Zimbabweans. They began working as interpreters in churches and other various settings where Deaf people needed communication access. These young Zimbabweans were typical of their generation in being educated, globally aware, and curious about their own culture and the cultures of the world. We treated them to a dinner at a restaurant of their choice in recognition of taking on the hard work of learning a new language and making their community more accessible for Deaf people with little financial compensation. They chose what they termed an American-style restaurant, which piqued my curiosity as to what made their choice of restaurants "American." The restaurant they chose was attached to an American-owned hotel chain and featured décor that could have been assembled from the props department of 1950s Hollywood Westerns. Hearing people informed me that the background music was a mix of current American pop and Motown tunes. But what made this restaurant American style for our young Zimbabweans was the presence of a salad bar. Comments from some of the older Zimbabweans on the evening revealed concerns around the nickname of *masalala*. The lure of Western culture and globalization and the effects they might have on the grounding of younger Zimbabweans in their own culture were on their minds. The nature of selecting what one liked off a display of attractive choices to create something new and personalized

10. Mucherera, *Counseling and Pastoral Care*, 8.

seemed to go beyond food preferences and apply to many aspects of young Zimbabwean lives.

The *masalala* tag also could be applied to the young Deaf Zimbabwean adults with whom we worked. But the ingredients, facilitated by other influences, were somewhat different. While their educational levels and global awareness were much lower than their hearing peers, they exhibited the same thirst for global connection. The DEAF-SAME connection our friendships exhibit became a conduit for their exposure to the ways that Deaf communities in the United States talk about our cultural identities, history, and how we organize to achieve our goals for equity and inclusion in churches and society. These ingredients off the global Deaf salad bar became a part of their own salad as they develop self-understanding, community identity, and organizational strategies to address areas of ministry and mission in their world. Yet, they also retain the influence of unique ways the UMC in Zimbabwe is organized, Shona cultural patterns of family and community life, and other elements that those of us from the United States do not fully understand. Yet, our friendships facilitate the continued effort to understand one another and support our mutual flourishing. This mixture of ingredients across the bonds of friendship is evident in how this Deaf Zimbabwean community has grown to address some of the issues that framed my 2012 study in *Making Sadza with Deaf Zimbabwean Women*.

A GROWING GRAPEVINE

During our mission partnership visits from 2000 to 2006, I became aware of a number of ways that Deaf Zimbabwean women expressed their pain and concern with regard to their role in raising their own hearing children. Because most deafness is not caused by genetic markers, most deaf people will have hearing parents and their children will be hearing. For Zimbabwean women, this created barriers to their involvement in raising their own children. Maria Chiswanda has explored many of the dynamics between hearing mothers and their deaf children in Zimbabwe in her study on mediated learning experiences.[11] She notes the disconnection in communication and fears regarding the transmission of significant cultural knowledge between hearing mothers and their deaf children. What I observed was the consequences of these disconnections as Deaf women gave birth to hearing children of their own. Chiswanda notes that it is not unusual for Zimbabwean children to spend a significant portion of their childhood with their

---

11. Chiswanda, "Hearing Mothers."

grandparents.[12] What seemed to differ for many Deaf mothers was that the communication gap with their own mothers meant their own bonds with their children became complicated by an ease of spoken communication between their hearing children and those children's hearing grandparents that bypassed their mothers' signed language communication. This compounded the concerns that hearing grandmothers had about whether their Deaf daughters had received all the cultural information needed to be a good mother and often resulted in Deaf women expressing frustration that they were not as much a part of their children's lives as they wished.[13]

Often their frustrations were expressed with a polyvalent question of, "What should we do?" The "we" in this question was often framed in a multitude of ways from individual choices specific to the women sharing their stories, to the women as a collective whole, to their extended families as a unit of sociocultural transmission, to their churches as a resource of women's groups and support. This was the dilemma that ignited my 2012 study *Making Sadza with Deaf Zimbabwean Women*. While that study was attempting to work out the ways in which a community such as these women could be empowered to address this complex situation, it was outside the scope of that study to go beyond methodological questions and implement actions.

The years that followed the 2006 visit were difficult for my Zimbabwean friends as their nation struggled with economic and political troubles that prevented their American friends from being able to be present with them for ten years. However, these barriers did not end our friendship or their work. In 2018, I was privileged to see the fruit of their organizing in the graduation ceremonies of a Grapevine Dream camp for Deaf women held at the Nzeve Deaf Children's Centre. This camp was a well-organized response to problems they faced as Deaf women in their families and churches. During our 2000 visit, a hearing mother stood up at a meeting of community stakeholders to express her worries that she would be unable to communicate important information to her deaf daughter about keeping herself safe and happy as a woman. This was her way of explaining that she was worried her daughter did not know a variety of skills relevant to contemporary Shona womanhood including safety against sexual predators, self-care and hygiene, pregnancy and childbirth, being a mother and wife, and running a household. These were topics she felt obligated as a mother to teach her daughter but felt unable to do so because she could not sign and had no opportunity to learn. The team from the United states was at a loss of

12. Chiswanda, "Hearing Mothers," 19–20.

13. See VanGilder, *Making Sadza,* for a fuller account of these dynamics.

how to answer these questions with our limited knowledge of Shona culture and Zimbabwean Sign Language. We did our best to assemble a small team of Zimbabwean and American women, both Deaf and hearing, who had the needed experience and knowledge among them. It quickly became a moment where Deaf Zimbabwean mothers were sharing their knowledge with this woman's Deaf daughter as interpretation teams facilitated communication to keep her hearing mother in the conversation. This was a limited solution to a single family but provided a window into a much larger need.

In the intervening eighteen years, the Deaf community in Mutare formed a club, ministries connected with United Methodist churches throughout the area, and a work project for incoming-generating skills and trades. Their coordination with the Nzeve Deaf Children's Centre, friendships built through mission visits, and growing relations with international development agencies allowed their plans to come to life. The rapid growth of Deaf community organizing was led by Deaf Zimbabweans motivated to improve their skills and create opportunities. The role of hearing and Deaf friends in Zimbabwe and the United States was primarily connecting Deaf Zimbabweans to resources, thinking through ideas together, and trainers for specific things like running meetings and elections for club officers that equipped Deaf Zimbabweans to flourish. This dynamic environment saw the emergence of several Deaf ministries in hearing churches, Deaf-led outreach to identify and teach life skills, HIV prevention and other health information for Deaf people in rural areas, and connections with emerging Deaf clubs and groups in other cities across Zimbabwe.

Our mission team in 2018 was informed that our arrival was at the end of a Grapevine Dream Camp for Deaf women and they wouldn't be able to do anything special for us until that was completed. We were delighted that their clear communication reflected autonomy and agency. Upon arrival, I was moved to discover that this camp was the culmination of a series of week-long camps for Deaf women in rural areas where they were isolated from the opportunity to attend the Deaf club gatherings, where they might learn things that worried the hearing mother who sat in that very room eighteen years prior. These workshops were also aimed at equipping women to be educators for others they encountered in outlying areas. This was the grapevine they designed to grow and spread their knowledge and skills. As I watched their graduation ceremony, which included many of the education skits they had developed for teaching, I saw the friendship between these young Deaf women and their older Deaf mentors. The families of these young Deaf women were invited to come to the ceremony and see what their daughters had learned in relation to everything from sexual assault safety to household management and budgeting and be assured that their daughters had learned well. When the time for pictures came, they were to be "family only," and Deaf mentors were to stand aside for the picture, but the hearing parents of these young Deaf women insisted that their mentors be included. In one instance, a young camper's family was unable to come, which led to a rush of all the mentors standing in for her family for the picture—and a few mothers of other campers ran up to join! The grapevine had clearly grown strong through friendships and had even older roots in the mission partnerships where seeds were planted. In many ways, this illustrates that friendship is an essential ingredient to the metaphorical *sadza* I was working to create years earlier. Without friendships, mission partnerships risk becoming stale and mere means to ends. Friendship brings vibrancy and vitality that turns relationships into self-sustaining processes of transformation.

MAKING GRAPEVINE SALAD WITH CHRISTIAN FRIENDS

Making Sadza with Deaf Zimbabwean Women presents three strategies which bubbled up to the surface of this metaphorical cooking pot that aimed at enabling us to connect across considerable gaps in language, culture, race, education, nationality, and socio-economic opportunity. First, I examine a strategy of enacted theology, which attends to the patterns of ritual and social interactions and fosters the virtue of creativity through shared actions that address issues at hand. Second, I suggest a need for a system of checks and balances that allows us to listen to one another across our differences. This practice of "checking in" with our perceptions of how we are talking about others fosters the virtue of humility within us that might help counter the imbalance of power and privilege that exist between us. Third, I seek to save room for God's grace and extending that grace to one another. Such grace acknowledges bridges of commonality and community that allow us to connect with one another in intentional ways that move our relationships beyond mere transactional exchanges.

The qualities of my original study—creativity, humility, and grace—have served our American teams well as we worked in partnership with Deaf Zimbabweans through the years. These qualities become virtues that make us better people in our shared mission. What has emerged as the most salient virtue through all of our partnerships is the virtue of friendship. I typically favor the use of "mission partnership visits" over "mission trips" as an intentional decision to reframe the spirit and intent of our relationships with Deaf Zimbabweans. A "trip" implies something akin to a vacation or pleasure tour, "mission partnership" communicates a shared purpose to our being together. Framing of our relationship as a partnership is an effort to recognize the agency of those with whom we work. It brings a more humanizing lens to the nature of our work together than describing such cooperative efforts as a "project." Describing the moments where face to face interaction and cooperation are possible as "visits" implies a familiarity to our purpose that softens the perception of "partnership" as a purely transactional relationship. One "visits" friends and family, but one "takes a trip" when going on a vacation or business. Dana Robert notes the emergence of "mission trip" nomenclature as she observes the rise of short-term missions as a dominant form of Christian mission in the twenty-first century.[14] While she presents the purpose of such mission trips to be the formation of global friendships, I remain concerned by the unreflective dynamic of some short-term missions that fails to prepare people to sustain these friendships. Such failure results in much of the benefit of these trips being one directional to those who experience travel as a thrill rather than something that leads to substantial change in the lives of those hosting visitors. Yet, the example of DEAF-SAME bonds in deepening and sustaining temporary encounters into meaningful friendships offers an intriguing model for examining how short-term missions might better achieve global friendship.[15]

Dana Robert's work on friendship in mission gives me pause with regard to the use of "partnership" at all and suggests that I might be better served by returning to an older term, "friendship." Taking her cues from a speech made by V. S. Azariah at the 1910 World Missionary Conference in Edinburgh, Robert presents a reframing of mission as friendship that took hold after World War I.[16] Such friendships were able to transcend many of the racist ideologies that dominated colonialist policies and practices. However, the use of friendship as a conduit for mission came under critical scrutiny in the postcolonial era as, too often, paternalistic attitudes within friendships led to the continued marginalization of people who have experienced the traumas of colonization.[17] Concerns over paternalism in friendships across differentials in power and privilege are valid. Yet, with careful self-examination and attention to the dynamics of one's friendship, mutuality can be established and maintained that allows for marginalized people to flourish by their own agency. Humility becomes a key component in friendships. Being a good friend forces us to attend to the needs and cares

14. Robert, "Global Friendship," 181.

15. I explore these dynamics in VanGilder, "Exploring the Contours," 140–49.

16. Robert, "Cross-Cultural Friendship," 100–101.

17. Robert, "Cross-Cultural Friendship," 103.

of those with whom we are friends and take the stance of John the Baptist in "preparing the way" without speaking on their behalf.

In *The Four Loves*, C. S. Lewis explores the topic of friendship to discuss how it can be a mechanism of improving our character. Lewis seeks to make a modern recovery of an older understanding of friendship as a mutual form of love between equals that, instead of being focused on the other person, is focused on a common interest.[18] The transnational Deaf friendships evidenced between Deaf people from the United States and Zimbabwe bear witness to this idea. While we share a commonality of being Deaf that draws us together, we also share a common interest of care for our Deaf communities. This common interest of care, grounded in Christian mission, becomes the task that forms our bonds in friendship. The commonality of our experiences leads us to this common task rather quickly. For Lewis, the love between friends was something not attached to our nerves and emotions as much as our voluntary connections with another. Thus, the love in friendships "seemed to raise you to the level of gods or angels."[19] Yet Lewis was also aware of the risks of friendships. While he agreed with ancient Greek philosophers that friendship could be a school of virtue where the practice of friendship makes us more excellent people, he also saw the potential for friendship to be a school of vice.[20] We must take care to maintain mutuality between friends in mission together and practice humility. Missiology would do well to learn from Deaf experiences with friendships and explore other avenues that foster friendship as a key principle of mission encounters.

I now look at my original thinking on mission and practical theology and notice how characteristics of creativity, humility, and grace are bound by a type of carefully considered friendship. Friendship in mission becomes a key component to keeping a check on the potential for power differentials to damage missionary relationships. The success of the Grapevine Dream Camps in preparing young Deaf Zimbabwean women for womanhood is rooted in the friendships created between these women. Such friendships become a conduit for knowledge, skill, and self-confidence to grow. They do not require the direct participation of Deaf people from the United States to operate. However, a missional friendship between Deaf Zimbabweans and Deaf people from the United States was a catalyst for Deaf Zimbabwean women to identify their issues and develop this grapevine. As one friendship blossoms and grows, so it begets another friendship on the same vine.

18. Lewis, *Four Loves*, 91.

19. Lewis, *Four Loves*, 89.

20. Lewis, *Four Loves*, 115.

These vines grow and branch on their own, creating new vines that take root in unexpected places until they bear the fruit that makes our salad a rich and vibrant feast. The discovery that friendships can become a source of empowerment and transformation across the divides of transnational differences creates new ways of thinking and reshapes mission as a process that starts from the simplicity of being together.

BIBLIOGRAPHY

Chicago Mission for the Deaf. "Mission Notes." *Silent Herald* 5.11 (1907) 4.

———. "Mission Notes." *Silent Herald* 36.3 (1937) 2.

Chiswanda, Maria. "Hearing Mothers and Their Deaf Children in Zimbabwe: Mediated Learning Experiences." DSci diss., University of Oslo, 1997.

Gulliver, Mike. "The Emergence of International Deaf Spaces in France from Desloges 1779 to the Paris Congress of 1900." In *It's a Small World: International Deaf Spaces and Encounters*, edited by Michele Friedner and Annelies Kusters, 3–14. Washington, DC: Gallaudet University Press, 2013.

Kusters, Annelies, and Michele Freidner. "Introduction: DEAF-SAME and Difference in International Deaf Spaces and Encounters." In *It's a Small World: International Deaf Spaces and Encounters*, edited by Michele Friedner and Annelies Kusters, ix–xxix. Washington, DC: Gallaudet University Press, 2013.

Lewis, C. S. *The Four Loves*. New York: Harcourt, Brace, Jovanovich, 1960.

Mucherera, Tapiwa. *Counseling and Pastoral Care in African and Other Cross-Cultural Contexts*. Eugene, OR: Wipf & Stock, 2017.

Robert, Dana L. "Cross-Cultural Friendship in the Creation of Twentieth-Century World Christianity." *International Bulletin of Missionary Research* 35.2 (2011) 100–107.

———. *Faithful Friendships: Embracing Diversity in Christian Community*. Grand Rapids, MI: Eerdmans, 2019.

———. "Global Friendship as Incarnational Mission Practice." *International Bulletin of Missionary Research* 39.4 (2015) 180–84.

VanGilder, Kirk. "Deaf America's Encounter with Methodism: A Brief Look at a Culture and a Church." *Methodist History* 26.4 (1998) 239–49.

———. "Exploring the Contours of DEAF-SAME Kinship Bonds in United Methodist Short-Term Missions." In *It's a Small World: International Deaf Spaces and Encounters*, edited by Michele Friedner and Annelies Kusters, 140–49. Washington DC: Gallaudet University Press 2015.

———. *Making Sadza with Deaf Zimbabwean Women: A Missiological Reorientation of Practical Theological Method*. Gottingen: Vandenhoeck and Ruprecht, 2012.

Mentoring for Missional Colleagueship and Friendship in the Lord

MARGARET ELETTA GUIDER, OSF

My motivation for writing this essay is rooted in a personal and professional conviction about the importance of colleagueship and friendship in the lives that we live and the work that we do. That being said, the goal of the essay is to make a related and more explicit claim: critical to the work of missiology and to the formation of a new generation of missiologists is the cultivation of *missional colleagueship* and *friendship in the Lord*. By *missional colleagueship*, I mean a colleagueship that is historically Christian; attentive to the particularities of vocation, location, and participation in the *missio Dei*; oriented by an evangelical commitment to missionary discipleship; and committed to a vision of the church that goes forth.[1] By *friendship in the Lord*, I mean possessing a conscious awareness that we are inextricably bound together by our relationship to Jesus Christ who has called us friends (John 15:15) and that, imperfect and incomplete as our unity may be, we are part of an unfolding fulfillment of Jesus's prayer "that all may be one" (John 17:21).

The first part of this essay begins with a challenging claim made by interdisciplinary researchers studying colleagueship and friendship, namely: the subject matter merits more attention from scholars than it tends

---

1. I offer this explanation of the term *missional* mindful of the discussions, debates, and differences of theological opinion regarding a word that, despite its frequent use in missiological circles, has no one agreed upon definition. My own definition is informed and influenced by the missiological thinking of Pope Francis in the apostolic exhortation encyclical *Evangelii gaudium*. See Francis, *Joy of the Gospel*.

to receive. True as this claim may be for a wide range of professions and disciplines, I venture to say it holds true as well, with some noteworthy exceptions, in the field of world mission studies. Simply stated, more needs to be done when it comes to recognizing the value of colleagueship and friendship and appreciating the ways in which the interactive dynamic that exists between them contributes to the pursuit of knowledge and to human flourishing. Although the amount of research conducted on colleagueship and friendship may be somewhat limited, the findings identify the vital role played by positive personal relationships among colleagues, not only in terms of the work they do, but also in terms of the lives they live.

Mindful of the diverse contexts of Christian faith and practice that give rise to the emergence of missiologists and the multifaceted discipline of world mission studies, I go on to discuss how our faith-based commitments and vocational self-understandings inform and influence our colleagueship and our friendships. For many missiologists, creating and cultivating such relationships is about more than advancing theoretical knowledge regarding countless manifestations of the *missio Dei*. It also is about bearing witness to the ways in which, through missional colleagueship and friendship in the Lord, we are inspired, sustained, and transformed by God's grace and renewed in the conviction that it is the love of Christ that urges us on (2 Cor 5:14).

Looking to the future in the light of our past and present relationships, the second part of the essay reflects on the importance of sowing seeds of desire and hope in the hearts and minds of those whom we teach and mentor through the processes of integral formation—human, spiritual, intellectual, and ministerial. By way of example, I draw upon the life and wisdom of the twelfth-century Cistercian monk, Aelred of Rievaulx, and his treatise on *Spiritual Friendship*. While the text contains numerous insights worthy of retrieval and consideration by those engaged in mentoring as well as those being mentored, I briefly identify six insights that lend themselves to contemporary reflection on specific aspects of friendship in the Lord and missional colleagueship.

With those insights in mind, in the final section of the essay, I offer some concluding thoughts, by way of two personal narratives, on the importance of encouraging, fostering and persevering in the sometimes arduous and transformative work of missional colleagueship and friendship in the Lord—across the lifespan. By observing some of the particular ways in which the interactive dynamic of missional colleagueship and friendship in the Lord informs and influences the missiological consciousness and missionary imagination of those engaged in the study and practice of Christian mission, I consider two expressions of missionary discipleship: bold humility and resilient vulnerability. As we venture into the future, described by some as a post-ecumenical era, I propose that these expressions, perhaps better understood as graces, are as important for a new generation as they have been for past generations.

COLLEAGUESHIP, FRIENDSHIP, AND MISSIONARY DISCIPLESHIP

A review of interdisciplinary research on the subject of colleagueship and friendship provides a point of reference for understanding the significance of this interactive dynamic in diverse professional settings. Focusing specifically on the realm of higher education, the work of Leslie Gonzalez and Aimee Terosky offers an interesting overview of the state of the question: How important is colleagueship and friendship among academics? What are the potential benefits and advantages? What are the potential detriments and disadvantages? The following summary statement captures their findings:

> Higher education researchers assert that the relationships that faculty members hold with their colleagues are connected to work satisfaction, organizational commitment, productivity, and self-efficacy (Niehaus and O'Meara 2014; Ponjuan, Conley, and Trower 2011; Stupinsky, Weaver-Hightower, and Kartoshkina 2015). Specifically, research shows that access to relationships can lead to more research opportunities (Fox 2010), foster creative and/or interdisciplinary approaches in one's thinking (Lewis, Ross, and Holden 2012), and enhance one's sense of belonging (Núñez, Murakami, and Gonzales 2015) . . . most of the literature on faculty relationships assumes that faculty approach their relationships instrumentally or only as a means to an end. However, workplace and human relations scholars have found that workplace relationships frequently evolve to serve more social purposes, and sometimes that they even evolve into friendships, rendering benefits that belie a transactional framework (Markiewicz, Devine, and Kausilas 2000; Morrison and Nolan 2007). However, most higher education studies of faculty relationships do not consider this angle.[2]

In other words, friendships matter a good deal, both professionally and personally, though their importance is often overlooked.

Claims about the power of friendship are echoed in ministerial reflections on mission as well as missiological writings devoted to more technical

---

2. Gonzales and Terosky, "Colleagueship," 1378.

research in the theological disciplines and the social sciences. Though seldom addressed directly, friendship is often just beneath the surface. Writings about a missioner's life often emphasize the importance of having true friends at home and abroad[3] and of "build[ing] close and loving friendships with people outside the family of God,"[4] not for reasons that are utilitarian, but for reasons that are profoundly vocational. As is often observed, mutual affirmation, trust, communication, vulnerability, and an investment of time and energy are essential elements of such friendships, occasioned as they are by the call to mission.[5]

Conversely, to find oneself in mission *without* friends is also not something that is readily acknowledged or admitted. However, it is a reality that is extremely consequential on one's life and witness. As Karl Dahlfield notes, "There are lots of reasons why missionaries go home. . . . But one of the reasons that I rarely hear is a lack of friends. Of course, it would be difficult for anyone to really admit that a lack of genuine, deep, friendships on the mission field is the reason they are going home."[6] As impressionistic evidence about the need for friendship suggests:

> A few close friendships with other missionaries can bring life-giving joy to ourselves that will help us get through the rough times, and not only survive on the mission field but also thrive. Do it for yourself. Do it for your friend. Do it for your family. Do it for your ministry. Do it for the church. Do it for the glory of God and the renown of our Lord Jesus Christ.[7]

Friendship is never far from mission. Frequently, it seeps into personal reflections. This fact is borne out in a series of forty-eight articles published in the *International Bulletin of Missionary Research* between 1987 and 2014 entitled "My Journey in Mission."[8] Written as brief memoirs by mission scholars and missionaries, these essays almost always point to particular relationships as being crucial to the authors' respective vocations. To some extent, colleagueship and friendship in the Lord played a significant role in almost all of these autobiographical narratives. Friendship is interlocked with mission.

---

3. M., "Finding Friendship in Unexpected Places."

4. Anne, "Evangelicals and Missionary Friendships." See also Harney, "Seven Surprising Ways."

5. Koteskey, "What Missionaries Ought to Know."

6. Dahlfred, "Friends."

7. Dahlfred, "Friends."

8. See vols. 11–39 of *International Bulletin of Missionary Research* (1987–2015).

Friendship is also a gift, I would argue, to world mission studies. Since many scholars (a number of whom are theological educators as well) are former missioners themselves, their investigations and inquiries rarely take up questions that are generated by some sort of decontextualized theoretical speculation. Rather, it is precisely within the missional context of their commitments *and* their friendships in the Lord that they have been given new eyes with which to see and new ears with which to hear (Isa 6:10; Matt 13:15–16). These new ways of seeing and these new ways of hearing are key factors in understanding some of the reasons why colleagueship and friendship, and more specifically, missional colleagueship and friendship in the Lord, are foundational for what a number of us experience as our *preferred* way of proceeding.

If friendship is important to the study of world mission, it is that much more important to the practice of world mission. Since becoming a true disciple involves being a friend of Jesus (John 15:15), the consequences and demands of such relationships are life-altering and transformative. Extending beyond the Judeo-Christian tradition, we are reminded that "friendship with God teaches us and inspires us to be a true friend to others."[9] As Anthony Strano observes, "Even if there is a difference in abilities, roles or positions, there is a vision of equality that does not allow any feeling of either superiority or inferiority."[10] For those who adhere to the Gospel message of Jesus, this connection with others is exemplified by Jesus' self-giving and willingness to lay down his life for his friends and similarly so, for the many as well (John 10:18; 15:13; Matt 26:28; Mark 14:24; Luke 22:20).

It is precisely this self-giving, this friendship in the Lord, that has been a hallmark of all that is good in relationships—very often cross-cultural and inter-cultural—that informs and influences participation in the *missio Dei*.[11] Commenting on the evolution and growth of world Christianity during the twentieth century, Dana L. Robert affirmed that "behind the scenes, amid revolutionary changes, cross-cultural friendships quietly continued to shape the unfolding story of world Christianity."[12] Similarly, other works by

9. Strano, "Divine Friendship."

10. Strano, "Divine Friendship."

11. See Robert, "Cross-Cultural Friendship," 100–101: "One key that unlocks the history of missions from the 1910 World Missionary Conference to the mid-twentieth century is that of cross-cultural friendships. Christian community depends upon personal relationships, and missionary failures can be traced to their lack. Cross-cultural friendship is a hidden component of twentieth-century missions. [V. S.] Azariah's plea 'Give us FRIENDS!' was prophetic because, despite human limitations, friendship made possible Christian community."

12. Robert, "Cross-Cultural Friendship," 105.

Robert and by Christopher L. Heuertz and Christine D. Pohl give voice and visibility to the impact on mission practice of this important dimension of Christian life.[13]

Given the awareness of how crucial friendship in the Lord is for mission, our responsibility as mission scholars for mentoring a new generation of mission scholars and practitioners in the pathways of missional colleagueship becomes all the more urgent. It is a responsibility that calls forth from us courage, compassion, and conviction.

MENTORING AND FORMATIVE SPIRITUALITY FOR MISSION: A MONASTIC RESOURCE FOR INTERGENERATIONAL REFLECTION

The call to mentor the younger generation in friendship in the Lord is clear. Yet, since the subject has received insufficient attention, the path forward to answering that call is not always as clear. There is a dearth of good resources on friendship. Yet, with a certain creativity and curiosity, we can explore and retrieve relevant resources on friendship from the history of Christian spirituality. In thinking about this topic, one resource that comes to mind is a medieval treatise on *Spiritual Friendship*, composed by Aelred of Rievaulx, a twelfth-century Cistercian monk and abbot.

Aelred was born in Hexham, Northumbria, England in 1110. He came from a long line of married priests at a time when clerical celibacy was being enforced throughout England. During his adolescence, he served in the court of King David I of Scotland. Gradually, he assumed more responsibilities in service to the king. As the king's financial steward, Aelred endeavored to be the "dependable dispenser, the discerning distributor, the prudent provider."[14] In what seems to have been an experience of conversion, he left Scotland in 1134, and, with the support of benefactors and friends, he entered the relatively new monastery of Rievaulx, in Yorkshire, England. Within a decade, he became the novice master and then the abbot of another Cistercian monastery at Revesby. In 1147, he returned to the Abbey of Rievaulx and became the abbot. During his years of spiritual leadership, the abbey flourished in its number of members as well as social influence. In his evangelizing mission as a spiritual leader, religious reformer, and experienced diplomat, Aelred was found worthy of trust as a friend of God. It was this friendship that served as a basis for all others. Despite a serious

13. See Robert, *Faithful Friendships*; Heuertz and Pohl, *Friendship at the Margins*.
14. Dutton, "Introduction," 14.

medical condition that caused him significant suffering during the final ten years of his life, he remained committed to the mission entrusted to his care, devoted to his brother monks, and dedicated to the process of making his spiritual, theological, and biblical treatises available to the people of God. In 1167, Aelred of Rievaulx died at the age of fifty-seven.[15]

Aelred's most popular treatise, *Spiritual Friendship*, written sometime between April of 1164 and his death in January of 1167, contains a prologue and three books made up of dialogues between an elder monk, Aelred, and three inquisitive younger monks: Ivo, Walter, and Gratian. *Spiritual Friendship*, as Marsha L. Dutton observes, gives expression to the "sacramental essence of friendship—the way in which men and women may by loving one another embrace Christ in this life and enjoy eternal friendship with God in time to come."[16] In the prologue, Aelred lays out his primary sources, some of which include Cicero's *On Friendship*, Ambrose's *On the Duties of the Clergy*, Augustine's *Confessions*, and the Bible.[17] Aelred also uses the prologue to identify himself, his credentials, his arguments, and his reflections on friendship that are informed and influenced by classical philosophical texts as well as classical Christian texts.[18] In the three books, the three young monks enter into dialogue with Aelred. Through a series of questions and answers, they explore and examine the essence and origin of friendship, the value and limits of friendship, the choice and trial of friends, and finally, the excellence and practice of friendship.

As with many texts coming out of various periods of history, there are aspects of the treatise that lend themselves to any number of modern criticisms. Yet, I contend that one of the values of the text has to do with the manner in which the dialogues unfold to reveal some perennial wisdom regarding formative faith-based mentoring that includes a recognition of equality in relationship before God, a reverence for the uniqueness of each vocation, and an acknowledgement of what it means to be a steward of the God-given gifts that are received individually and collectively.

In proposing *Spiritual Friendship* as a resource for inter-generational reflection on mentoring, missional colleagueship, and friendship in the Lord, I am mindful of the fact that we are separated in time and space from the monks of Rievaulx by much more than eight hundred years. At the same time, there is something that holds us together as friends of the

---

15. For more complete details on Aelred's life and legacy, see Dutton, "Introduction," 13–50. This paragraph is a summary of some of her central biographical insights.

16. Dutton, "Introduction," 22–23.

17. See Dutton, "Introduction," 25–32.

18. Dutton, "Introduction," 33–34.

Lord—whether in a medieval monastery or a modern-day collegium of actual and aspiring scholars of world mission studies and missionary disciples. What follows are six selected insights of Aelred that merit retrieval and consideration. These include: beginning in Christ, discovering and fostering characteristic qualities of friendship, cultivating friendships built on equality before God, creating and sustaining the conditions for authentic dialogue with a new generation, remembering the lives and legacies of friends in the Lord, and focusing on Christ.

In the second book of *Spiritual Friendship*,[19] Aelred speaks about the importance of beginning in Christ. Unlike students and scholars in most other disciplines, there is a way in which, as colleagues, we can assume this common beginning. And it is precisely this common beginning, this experience of friendship in the Lord, that makes our colleagueship missional.

Aelred's discussion of the four qualities characteristic of friendship as described in the third book of *Spiritual Friendship* resonates to a great extent with what many have witnessed in the company of missional colleagues.[20] Love, affection, reassurance, and joy are manifested in countless ways. Despite our differences in traditions, cultural and racial backgrounds, countries of origin, and social location, there is a way in which a heart transformed by participation in the *missio Dei* is often a heart that has been broken open. In the intuitive process of mutual recognition, there is a common experience of evangelical joy that is life affirming and convicted in the belief that Christ is our reason for being in relationship.

No stranger to the management of strained, competitive, envious, and divisive relationships in the monastery, Aelred takes up the theme of equality before God as the foundation for cultivating friendships where the practices of loyalty, simplicity, constancy, and unity are present.[21] In all three

19. "In friendship, then, we join honesty with kindness, truth with joy, sweetness with goodwill, and affection with kind action. All this begins with Christ, is advanced through Christ, and is perfected in Christ. The ascent does not seem too steep or too unnatural, then, from Christ's inspiring the love with which we love a friend to Christ's offering himself to us as the friend we may love . . . hence a friend clinging to a friend in the spirit of Christ becomes one heart and one soul with him (Acts 4:32; 1 Cor 6:17)" (Aelred, *Spiritual Friendship* II.20–21, 75).

20. "Four qualities seem to be especially characteristic of friendship: love and affection, reassurance and joy. To render service with good will pertains to love, an increasing inner delight pertains to affection, and a communication of all secrets and plans, without fear or suspicion, pertains to reassurance. But what pertains to joyfulness is a kind and friendly exchange about all events whether happy or sad, about all one's thoughts whether harmful or helpful, and about all the lessons one has learned or taught" (Aelred, *Spiritual Friendship* III.51, 99).

21. "Moreover, thanks to the influence of friendship, the greater and the less become equal . . . reverting to our first origin and probing deeply, let both parties set store by the

books, several references to Acts 4:32 can be found underscoring the importance and value of the many becoming one.

In all three books of *Spiritual Friendship*, Aelred offers examples of diverse ways of engaging and being engaged by those we teach and mentor. It
is true that the use of dialogues was a common genre of the time, yet there is
something particularly moving in the final twenty paragraphs of Book III.[22]
In these paragraphs, Aelred speaks freely and openly about realizations that
he had come to in his own life. Looking back on experiences, he specifically
relates experiences of friendship and the demands of being in leadership.
To the attentive young monks, a certain knowledge ordinarily acquired by
direct experience is acquired vicariously through Aelred's honest sharing
and interpretation, often done through the lens of Scripture. While there is
no sufficient way to supply for the inexperience of age or lack of authority,
missional colleagueship, like friendship, is deepened when reflections on
one's own experiences of bold humility and resilient vulnerability are not
reserved only to peers, but appropriately shared with those who are on the
path, no longer of only students, but missional colleagues in the process
of becoming. As Aelred says to Walter, if what "I have introduced by way
of example, you discover something to imitate, make it serve your own
progress."[23]

Speaking of two of his treasured friends, "who although no longer
among the living are still alive for me and always will be,"[24] Aelred gives
voice to a value deeply shared by missional colleagues, namely our remembrance of those who have gone before us in faith. With every journey home
to God, we are entrusted with their legacies, not only the legacies of their
scholarly contributions, but the legacies of their lives, their witness as missionary disciples, and, yes, their friendship in the Lord. As we remember
them, we can say with Aelred, "What an advantage it is, then, to grieve for
one another, to work for one another, to bear one another's burdens."[25]

As Aelred concludes Book III, he observes "how delightful friends
find their meetings together, the exchange of mutual interests, the exploration of every question."[26] Reading this phrase, it is easy to be reminded of

---

equality that nature grants . . . in friendship, then, which is the best gift of nature and of
grace together, the lofty steps down and the lowly steps up, the rich one is impoverished
and the poor one enriched. Thus, they communicate to one another their own state,
with a resulting equality (2 Cor 8:15)" (Aelred, *Spiritual Friendship* III.90–91, 110–11).

22. Aelred, *Spiritual Friendship* III.115–34.

23. Aelred, *Spiritual Friendship* III.127, 124.

24. Aelred, *Spiritual Friendship* III.119, 121.

25. Aelred, *Spiritual Friendship* III.132, 125.

26. Aelred, *Spiritual Friendship* III.132, 125.

the local, regional, national, and international meetings where scholars of world mission studies and missionary disciples assemble, as missional colleagues, to commemorate our efforts, to celebrate our milestones, to mourn the passing of our beloved friends in the Lord, and to welcome into our midst a new generation. While Aelred's observation captures our attention, he masterfully redirects our focus before concluding his treatise. He goes on to say that "surpassing all this is prayer for each other. In remembering a friend, the more lovingly one sends forth prayer to God, with tears welling up from fear or affection or grief, the more effective that prayer will be. Thus praying to Christ for a friend and desiring to be heard by Christ for a friend, we focus on Christ with love and longing."[27]

MENTORING A NEW GENERATION FOR MISSIONAL COLLEAGUESHIP AND FRIENDSHIP IN THE LORD

For many years, discussions and debates have ensued regarding a series of related questions, some of which include: Can spirituality be taught? Can empathy be taught? Can solidarity be taught? Can resiliency be taught? To these questions, and others like them, I would add: Can missional colleagueship be taught? Can friendship in the Lord be taught? Moreover, as longstanding battles wage on over nature and grace and nature and nurture—in communities of faith, in the academy, and in society—another question, perhaps prior to all of the others, arises: Does mentoring matter?

Aelred would answer these questions in the affirmative. Friendship in the Lord can be taught, and mentoring matters in that process. Both his essay and his life make this conviction plain. I, too, would like to think that missional colleagueship and friendship in the Lord can be taught through mentoring, and for one simple reason: teaching by example works. To quote an adage often attributed to Saint Francis of Assisi: "Teach by example and, when necessary, use words." My faith in the power of teaching by example stems from my own professional experiences of mentoring and being mentored.

Since the mid-1980s, I have participated in annual meetings of the American Society of Missiology.[28] As a graduate student, beginning doctoral studies in Religion & Society at Harvard Divinity School, I was fortunate

---

27. Aelred, *Spiritual Friendship*, III.132–33, 125–26.

28. Eventually, my experiences of the guild were enlarged by my engagement with the Association of Professors of Mission, the Eastern Fellowship of the American Society of Missiology, and the International Mission and Ecumenism Committee of the Boston Theological Institute.

to be invited and introduced to this guild by five of my mentors and teachers from the Catholic Theological Union and the Lutheran School of Theology: William Burrows, Robert Schreiter, Anthony Gittins, Lawrence Nemer, and James Scherer. Attending my first meeting, I felt a bit like Lucy Pevensie as she passed through the wardrobe door and ventured into Narnia.[29] The location was Techny Towers, a conference center of the Divine Word Missionaries, and it was there that I had my first experience of aspiring to be a colleague in the ecumenical world of mission and mission studies.

Sitting in the back corner of the assembly hall, I found myself in proximity to missiologists and missionary leaders whose work I had read in class and in preparation for my comprehensive exams: Gerald Anderson, Samuel Escobar, Mary Motte, Ruth Tucker, Joseph Lang, Lamin Sanneh, and Janet Carroll. Generously, they, along with others, invited me to move from the periphery of their conversations to the center. As Aelred advised, they invited me, as a member of a new generation, into authentic dialogue with them. Later that evening, as the annual banquet was about to get underway, I found myself included at a table of missional colleagueship and friendship in the Lord. My graduate student aspiration—namely, to become their colleague one day—was on the way to being realized.

Far beyond the possibility of colleagueship that I was only beginning to imagine, these women and men foresaw something in me that I had not yet fully recognized in myself. At that meeting, I was being invited into something much more than colleagueship. I was being invited into an intergenerational relationship of friendship in the Lord that was grounded in a shared passion for participating in the *missio Dei*. It was a friendship begun in Christ and focused on Christ, as Aelred recommends. Truly, being mentored in this way was a dynamic experience of the Spirit that transformed my way of proceeding in the future that awaited me. Over the course of more than three decades of ongoing missional colleagueship and friendship in the Lord, I continue to be inspired and sustained by a vision grounded in the praxis of Jesus (Matt 18:20; John 15:15) and built upon the praxis of missionary discipleship (Rom 12) that I have been privileged to witness and experience, year after year, annual meeting after annual meeting. Along the way, I have experienced again and again the qualities of friendship named by Aelred: love, affection, reassurance, and joy. Now, as I find myself in a more senior position within the society, I aspire to do for my students and the students of my colleagues exactly that which was done for me by way of mentoring.

---

29. Lewis, *Lion, the Witch and the Wardrobe*.

Central to my attempts to live out this aspiration to mentor others has been an awareness of the ongoing need for critical reflection on missiology and its teaching. A few years after my introduction to the circle of missional colleagueship at Techny Towers, in the early 1990s, David Bosch proposed a postmodern vision for mission and missionaries that expanded my understanding of mission and of friendship in the Lord.[30] It was invigorating, and I embraced it, allowing it to influence and enlarge my own Roman Catholic understanding of what it meant to live out the Great Commission and the Great Commandment. Bosch recommended that mission needed to proceed in bold humility.

However, as I team-taught a course on mission with Ian Douglas, we—along with others—began to recognize deeper challenges to Bosch's "emerging ecumenical paradigm." It was not that his argument was wrong, so much as we were concerned that the students before us might not have the formation or inner capacities to live out the complexities of mission, which Bosch described so elegantly, in meaningful ways.[31] It was one thing to promote bold humility, but it also became clear that students also needed something else to pursue Aelred's goal of cultivating enduring friendships built on equality before God and focused resolutely on Christ. While Douglas and I shared a common vision of missionary discipleship guided by bold humility (Mark 10:41–45; Acts 4:23–31) and gave testimony to its permanent validity, just as Aelred shared honestly with his three monastic interlocutors, we could not help but do a missional reality check about resiliency and vulnerability in our students.

As we looked out into the faces of the students and envisioned the futures that awaited them as ministers, scholars, and theological educators in Pakistan, Ivory Coast, Myanmar, Cameroon, East Timor, Rwanda, India, Ukraine, China, Turkey, Kenya, El Salvador, the Philippines, Brazil, New York City, Houston, Miami, Los Angeles, and Minneapolis, we could see individual boldness and personal humility. But, I wondered, in the midst of chaos, conflict, corruption, persecution, and disaster, would the grace of bold humility suffice? Or was there another experience of grace needed in order to hold fast to authentic gospel hope, given the predictable, perhaps inevitable, allures of presumption, temptations to despair, and experiences of futility that can lead to resignation? How could we mentor students to form friendships in the Lord that would continue to produce the love, affection, reassurance, and joy necessary to continue in mission, even amidst the challenges of the world?

30. Bosch, *Transforming Mission.*
31. Guider, "Transforming Missionaries."

My response to the questions articulated above is straightforward. Bold humility is not enough. It needs to be supplemented with the grace of resilient vulnerability (Luke 12:22–34; 2 Cor 4:7–18). Over time, I have discovered that just as missiological consciousness and missionary imagination contribute to bold humility, so too, missional colleagueship and friendship in the Lord create the conditions for resilient vulnerability. On the one hand, the grace of bold humility sustains a discerning commitment to integrity and competency as reflected in a readiness to meet foreseen challenges—a commitment that is characterized by an evolutionary sense of a future that is continuous with the present and the past. Here, Aelred's advice about remembering the lives and legacies of friends in the Lord is relevant, as it helps us see the continuities between past, present, and future.

On the other hand, the grace of resilient vulnerability gives rise to a charismatic *disponibilité* that enables us to make ourselves available for risk-taking and innovation. This resilient vulnerability is manifested in an intuitive capacity to live in anticipation of the unexpected that is characterized by an apocalyptic sense of an advent of something new, or at least unknown, breaking into human history in uncertain, unprecedented, and uncharted ways. It is a grace that makes possible an experience of embodied solidarity with the created world and with others—just as they are and just as they are becoming. Grounded theologically in an incarnational conviction that God became human to be *God-with-Us*, resilient vulnerability goes to the very heart of what it means to participate in the *missio Dei*. It is the means by which missional colleagueship and friendship in the Lord yield the many benefits for world mission study and practice mentioned earlier in this essay.

CONCLUSION

As I reflect upon the evolution that has taken place in theological education over the course of the past thirty years,[32] specifically in the field of world mission studies, and as I think about the students I have been privileged to teach, many of whom are now scholars, theological educators, church leaders, and missioners throughout the world, I am more and more convinced that the task entrusted to those of us privileged to be mentors is about much more than heightening, widening, deepening, and enlarging missiological consciousness and missionary imagination into a curriculum. It also is about infusing into mentoring relationships, with intentionality, an awareness and appreciation for missional colleagueship and friendship in the Lord. While the former opens us up to the grace of bold humility, the latter

---

32. See Pieterse, *Locating US Theological Education.*

opens us up to the grace of resilient vulnerability. Indeed, these grace-filled experiences of bold humility and resilient vulnerability make missional colleagueship *and* friendship in the Lord possible from generation to generation, which is the reason why mentoring is so important. Though every age has its own trials and tribulations, disputations and divisions, controversies and constraints, credible missionary discipleship always has involved, indeed required, remembering why Jesus called his disciples friends (John 15:15) and why he prayed "that all may be one" (John 17:21). Such remembrance has demanded much of past generations, perhaps, in more ways than they were able, equipped, or disposed to take to heart. Most certainly, going forward from where we find ourselves today, such remembrance may demand even more of present and future generations. As beneficiaries of the mentoring we have received and as stewards of the legacies entrusted to our care, whether that of Aelred or those of our own teachers, with God's grace, let us be intentional about leaving to those who will come after us a legacy that includes an enduring commitment to missional colleagueship and friendship in the Lord.

BIBLIOGRAPHY

Aelred of Rievaulx. *Spiritual Friendship*. Edited by Marsha L. Dutton. Translated by Lawrence C. Braceland. Collegeville, MN: Cistercian, 2010.

Anne, Libby. "Evangelicals and Missionary Friendships." *Patheos* (blog), March 28, 2019. Online. https://www.patheos.com/blogs/lovejoyfeminism/2019/03/evangelicals-and-missionary-friendships.html.

Bosch, David J. *Transforming Mission: Paradigm Shifts in Mission Theology*. Maryknoll, NY: Orbis, 1991.

Dahlfred, Karl. "Friends: A Key to Survival on the Mission Field." *Gleanings from the Field* (blog), January 22, 2014. Online. https://www.dahlfred.com/index.php/blogs/gleanings-from-the-field/691-friends-a-key-to-survival-on-the-mission-field.

Dutton, Marsha L. "Introduction." In *Spiritual Friendship*, by Aelred of Rievaulx, 13–50. Edited by Marsha L. Dutton. Collegeville, MN: Cistercian, 2010.

Francis. *The Joy of the Gospel (Evangelii Gaudium)*. New York: Random, 2014.

Gonzales, Leslie D., and Aimee L. Terosky. "Colleagueship in Different Types of Postsecondary Institutions: A Lever for Faculty Vitality." *Studies in Higher Education* 43.8 (2018) 1378–91.

Guider, Margaret Eletta. "Transforming Missionaries: Implications of the Ecumenical Paradigm." In *Mission in Bold Humility: David Bosch's Work Considered*, edited by Willem Saayam and Klippies Kritzinger, 151–61. Maryknoll, NY: Orbis, 1996.

Harney, Kevin G. "Seven Surprising Ways to Prepare Yourself to Share the Gospel." *Christianity Today*, March 22, 2019. Online. https://www.christianitytoday.com/edstetzer/2019/march/seven-surprising-ways-to-prepare-yourself-to-share-gospel.html.

Heuertz, Christopher L., and Christine D. Pohl. *Friendship at the Margins: Discovering Mutuality in Service and Mission.* Downers Grove, IL: InterVarsity, 2010.

Koteskey, Ronald L. "What Missionaries Ought to Know about Relationships." *Missionary Care.* Online. http://www.missionarycare.com/relationships.html.

Lewis, C. S. *The Lion, the Witch and the Wardrobe.* London: HarperCollins Children's, 1998.

M., Rachel. "Finding Friendship in Unexpected Places." *Missionary Life* (blog), May 18, 2019. Online. https://missionarylife.org/2019/05/18/finding-friendships-unexpected-places. Excerpted from Rachel M., *"Pack Up Kids! Let's Go!": Encouragement for Families Living Cross-Culturally.* Self-published, 2015.

Pieterse, Hendrik R., ed. *Locating US Theological Education in a Global Context: Conversations with American Higher Education.* Eugene, OR: Pickwick, 2019.

Robert, Dana L. "Cross-Cultural Friendship in the Creation of Twentieth-Century World Christianity." *International Bulletin of Missionary Research* 35.2 (2011) 100–107.

————. *Faithful Friendships: Embracing Diversity in Christian Community.* Grand Rapids, MI: Eerdmans, 2019.

Strano, Anthony. "Divine Friendship." *HuffPost* (blog), November 7, 2012. Online. https://www.huffpost.com/entry/friendship_b_2089025.

SECTION IV

Friendship and Dana L. Robert

Dana L. Robert as Friend and Scholar

The preceding essay by Meg Guider reminds us of how we are shaped by the lives and legacies of friendship and mentoring that we experience from our colleagues and teachers. This volume is a celebration of the life and legacy of one particular scholar: Dr. Dana L. Robert. Thus, this chapter shares a series of commendations by Robert's colleagues and former students, testifying to her particular knack for friendship and mentoring.

JONATHAN BONK

Founding Director Emeritus, Dictionary of African Christian Biography

I have been invited to reflect briefly on Dana Robert as a friend. Of course, she is not only a friend to me, but a valued colleague, a peer, and in many ways—despite my being eleven years her senior—a mentor from whose friendship I have benefited immensely. I cannot recall when first I met her, but I suppose it must have been at an annual meeting of the American Society of Missiology, an organization that was founded in 1972, the year that I graduated from Trinity Evangelical Divinity School.

Prolific author of at least a dozen books and scores of articles, her scholarly writing is characteristically uncluttered by academese, making it accessible to readers both within and outside of the academy. She served as an active member of the Board of Trustees of the Overseas Ministries Study Center from 2000–2009, when the organization flourished as a hub of world Christian scholarship, missiological publications, and international art. She was a key member of Lamin Sanneh's Oxford Studies in World Christianity group that met annually at OMSC and issued in a stream of significant books. When in 2011–2012, the *Dictionary of African Christian Biography* began to explore formal affiliation with a major university, she took active steps to ensure that the enterprise found a home in the Boston University School of Theology's Center for Global Christianity and Mission, where it flourishes today. She serves as a member of its Editorial Committee and as a contributing editor to the *Journal of African Christian Biography*, launched in June 2016. It now has more than two thousand subscribers, no small feat for an academic journal!

She has mentored many a dissertation, working diligently and effectively with the scholars to produce some of the more outstanding mission-related scholarship of her generation. But as impressive as her academic acumen and productivity might be, these are merely compliments to her qualities as a person, a spouse, a mother, a friend, and a colleague. I have not been given space to elaborate, but those whose contributions you read in this volume will readily attest and illustrate both the truth and the inadequacy of the list of attributes that immediately came to mind when I was asked to contribute these remarks. The qualities that make her an outstanding scholar also make her an extraordinary friend and colleague. In no particular order, these include warmth, friendliness, graciousness, and generosity of spirit; diligence, self-discipline, and intellectual rigor of mind; candor, honesty, and clarity in speech and writing; and empathy, collegiality, and loyalty in relationships with family, friends, colleagues, and students. Each of these could be illustrated and elaborated upon by anyone who knows her.

To have known Dana as a friend and colleague over the course of much of my own academic life is a privilege indeed!

ANDREW F. WALLS

Professor of the History of Mission, Liverpool Hope University; Honorary Professor, University of Edinburgh; Research Professor, Africa International University Center for World Christianity; and Professor Emeritus, Akrofi-Christaller Institute of Theology, Mission, and Culture

Dana Robert has been one of the scholars who has shaped the developing field of the study of World Christianity. Her contributions have constantly illuminated the interconnections between Christian developments in the West and in the rest of the world. Her influence in the field of mission history has been immense. More than anyone else, she has demonstrated the extent to which Western missions became a women's movement, sustained and carried forward by women. Her invaluable studies of such figures as A. T. Pierson and A. J. Gordon demonstrate how preachers' exposition of Biblical themes could galvanize and mobilize young people and how extra-ecclesial patterns of Christian organization developed as an outcome. There has been much discussion in some circles of "church history as mission history"; Dana's work reveals mission history as church history. Followed through, that insight could have huge implications for the theological academy, where the missionary movement has had a marginal place, if any place at all, in the study of the Western church. In the setting of the history of World Christianity as a whole, it is arguably the most important development in the modern history of the church in the West.

Dana has been a builder in other important respects also. She has developed an outstanding program in World Christianity—and there are not too many of them—in a major Western theological institution. Such achievements require the fusion of the qualities of the diplomat and the warrior, and she has both. Valuable and innovative research has flowed from the program. With her husband, Inus Daneel, she has secured the future of crucially important records relating to African Christianity. She has furthered the progress of vital scholarly tools such as the *Dictionary of African Christian Biography*.

Her influence as a kindly, generous, supportive friend and encourager of others has paralleled her personal contributions to scholarship. From the experience of four decades or more, I hereby give my grateful testimony.

GERALD H. ANDERSON

Director Emeritus, Overseas Ministries Study Center, and former Editor, International Bulletin of Mission Research

I know I am a better person because Dana Robert is my friend. Of course, she has many friends; it is a distinguishing feature of who she is.

In her book, *Faithful Friendships: Embracing Diversity in Christian Community*, she makes a powerful case for the importance of friendship. It "forms Christian identity," she says, and "the model for friendship is the life of Jesus and his disciples."[1] Therefore, "Christians have the responsibility to make friends across divisions that separate us from one another. For

---

1. Robert, *Faithful Friendships*, 4.

Christians today the cultivation of risk-taking friendships is an ethical and spiritual imperative."[2] "It points to God's kingdom."[3]

She explores and describes other models of friendship from different cultures, societies, and even some other religions around the world. It is impressive.

In addition to the importance of friendship in Dana's work is the fact that she is a prominent scholar who serves as the Truman Collins Professor of World Christianity and History of Mission, and Director of the Center for Global Christianity and Mission at Boston University School of Theology.

Among the vast array of published books and articles she has produced, one that stands out is her article in the April 2020 issue of the *International Bulletin of Mission Research,* "Naming 'World Christianity': Historical and Personal Perspectives on the Yale-Edinburgh Conference in World Christianity and Mission History." It is a classic survey that charts "the historical development of the interlocking academic discourses of mission studies and World Christianity . . . within North American Protestant academia since 1910."[4] This should be required reading in all mission courses.

It is important to know that it was Dana with her husband, M. L. "Inus" Daneel, an expert on African Indigenous Churches in Zimbabwe, who actually started the Center for Global Christianity and Mission at Boston University School of Theology in 2001 and helped nourish it all these years to what it has become.

To God be the glory.

WILBERT R. SHENK

Senior Professor of Mission History and Contemporary Culture, Fuller Graduate School of Intercultural Studies

Two things stand out as I recall the 1984 annual meeting of the American Society of Missiology held at Princeton Theological Seminary the third week of June. The first memory worth noting is the moving address to the final session on Sunday morning by a relative newcomer, Dr. Lamin Sanneh, then teaching at Harvard Divinity School. That morning Sanneh recounted his faith journey. As a young boy he observed his devout Muslim father reading the Koran and praying as day was breaking. His inquiring mind led him to begin asking questions and searching. Eventually in his teenage years

2. Robert, *Faithful Friendships*, 3.

3. Robert, *Faithful Friendships*, 6.

4. Robert, "Naming 'World Christianity,'" 12.

he began reading the New Testament. In a transforming moment he felt compelled to accept the claim that Jesus Christ's love embraced all people, "even me!" This became a holy moment for the audience. A hush seemed to envelop us. As Sanneh took his seat, I overheard someone sitting nearby say, "that was St. Augustine speaking!"

The second memory I associate with the 1984 ASM meeting was becoming acquainted with a young Yale doctoral student, Dana Robert. I counted among my friends Professor Charles W. Forman, and he was pleased to inform me that he was Dana's "doktor-vater." Two years later, immediately following the 1986 ASM meeting, held at North Park Seminary, Evanston, Illinois, a group of us caucused to lay plans for a multivolume retrospective to mark the bicentennial of the launch of the modern mission movement, using William Carey's 1792 departure for India as the symbolic starting point. Dana was an important part of that group. Out of that initiative came her landmark volume, *American Women in Mission: A Social History of Their Thought and Practice* (1996). Her superb scholarship has done much to retrieve the indispensable role women have played in the history of Christian missions: pioneering new dimensions of mission, overcoming prejudice, demonstrating extraordinary courage, expertise, and compassion that this largely unsung multitude of women sacrificially contributed to the Christian mission.

Each year I have looked forward to the ASM annual meeting and the opportunity these occasions have afforded for a good conversation with Dana, catching up on our mutual preoccupations. The year 2020 has been filled with surprises and some disappointments, including cancellation of the ASM annual meeting. But friendship transcends the momentary. I am ever grateful for Dana's friendship these thirty-six years. Thank you, Dana, for the gift of friendship you have given to your students and colleagues.

DAVID HEMPTON

Dean, Harvard Divinity School

I first met Dana Robert over twenty years ago when I interviewed for a position in the School of Theology at Boston University (BU). In truth, it was a position I had little intention of accepting even if offered. As part of the interview process, I remember giving a lecture on the Methodist tradition to a BU class, and Dana sat unobtrusively at the back. Although there were many reasons why I ended up changing my mind and accepting a position at BU, interacting with Dana over the interview process played a significant part. Over my eight plus years at BU, Dana became a close and deeply valued colleague. My expertise was located mostly in transatlantic traditions of popular evangelical religion, but my knowledge of the rest of the world was limited. Over the years at BU, Dana and I shared many doctoral students working on historical projects in the United States and missiological topics around the world. I came to admire her combination of impeccably high standards and compassionate engagement with our students. She was a model doctoral adviser, a devoted teacher, and a formidably talented scholar. I learned a great deal from her. Many years later, when I had to write a global history of early modern Christianity for the IB Tauris series on the History of the Christian Church,[5] I drew deeply on Dana's brilliant corpus of published work, our shared doctoral supervisions, and our many casual conversations. Dana's respect for the Methodist tradition, her awareness of the complexity of the issues at stake in the global dissemination of Christianity, and her small army of doctoral students over the years make her one of the world's most distinguished and influential missiologists. I am delighted to pay tribute to her contribution to church, academy, and wider world and to wish her well in all her future endeavors. Thank you for being such a great colleague and friend.

SCOTT W. SUNQUIST

President and Professor of Missiology, Gordon-Conwell Theological Seminary

The fellowship of missiologists is like nothing I have experienced in any other academic field. Scholars care about the implications of the Christian message for real people embedded in earthly cultures. We love to talk about different communities, and we find great satisfaction in making connections—personal, theological, cultural, theoretical—and finding common love for God's mission. Missiological friendships bridge divides than most churches, seminaries, academic disciplines, or languages could never unite.

Dana Robert has been for me one of the noble examples of a missiological friend. We shared through scholarship, panel discussions, and she even wrote nice things about one of my books.[6] I, however, have been the greater beneficiary of this friendship, for I have relied on her books and even lectures in my teaching and research. Friendships rely on trust, and trust can be expressed through scholarship. There are certain scholars we

5. Hempton, *Church in the Long Eighteenth Century.*
6. Sunquist, *Unexpected Christian Century.*

can always trust. Dana is one of them. But even more than this, we can trust Dana to be respectful, attentive, and pleasant. Friendships like this make life in God's mission a foretaste of the Kingdom.

TODD M. JOHNSON

Eva B. and Paul E. Toms Distinguished Professor of Mission and Global Christianity and Co-Director of the Center for the Study of Global Christianity, Gordon-Conwell Theological Seminary, and Visiting Research Fellow at Boston University's Institute for Culture, Religion, and World Affairs

Dana Robert was a friend from the start. Shortly after I arrived in Boston in 2003 to set up a new research center on global Christianity, Dana called and arranged for us and our respective deans at Gordon-Conwell Theological Seminary and Boston University to meet over lunch. As the four of us enjoyed our meals, Dana celebrated my arrival, placing my work in context with similar initiatives of universities in the area. Not only did she welcome me, but she also gave me a sense of how I belonged in the broader academic community in the Boston area. That first meeting was followed by dozens more over the next seventeen years, as we labored together in the International Mission and Ecumenism faculty committee of the Boston Theological Institute (BTI). I grew to cherish those monthly meetings of the BTI, along with the hours Dana and I spent over coffee every summer to catch up on life, family, and vocation.

It did not take me long to realize that Dana was a bridge between generations of scholars in the field of World Christianity. Having studied with the great scholars of the field, Dana embodies their legacies for a younger generation of scholars. But she is also a pioneer with a legacy of her own. Dana is a unifying figure in the field by her insistence that World Christianity or Global Christianity is not simply thousands of unrelated "Christianities" around the world. She has consistently and compellingly emphasized the interconnectedness of Christians worldwide, advocating for unity in diversity. Dana Robert has been a prophetic voice in what World Christianity means for each of us, but especially for women, who have done most of the work of building a truly global Christian family.

Shortly after Dana's book *Faithful Friendships: Embracing Diversity in Christian Community* was released, we were, for the first time, co-teaching a course on global Christianity at Boston University. After all these years, we had never listened to each other teach in the classroom, and it was in this context I realized more fully how faithful of a friend Dana had been to me. As it turned out, we were working shoulder to shoulder when the pandemic struck in the middle of the semester. While we scrambled to continue the class remotely, we were able to face this challenge together, and that made the experience more rewarding. It struck me that she was the perfect person to write on friendship since it was a skill that she so adeptly employed. So many of us have been beneficiaries of Dana's magnanimous and generous spirit—it is through her care and thoughtfulness that we've become better versions of ourselves.

ARUN W. JONES

Dan and Lillian Hankey Associate Professor of World Evangelism, Candler School of Theology, Emory University

I first encountered Dana Robert at a missionary gathering in 1980 or 1981. It was, I believe, a gathering of missionaries who were being prepared to be sent out for service. Dana was a graduate student at Yale University and had come to talk to actual missionaries—since she was going to be studying the history of Christian missions. Newly out of college, I was impressed that someone studying for the PhD would be interested in run-of-the-mill mission workers. Little did I realize back then that this was a sign of the type of academician that Dana would become.

As we all know, Dana is a ground-breaking, incisive, thoughtful, and prodigious scholar. I marvel not only at the sheer output of her work, but her amazing capacity both to broach fresh topics as well as pithily and aptly summarize the state of a particular field of research. I call her the "dean" of Methodist and Wesleyan missiologists and include her as one of the top five scholars in the fields of missiology and world Christianity of our generation.

Yet, to my mind, what truly sets Dana apart is her ability to hold together three distinct, even competing characteristics. First, she is thoroughly grounded in the matters of everyday life; second, she is passionate in her commitments; and third, she brings her powerful intellect to bear upon the subject she is studying. Scholars usually are known for one, or at most two, of these traits. Dana Robert brings all three together in her scholarship, teaching, and service to the church and academy, with marvelous results. It is these qualities that led her to interview a group of United Methodist missionaries as a student in graduate school. And it is these qualities that have continued to make her a source of deep wisdom and abundant blessing to so many in our world today.

RODNEY PETERSEN

Executive Director, Cooperative Metropolitan Ministries; Executive Director, The Lord's Day Alliance of the U.S.; Visiting Researcher, Center for Global Christianity and Mission, Boston University School of Theology; and former Executive Director, Boston Theological Institute

Faithful Friendships: Embracing Diversity in Christian Community is the title of one of Dana Robert's recent books. It might be seen to mark her life's journey.

My most direct encounter with Dana Robert around the idea of friendship was through the Boston Theological Institute (BTI) from the years 1990–2014. She was the animating spirit behind the certificate offered by the BTI faculty committee in International Mission and Ecumenism (IME). Through this committee, students at the BTI schools were encouraged to take courses in the diverse schools of the consortium. What made such cross-registration work possible were the faculty friendships between Sister Margaret Guider (Weston Jesuit School of Theology) and Dana Robert, between Ian Douglas (Episcopal Divinity School) and Dana Robert, between Todd Johnson (Gordon-Conwell Theological Seminary) and Dana Robert, between Nimi Wariboko (Andover Newton Theological School) and Dana Robert, between Fr. Ray Helmick, SJ (Boston College) and Dana Robert, between Fr. George Papademetriou (Holy Cross Greek Orthodox School of Theology) and Dana Robert, between Fr. John McGinnis (St. John's Seminary) and Dana Robert, between Harvey Cox (Harvard Divinity School) and Dana Robert—and this is only the beginning of the list.

These patterns of relationship validated similar patterns among the students of the BTI schools. They promoted cross-registration, if only out of sheer curiosity about the "other," stimulated research nurtured in cross-institutional settings and opportunities, and added to MBTA revenues as students moved around from one school to another. It was like moving from one country to another. Again, Robert's idea of friendship was an animating force.

When we began the overseas workshops in 1991, we brought twenty-five students to the offices of the World Council of Churches in Switzerland and to other ecumenical sites. Upon our return to Boston, Fr. Helmick, SJ turned to me and said, "Rodney, next year let's visit my friends in Rome." We were promptly invited to a private audience with Pope John Paul II and an opportunity to visit the various dicasteries and operations of the Roman Catholic Church. Upon our return to Boston, Fr. George Papademetriou turned to me and said, "Rodney, next year we have to visit my friends in Constantinople/Istanbul." So began BTI workshops in over twenty-six countries from 1991–2014. Dana Robert was often the animating force behind these rich educational experiences and their on-going eddies in places as diverse as Ireland, Russia, Rwanda, South Africa, Ghana, and Colombia, to name but a few.

Friendship inspires institutional growth and innovation. This was the inspiration which led to the 1910 Edinburgh mission conference which led, in turn, to the founding of the World Council of Churches. Friendship was foundational to the Moral Re-Armament (MRA) movement and efforts toward peace in the twentieth century. Friendship between German Federal Chancellor Konrad Adenauer and French Foreign Minister Robert Schuman led to Franco-German reconciliation and eventually to the European Union. Who knows what the gift of friendship can bring to our world today?

C. S. Lewis describes "four loves" in his book of that title, *storge*, *eros*, *filia*, and *agape*. Each has its own properties and role to play. In stimulating friendship (*filia*), Dana Robert has pointed the way forward: Good friendships make for good people. Good people make for good organizations. Good organizations make for human flourishing.

JOEL CARPENTER

Senior Research Fellow, Nagel Institute, Calvin University

I first met Dana Robert in June of 1986, when she gave a paper for a conference on American evangelicals and foreign missions at Wheaton College. Dana presented on premillennialism as a driver of missionary commitment. That paper became an important chapter in *Earthen Vessels: American Evangelicals and Foreign Missions.* My first impression of her was not just the quality of her work, however. I was struck by her Southern charm, as she arrived in a stylish summer dress and hat. She seemed like an exotic flower on our austere Midwestern campus.

Through the years I have seen that my friend and colleague is indeed a steel magnolia. She is full of warmth and courtesy, with a Southern lyricality to her voice, but before long you will see her grit as well as her grace. She has a remarkable ability to see through surfaces and get to the deeper truth. Most of her writing has been discovery-driven rather than critical, but she has come to fresh conclusions because she can sweep away dust and sort out the gold.

We have served together quite a few times, and I have learned to wait for the one-sentence sidebars that she offers to get to the heart of the matter, which often come with an imperative: "Joel, we need to . . . " I have spent much of my career following up on these things. One of them: a joint mission as longtime members and sometime leaders in the American Society of Church History, to keep up the pressure on the Society to be more oriented toward world Christianity. We have recruited others and persisted, and we have seen some positive changes.

Persistence is a keen measure of friendship. We need to stay true to relationships and callings by following through on what God gives us to be and do. Dana was given much, not least to be a mentor of doctoral students studying the history of missions and world Christianity at Boston University. Over the years, she has mentored more than 60 doctoral students, either as primary advisor or as a reader on dissertations. What an amazing feat, and what a powerful influence on our field of inquiry. A doctoral advisor is a peculiar kind of friend, one with a clear imbalance of power. But it allows one to be what we Midwesterners call a "Dutch uncle" (or Dutch auntie?), speaking the truth bluntly, but in love, and seeing someone grow stronger as a result. Dana has given of herself sacrificially to several dozens of those who are now our colleagues and our friends. What a friend she is to us all.

RUTH PADILLA DEBORST

Resonate Global Mission, Christian Reformed Church of North America, and the International Fellowship for Mission as Transformation (INFEMIT)

"Hurry up and be done! That way we can simply be friends, without these curricular requirements between us!" I cannot recount how often those words slipped from Dana's mouth during the years between 2008, when I finished my course work, and 2016, when I finally completed my PhD. Not that academic formalities *actually* interfered in what would become one of my most treasured friendships! While I lived in Cambridge, the Au Bon Pain in Davis Square witnessed many a deep, honest, and life-giving conversation between us, ranging from marital matters to parenting and balancing professional and family life, from being women in leadership to life in distant lands, from the burdens of others' pain to personal challenges. And drives down to Maryknoll for the ASM Eastern Fellowship meetings became annual highlights, not less because of Dana's obligatory bagel stops along the way! Once I had moved back to Central America and my studies required that I return to the Boston area, Dana warmly welcomed me into her home for several overnight stays, and our heart-to-heart conversations continued at her unpretentious kitchen table. Indelibly impressed in my heart is her willingness to enter my Latin American ministry context and to honor the Latin American Theological Fellowship by speaking at CLADE V, our 2012 congress in Costa Rica, where she proposed friendship was at the heart of mission. In time, the annual meeting of the American Society of Missiology became an anticipated opportunity to catch up, laugh, lament, and encourage one another over a shared meal. For all these gifts, I am profoundly grateful.

Of course, the familiarity of friendship never dulled my deep respect and admiration for Dr. Robert as a scholar and professor. Her rigorously disciplined research and writing practices and her strong work ethic are woven together with an unswerving commitment to her students and deep pastoral concern for the laity of her church into a beautiful tapestry of the consummate scholar-practitioner. As if this balancing act were not in itself exemplary enough, the addition of navigating historically male-dominated spaces as a woman and coupling the academy with mission involvement in Zimbabwe along with her beloved Martinus Daneel and raising two children, makes Dana's multi-tasking capacity and prolific academic production all the more admirable. I undoubtedly join many dozens of Boston University PhDs who owe Dr. Dana Robert not only wise mentorship in their scholarly trajectory but also the joy of fruitful friendship. For all that, thanks to Dana and to the God she so generously reflects!

GINA A. ZURLO

Co-Director, Center for the Study of Global Christianity,
Gordon-Conwell Theological Seminary

As my PhD advisor from 2012 to 2017, Dana Robert drew sad faces on my papers when my writing was sloppy. One time, she told me chapter 2 of my dissertation was only worthy for the bottom of her birdcage. Tough love, as they say, is needed during a PhD program, and Dana certainly delivered. And yet, that same tough love challenged me to think beyond what I thought I knew and to see history from other perspectives. Though I often entered her office with fear and trembling, working with Dana gave me confidence in knowing that whatever happened, I was becoming a better scholar. Like a good friend, I could always count on Dana's unsparing honesty.

Dana's love was balanced with gentle nurturing. Showing sincere care and concern for my personal life, she saw me as a human being. During the five years of my program I divorced my first husband, was a single mother to a special needs toddler, got remarried, and had a baby. Through it all, Dana was more than my academic advisor—she was a consistent friend. We bonded over shared life experiences. She regularly asked how my daughter was doing. She came to my wedding! She was a source of emotional support that I desperately needed.

Dana's holistic view of friendship and scholarship continues to be a model as I build relationships with my own students. I try to replicate her balance of tough love and gentle nurturing. Her personal example of holism was much like the women we studied in mission history—no separation between spiritual and physical needs, a commitment to care and concern for all who needed it. She contextualized her interactions with students according to their circumstances, needs, and spiritual inclinations because she saw people for who they were and for who they were capable of becoming. I'm grateful for Dana's mentoring and the honor of calling her my friend.

SUNG-DEUK OAK

Dongsoon Im and Mija Im Endowed Chair Associate Professor of Korean Christianity, UCLA

Memory starts with meetings. I met Prof. Dana Robert as one of her earlier Korean doctoral students in September 1994. When I searched for the doctoral program for the history of Korean Christianity, Dr. Samuel H. Moffett of Princeton recommended me to study under Prof. Robert. I was accepted with full scholarship and moved to Boston with my wife and three little children. Dr. Robert introduced me to a new idea of "world Christianity." As I had written two books on the history of Bible translation in Korea before coming to America, I could readily agree to the newly rising study of world Christianity, in which Prof. Robert was a rising and leading scholar. Her explicit and vibrant lectures and discussion sessions inspired me with missional imagination.

Memory goes on with mind and heart. Dr. Carter Lindberg was my first advisor and then Dr. Dana Robert after the course work. She carefully guided my dissertation on the history of Protestant missionaries' attitudes toward traditional Korean religions and the indigenization of Christianity in Korea from 1876 to 1910. A Pew Charitable dissertation scholarship enabled me to visit archives in New Haven; New York; Philadelphia; Madison, New Jersey; and Seoul. She read my dissertation draft line by line for two years. Every page was marked with her kind notes and sharp questions, which stimulated my reflection and continuous revisions. After September 11, I could leave BU with her blessing for my postdoctoral job at UCLA in 2002.

Memory travels with me. When my position was promoted from visiting assistant to adjunct assistant and from assistant to associate professor and Im Endowed Chair at UCLA in 2011, my mentor's moral unwavering support went with each step. She has always been one of the most delighted persons at my achievements. My dissertation was actually selected to be published by the American Society of Missiology in 2002, but I lost the opportunity. When my monograph, *The Making of Korean Christianity*, was published in 2013 as the first book of the series of the Studies in World Christianity of the Nagel Institute of Calvin College and Baylor University Press with her endorsement, the editor of the *Books and Culture* selected it as the book of the year in 2013. Finally, I could express my deep and official gratitude to my teacher Dana.

Good memory matters. We met as a teacher and a student when we were in our thirties. More than a quarter of a century has passed. My "old" good teacher remains in my heart always "young" in her early forties. Blessed are those who have a memory of a good and caring teacher-friend. They will have a lamp for their journey in their narrow and story-filled path of worshipping God.

SEPTEMMY LAKAWA

President of Sekolah Tinggi Filsafat Theologi Jakarta (Jakarta Theological Seminary)

As I was thinking of what to write that would adequately express my eternal gratitude and thanksgiving for being Prof. Dana L. Robert's student, I remembered a paragraph in the acknowledgments section of my dissertation, "Risky Hospitality: Mission in the Aftermath of Religious Communal Violence." This is what I wrote about her there:

> I find in her the highest excellence that a doctoral student could expect from her advisor . . . . The high expectations she has for my studies combined with her calm and reassuring presence, especially at many difficult stages of my journey, provides me with a challenging working environment without losing any of the joy and fascination I have for studying mission. The time we prayed together in her office is one of the profound moments of my journey. She played a crucial role in shaping my deep

interest in linking historical study, missiology, and anthropology. The wide access to mission networks, conferences, and seminars, both national and international, and the unending support she provided throughout my academic journey, shaped the formation of my understanding of what being in mission entails for a woman, a minister, and a scholar. I hope this dissertation reflects the enormous gratitude and joy that I have for the opportunity to be her student. She is a great role model.

Almost ten years later, this paragraph remains true to what I feel and understand about Prof. Robert. I celebrate her life as an inspiring and visionary woman who is transparent in her multiple roles and responsibilities. She is a great inspiration to her family. I am honored to call her my "guru"—she is one of the best scholars and leading mission historians and theologians in the world. Her work and ministry have shaped the future of mission studies across the globe, especially regarding women in mission. She has continued to support my work after I completed my studies at Boston University School of Theology, which shows her commitment to the flourishing of women scholars across boundaries. In her, I have found the meaning of "unlikely friend."

CASELY B. ESSAMUAH

Secretary, Global Christian Forum

One of my favorite Bible verses is a phrase from First Corinthians 15:10 that states as follows: *By the grace of God I am what I am.* I consider all of my life as flowing from God's grace. And there are several people whom the Good Lord has used to demonstrate his grace towards me. One of them is Prof. Dana L. Robert. I studied at Boston University School of Theology, 1998–2003, and Prof. Robert's mentorship and friendship has determined the course of my career ever since.

First of all, the academic rigor with which the research and writing process of my ThD thesis was subjected to made it into probably my most significant academic achievement. In my travels, when I see it on the bookshelves of Methodist church leaders all over the world, I give thanks to God for Dana. *Genuinely Ghanaian: A History of the Methodist Church Ghana, 1961–2000* is a story that is in many ways part of my own story too. It has been widely and positively received and is a recommended text not only in seminaries in Ghana, but for all who answer the call to become vocational Methodist ministers, in Ghana and among the Ghanaian diaspora.

Secondly, it was Prof. Dana Robert who invited me to a conference in Pretoria, South Africa in 1997. I was serving as an intern at Park Street Church, Boston (PSC) at the time, and a friend recommended that I inform the missions leadership of PSC of the trip and request funds to travel after the Pretoria conference and visit two of the church's missionaries, David and Deborah Bliss, serving in Cape Town, South Africa. Upon my return, I gave a report to PSC leadership. The warm and positive reception given to my report, both from leadership and the congregation, resulted eventually in my being asked to serve as Minister of Missions at PSC, which I gladly did from 1998–2005.

Thirdly, it was Prof. Robert who introduced me to the leadership of the Overseas Ministries Study Center in New Haven, and eventually I served on that board and became friends with many in the world of academic missiology and leaders of mission agencies. One such friend and mentor has been Prof. Tite Tienou, who was Dean at Trinity Evangelical Divinity School, and for whom, with one of his Kenyan former students, Dr. David Ngaruiya, I co-edited a festschrift, *Communities of Faith in Africa and the African Diaspora: Essays in Honor of Dr. Tite Tienou with additional essays on World Christianity*.

Lastly, but probably the most significantly, it was Prof. Dana Robert that I first consulted when a friend approached me to consider making myself available for the role of Secretary, Global Christian Forum. She patiently answered my questions, calmed my fears, and wrote a generous reference that ensured that the Search Committee, none of whom knew me but most of whom knew her from her plenary address at the Second Global Christian Forum Global Gathering in Manado, Indonesia, 2011, considered my application seriously.

And so, I am very grateful to Prof. Dana Robert for these significant introductions and guidance. I consider her husband, Prof. Inus Daneel, also as a mentor and was pleased to visit with him in Zimbabwe during better days. Yes, indeed, my life has been undergirded and enveloped by the grace of God, and Dana Robert has been used as a means of that grace.

BIBLIOGRAPHY

Carpenter, Joel A., and Wilbert R. Shenk, eds. *Earthen Vessels: American Evangelicals and Foreign Missions*. Eugene, OR: Wipf & Stock, 2012.

Essamuah, Casely B. *Genuinely Ghanaian: A History of the Methodist Church Ghana, 1961–2000*. Trenton, NJ: Africa World, 2010.

Essamuah, Casely B., and David K. Ngaruiya. *Communities of Faith in Africa and the African Diaspora: Essays in Honor of Dr. Tite Tienou with Additional Essays on World Christianity*. Eugene, OR: Pickwick, 2013.

Hempton, David. *The Church in the Long Eighteenth Century: The IB Tauris History of the Christian Church*. London: IB Tauris, 2007.

Lakawa, Septemmy. "Risky Hospitality: Mission in the Aftermath of Religious Communal Violence." PhD diss., Boston University, 2011.

Lewis, C. S. *The Four Loves*. New York: Harcourt, Brace, Jovanovich, 1960.

Oak, Sung-Deuk. *The Making of Korean Christianity: Protestant Encounters with Korean Religions, 1876–1915*. Waco, TX: Baylor University Press, 2013.

Robert, Dana L. *Faithful Friendships: Embracing Diversity in Christian Community*. Grand Rapids, MI: Eerdmans, 2019.

———. "Naming 'World Christianity': Historical and Personal Perspectives on the Yale-Edinburgh Conference in World Christianity and Mission History." *International Bulletin of Mission Research* 44.2 (2020) 111–28.

Sunquist, Scott W. *The Unexpected Christian Century: The Reversal and Transformation of Global Christianity, 1900–2000*. Grand Rapids, MI: Baker Academic, 2015.

"Evangelizing the Inevitable"

The Work of Dana L. Robert

DARYL R. IRELAND

"Evangelize the inevitable," Dana Robert told me when I explained that I did not believe in the value of digital projects. It was not the last time she brushed aside my reluctance or recalcitrance by quoting E. Stanley Jones's line from *The Christ of the Indian Road*. His words surfaced regularly in our conversations until I could anticipate them: don't watch the world change or, worse, stand on the sidelines and complain about the shifts; step into the action and dare to shape the world in Christ's name. Since Dana Robert has spoken those words to me so often, it is with a certain relish that I now turn them on her. However, I cannot use "evangelize the inevitable" to prescribe what she must do. I can only write them descriptively to explain what she has done. For almost forty years, Dana L. Robert has anticipated major trends and movements in the academy, so that when the rest of us arrive, we find that she has already been there.

Dr. Dana L. Robert
Source: Dave Green for Boston University Photography.

WORLD CHRISTIANITY

Because Dana Robert is often the first to arrive, it is impossible to accuse her of following academic fashions. Unlike E. Stanley Jones, who bumped into nationalism everywhere in India in the 1920s, Robert has often moved alone or as part of a small group. Her decades of work in what is now called World Christianity, for example, had no recognizable nomenclature in the late 1970s when she began graduate studies at Yale University. Robert could only express her interest in "Comparative Christianity," a term she invented to describe her attempts to understand Christianity as it took shape in different times and places.

Her curiosity about differences emerged in the Mississippi Delta. Born on October 9, 1956, Robert grew up in pre-Vatican II Louisiana. She observed, with a tinge of envy, that the Roman Catholic children were dismissed from school on Ash Wednesday and would return to class with smudges on their foreheads. Southern Baptists, meanwhile, were exempt from particular classes on hygiene and biology. Being Methodist, however, she "never got excused from school for any religious reasons whatsoever."[1] Religious identities mattered, Robert recognized, and they had real consequences. That is why she ultimately gave up the impulse to study literature at Louisiana State University. "The problems of the real world are so important, why would I want to spend my life on fake problems, which is to say, fiction?"[2] Instead, she majored in history and found ways to incorporate religion into everything she wrote, whether it was the French Huguenots, Russian Orthodoxy, or Daniel Berrigan and the American Catholic Left. What really sparked her imagination, though, was evangelicalism. It was a fascinating amalgamation of faith and action, religion and politics, Americans at home and abroad. After a short stint as a high school teacher, Robert departed for Yale to study the potent mix.

Sydney Ahlstrom, her PhD advisor, found Robert's interests boring. "Evangelicals have had no new ideas in that last two hundred years," he bluntly told her. He did not stand in her way, though, when she proposed studying A. T. Pierson and the matrix of the American missionary movement. Other forces at Yale were less kind. Her interests in mission had no clear home. The Department of Religious Studies had reorganized and dropped mission studies shortly before her arrival. Missions did not fit in the anti-colonial paradigm. Similarly, confidence in the secularization theory meant her proposal to take a fourth comprehensive exam in African

1. Robert, "Reflections on Historians," 88.
2. Robert and Hutchinson, "Interview."

Christianity had to be done entirely on her own. No one wanted to waste time on something assumed to be on the verge of extinction. Nonetheless, Robert carried on, and when Sydney Ahlstrom died of amyotrophic lateral sclerosis (ALS), she petitioned to move her work under the Divinity School's professor of mission, Charles Forman. She was the first PhD student at Yale in forty years—since the days of Kenneth Scott Latourette—to graduate under the direction of a mission professor.

No clear job market existed for someone like Robert, so she applied for a position in evangelism at the Boston University School of Theology. Except for being a United Methodist, she was not particularly qualified for the post. The Dean offered her an alternative. He had $10,000 a year from the sale of a Methodist church building, and he proposed using it for a non-tenure track position that would restart the school's curriculum in ecumenism and mission. Robert agreed, and when she began in 1984, she put forward her first course: The Emergence of Christianity in Asia, Africa, and Latin America.

It was an ambitious undertaking, especially since secondary literature was so rare. Piece by piece, Robert had to assemble a history of Christianity in the non-Western world for her students. She distilled the fruit of her labors in 1991 as an epilogue to a textbook, *Christianity: A Social and Cultural History*. The first of its kind, her epilogue—which, for the book's second edition, she expanded into an entire section of the volume—began to work out a postcolonial global narrative of Christianity.

Another early and ambitious undertaking was a study of American women in mission. In the late 1980s, Wilbert Shenk organized a project through the American Society of Missiology to create a series of books that would honor the bicentennial of William Carey's *Enquiry*, written in 1792. He asked Robert to write a volume on church-state relations, to which she agreed. In prayer, though, she realized that women in mission were being overlooked by missiologists again. "Unless *you* do women," she understood in prayer, "no one will." Boldly, Robert asked to change her topic and started working in women's history, which was new to her. The work would take ten years to complete. William Hutchison at Harvard Divinity School, Robert's third reader for her dissertation, told her that women had no mission theories; they just did things. She therefore bypassed writing a conventional intellectual history of mission, relying instead on the tools of social history to tease out the creative and remarkable role that both Protestant and Catholic women played in American missions.

Robert's attention to Christianity beyond the confines of Christendom and her inspired decision to write a history of American women in mission made her a valuable addition to the small team of people Gerald Anderson assembled in 1989 at the Overseas Ministries Study Center in New Haven, Connecticut. Joel Carpenter at the Pew Charitable Trusts had asked Anderson to lead SISMIC, the Scholars Initiative for Studies in Mission and International Christianity. Pew was looking for ways to build the infrastructure that could support new work in the academy about Christianity around the world. Contrary to popular expectation, Christianity had not shriveled or died when colonial structures no longer propped it up. Rather, freed from its colonial confines, Christianity was expanding rapidly in Africa and Asia, while Pentecostalism was reconfiguring religious adherence in Latin America. Over the next decade, Robert participated in the Research Enablement Program (REP), which channeled Pew money into more than one hundred different scholarly projects on all matters pertaining to Christianity around the globe, including the 1992 Yale-Edinburgh meeting that first introduced the term which summarized so much of her own scholarship, "From Christendom to World Christianity."[3]

As one of the few people who worked in World Christianity before it even had a name, Robert played a central role in the field's development. She was instrumental, for example, in making academic positions in the field of World Christianity a possibility. Personally, she has overseen more than seventy dissertations on the topic. Single-handedly, she gave Boston University its distinction as the research university that generates the most dissertations in Mission Studies and World Christianity in North America.[4] But Robert has done more than produce many of the scholars in the field, she has also written multiple tenure reviews for those who have taken the first posts. Robert has made World Christianity institutionally viable and credible. Meanwhile, her publications continue to demarcate the field of study. Her twelve single-authored or edited books and more than one hundred articles repeatedly cross boundaries and invite readers to see connections. Robert writes comfortably about Zimbabwe, Manchuria, Ireland, and Brazil. She looks at Catholics, Zionists, Methodists, and Pentecostals. The range of her publications is staggering, but its true quality is seen in its accessibility. Robert never hides ideas behind jargon or convoluted argumentation. Her thinking and her prose are clear, and readers have rewarded her determination to communicate well. Her book *Christian Mission: How Christianity Became a World Religion* is already in its twelfth printing.

In 2021, Christianity as a worldwide religion is not a unique concept anymore. Books have popularized the idea, conferences are replete with papers about Christianity in all parts of the globe, and professorships in

3. Robert, "Naming 'World Christianity,'" 119–21.
4. Priest and DeGeorge, "Doctoral Dissertations on Mission," 195–202.

World Christianity are multiplying. It only appears obvious, however, because Robert and a small cohort of other pioneers worked together to open the academy's eyes. We see Christianity around the world, and see it with depth and insight, because Dana Robert directed our attention to where and how we should look. She evangelized the inevitable or, more accurately, she made the idea of the academic study of World Christianity inescapable.

DIGITAL FRONTIERS

Evangelizing the inevitable does not mean you are an expert in it. E. Stanley Jones recognized Indian nationalism as a tide that could not be turned back, not because he was a historian of nationalistic movements or a seasoned veteran in social or political activism, but because he was alert to the forces that were remaking society around him. In the same way, Dana Robert was a pioneer in digital scholarship, not because she was an expert in technology or trained in computer science. She was simply aware, often before those around her, that the world was going digital.

In 2001, she and her husband, Professor M. L. Daneel, created the Center for Global Christianity and Mission at Boston University. At its inception, the CGCM was a virtual reality. Andrew Walls had counseled Robert to avoid heavy infrastructure. He warned that trying to fund a center can easily eclipse the work of a center. Therefore, the CGCM began with neither physical space nor any employees. The Center was a website maintained by research assistants. Even so, the CGCM managed to organize visits and lectures on mission and World Christianity. It found money to support international students who came to Boston University to study for a PhD in mission or World Christianity. And the virtual CGCM also sponsored theological education by extension for over one thousand Christian leaders in rural Zimbabwe.

Arguably, though, Dana Robert's real creativity was in the construction of the *History of Missiology* website (bu.edu/missiology). In 2007, the site was the very first Digital Humanities project launched at Boston University. It did two things simply and elegantly. First, it created hundreds of biographies on missionaries from all parts of the world. Second, it digitized and curated shelves and shelves of books on mission theology, theory, and practice, as well as some of the first ethnographic studies of people in primal societies and materials that recorded the encounters between western missionaries and people from Asia, Africa, and the Americas. Although the School of Theology library embraced the project, it met stiff resistance from other quarters. No one believed that people would read anything online;

they feared the costs of printing would explode as students would turn digital copies into paper. Nonetheless, Robert and the team in the library persisted, aware that they were indebted to the peoples and nations in the global south for much of the literature they were scanning. Digitizing the sources and providing global access through the Internet was, they hoped, a way to return Boston University's resources to those from whom they first came.

If wisdom is known by her children, then the History of Missiology project has been an extraordinary success. It set trends; others followed in its wake. The Hathi Trust Digital Library, for example, was founded in 2008, a year after Dana Robert made public an enormous digital library from Boston University. Also in 2008, the National Endowment for the Humanities institutionalized the term "Digital Humanities" to describe projects like the one Robert spearheaded. Of course, since its launch, digital book readers and software have multiplied, making it easy for people to read texts online. Today, the site is used in numerous courses across the globe and provides valuable resources to approximately 150,000 users every year.

Other pathbreaking digital projects followed. They included the *Dictionary of African Christian Biography* (DACB; dacb.org), which Robert negotiated to bring to Boston University when its director, Jonathan Bonk, retired. The DACB was a digital initiative Robert had first cultivated in the mid-1990s when she had been involved in the Pew Trust's Research Enablement Program. She also supported *In the Midst* (sites.bu.edu/midst), a multimedia autobiography of Barbara Beach Alter, a missionary who served in Northern India from 1945 to 1980. Robert launched *Old & New in Shona Religion* (sites.bu.edu/shonareligion) to curate the photographs, films, books, and stories of her husband's work among the African Initiated Churches and African Traditional Religious leaders of Zimbabwe. And it was Robert who inspired the application to the Henry Luce Foundation to work with twenty institutions worldwide to digitize, transcribe, translate, tag, and exhibit mid-twentieth-century Chinese Christian propaganda posters online (ccposters.com). These and other projects gave the Center for Global Christianity and Mission a digital signature. The CGCM runs more Digital Humanities projects than any other humanities or social science entity at Boston University, and because every program run by the CGCM has an online component, the Center's research receives more than one million views every year.

COLLABORATION AND FRIENDSHIP

Dana Robert recently published a book on friendship, the hidden dimension of mission. In the short span since its publication, other articles and books have come out on this topic. The sudden emphasis can make it look like friendship is a cottage industry. But let it not be forgotten that Robert was early to the study of close personal relationships. She had been writing about them for years before her book came out, and it was never far from any of her research or publications, probably because Robert was acutely aware of how she herself was embedded in and indebted to personal friendships.

From her earliest years, Robert worked collaboratively. Her study of American Catholic women in mission, for example, was only possible because of the long hours she spent with Maryknoll Sisters and the friendships that inevitably coalesced out of their time together. Her work with SISMIC and REP were team efforts. They prioritized annual workshops and building a movement around World Christianity by linking people from diverse disciplinary backgrounds and interests together. When she proposed the book *Gospel Bearers, Gender Barriers* to the women of the American Society of Missiology (published in 2002), she constructed the volume as a work not only of peers but also of friends.

As in her scholarship, so in her institution: Robert values and nurtures relationships and friendships. Whether it is a plea for her faculty colleagues not to give up meeting together regularly and informally, or her invitation for Visiting Researchers in the Center for Global Christianity and Mission to work in teams, Robert regularly champions friendship and collaboration. Boston University has noticed the power a research center like the CGCM has to form interdisciplinary networks. In 2018, the university's ten-year Strategic Plan included the suggestion that centers and interdisciplinary programs become core components of the university.[5] As Robert had demonstrated, centers are places within a university where institutional silos can dissolve and collaborative friendships form to cut across fields and disciplines.

In 2019, Dana Robert was asked by the Association for Theological Schools (ATS) to participate in a process of envisioning the future of theological education. Not surprisingly, she helped create a group intended to fund and support collaborative work, not just the efforts of individual scholars. She recognizes that she is moving against the stream. Collaboration is complicated: it can get expensive, requires humility, and takes time. Nonetheless, when cooperation among scholars becomes more common

5. Brown, "Envisioning Our Future."

across theological schools, maybe even making it appear "inevitable," let us remember that Robert helped make it possible. As in so much else, Dana Robert saw its power long before the rest of us.

CONCLUSION

The accomplishments of Dana L. Robert in the academy extend far beyond this brief summary, and they are widely recognized by her peers. The American Society of Missiology (ASM), for instance, bestowed its Lifetime Achievement Award on her in 2017, when she was just sixty. It came with the assurance that the ASM did not think Robert's contributions were over, but that she deserved the award—albeit somewhat prematurely in her career—for everything she had already done for mission studies. In 2018, Robert was inducted into the American Academy of Arts and Sciences, linking her to a small group of "leaders from every field of human endeavor to examine new ideas, address issues of importance to the nation and the world, and work together 'to cultivate every art and science which may tend to advance the interest, honor, dignity, and happiness of a free, independent, and virtuous people.'"[6] Robert is rightly honored in the academy for her meticulous and purposeful work, but maybe her greatest gift is her foresight. Time and again, Dana Robert has been among the first to "evangelize the inevitable." This book celebrates her perspicuity. By putting together a volume on the real but subtle intersections between mission and friendship, we—her students and friends—hope to demonstrate that Dana L. Robert's work is extraordinary because it is so generative.

BIBLIOGRAPHY

American Academy of Arts & Sciences. "About the Academy." Online. https://www.amacad.org/about-academy.
Brown, Robert. "Envisioning Our Future: Boston University in 2030." *Boston University*, April 25, 2018. Online. http://www.bu.edu/president/envisioning-our-future-boston-university-in-2030.
Jones, E. Stanley. *The Christ of the Indian Road*. New York: Abingdon, 1925.
Kee, Howard Clark, et al. *Christianity: A Social and Cultural History*. New York: Macmillan, 1991.
Priest, Robert, and Robert DeGeorge. "Doctoral Dissertations on Mission: Ten-Year Update, 2002–2011 (Revised)." *International Bulletin of Missionary Research* 37.4 (2013) 195–202.

6. American Academy of Arts & Sciences, "About the Academy."

Robert, Dana L. *Christian Mission: How Christianity Became a World Religion*. Malden, MA: Wiley-Blackwell, 2009.

———. "Naming 'World Christianity': Historical and Personal Perspectives on the Yale-Edinburgh Conference in World Christianity and Mission History." *International Bulletin of Mission Research* 44.2 (2019) 111–28.

———. "Reflections on Historians, Historiography, and the Confessional Divide." *Fides et Historia* 44.2 (2012) 87–91.

———, ed. *Gospel Bearers, Gender Barriers: Missionary Women in the Twentieth Century*. American Society of Missiology Series. Maryknoll, NY: Orbis, 2002.

Robert, Dana L., and Mark Hutchinson. "Interview with Dana L. Robert." Episode 5 of *Interviews on the Vocation of History*, May 28, 2020. Audio recording, 1:40:32. Online. https://soundcloud.com/mhutch58/sets/ivh-interviews-on-the-vocation-of-historians/s-d2eVv7ES8Zy.

The Writings of Dana L. Robert

BOOKS

Robert, Dana L. *Arthur Tappan Pierson and Forward Movements of Late Ninteenth-Century Evangelicalism.* Translated by Dal Jin Park. Seoul: Yang Seo Gak, 1988.

———. *American Women in Mission: A Social History of Their Thought and Practice.* Macon, GA: Mercer University Press, 1997.

———. *"Occupy Until I Come": A. T. Pierson and the Evangelization of the World.* Library of Religious Biography. Grand Rapids, MI: Eerdmans, 2003. [Korean: Translated by Yoonjong Yoo. Seoul: B & A, 2004.]

———. *Christian Mission: How Christianity Became a World Religion.* Malden, MA: Wiley-Blackwell, 2009.

———. *Joy to the World!: Mission in the Age of Global Christianity.* New York: Women's Division, General Board of Global Mission, United Methodist Church, 2010.

———. *Faithful Friendships: Embracing Diversity in Christian Community.* Grand Rapids, MI: Eerdmans, 2019.

EDITED, CO-EDITED, AND CO-AUTHORED WORKS

Robert, Dana L., Howard Clark Kee, Emily Albu, Carter Lindberg, and Jerry W. Frost. *Christianity: A Social and Cultural History.* 2nd ed. Upper Saddle River, NJ: Prentice Hall, 1998.

Robert, Dana L., ed. *Gospel Bearers, Gender Barriers: Missionary Women in the Twentieth Century.* Maryknoll, NY: Orbis, 2002.

Robert, Dana L., Gregor Cuthbertson, and H. L. Pretorius, eds. *Frontiers of African Christianity: Essays in Honour of Inus Daneel.* Pretoria: University of South Africa Press, 2003.

Robert, Dana L., ed. *Mission Churches.* Vol. 2 of *African Christian Outreach.* Pretoria: South African Missiological Society, 2003.

———. *Converting Colonialism: Visions and Realities in Mission History, 1706–1914.* Studies in the History of Christian Missions. Grand Rapids, MI: Eerdmans, 2008.

Robert, Dana L., Dwight P. Baker, and Wilbert R. Shenk eds. *Engaging Mission: Hospitality, Humility, Hope. Essays in Honor of Jonathan J. Bonk.* Special issue of *International Bulletin of Missionary Research* 39.4 (2015).

Robert, Dana L., ed. *African Christian Biography: Stories, Lives, and Challenges*. Editor. Pietermaritzburg, South Africa: Cluster, 2018.

OTHER MAJOR COLLABORATIVE WORKS

Anderson, Gerald H., ed. *Biographical Dictionary of Christian Mission*. New York: Simon & Schuster Macmillan, 1998. [Member of editorial advisory board.]

Thomas, Norman, ed. *International Mission Bibliography*. ATLA Bibliographies 48. Lanham, MD: Scarecrow, 2003. [Subeditor for section on mission history.]

ENTRIES IN DICTIONARIES AND ENCYCLOPEDIAS

Robert, Dana L. "Gordon, A. J." In *Dictionary of Christianity in America*, edited by Daniel G. Reid. Downers Grove, IL: InterVarsity, 1990. [Reprinted in *Dictionary of Baptists of America*, edited by Bill J. Leonard. Downers Grove, IL: InterVarsity, 1994.]

———. "Mount Hermon One Hundred"; "Pierson, A. T." In *Dictionary of Christianity in America*, edited by Daniel G. Reid. Downers Grove, IL: InterVarsity, 1990.

———. "Missions, Promotion of." In *New Twentieth-Century Encyclopedia of Religious Knowledge*, edited by J. D. Douglas. 2nd ed. Grand Rapids, MI: Baker, 1991.

———. "Anderson, Rufus"; "Judson, Ann"; "Lyon, Mary." In *The Blackwell Dictionary of Evangelical Biography, 1730–1860*, edited by Donald Lewis. Oxford: Blackwell, 1995.

———. "Gamewell, Mary"; "Missions"; "McKendree, John"; "Springer, Helen Emily (Chapman) Rasmussen"; "Swain, Clara"; "Thoburn, Isabella." In *Historical Dictionary of Methodism*, edited by Charles Yrigoyen Jr. and Susan Warrick. Lanham, MD: Scarecrow, 1996.

———. "Agnew, Eliza"; "Bennett, Belle Harris"; "Blackstone, William Eugene"; "Bridgman, Eliza"; "Butler, William and Clementina"; "Coppin, Fanny Jackson"; "Dodge, Grace"; "Doremus, Sarah"; "Edwards, Mary"; "Fernbaugh, Hettie"; "Honsinger Fisher, Welthy"; "Fiske, Fidelia"; "Frame, Alice Browne"; "Grant, Asahel"; "Grant, Judith Campbell"; "Judson, Ann Hasseltine"; "Lambuth, Walter Russell"; "Loveless, Sarah Farquhar"; "Pierson, Arthur Tappan"; "Reed, Mary"; "Rowe, Phoebe"; "Simpson, Albert Benjamin"; "Springer, Helen Rasmussen"; "Springer, John McKendree"; "Stewart, John"; "Vinton, Justus and Calista"; "Wade, Jonathan and Deborah"; "Woolston, Beulah and Sarah." In *Biographical Dictionary of Christian Mission*, edited by Gerald H. Anderson. New York: Simon & Schuster Macmillan, 1998.

———. "Premillennialism." In *Evangelical Dictionary of World Missions*, edited by A. Scott Moreau. Grand Rapids, MI: Baker, 2000.

———. "Missions, Foreign." In *Dictionary of American History*, edited by Stanley I. Kutler. 3rd ed. New York: Scribner's Sons, 2003.

———. "Missions." In vol. 3 of *Encyclopedia of Protestantism*, edited by Hans J. Hillerbrand. New York: Routledge, 2004.

———. "Foreign Missions and Revivals." In vol. 1 of *Encyclopedia of Religious Revivals in America*, edited by Michael J. McClymond. Westport, CT: Greenwood, 2007.

―――. "Gender Issues." In *Dictionary of Mission Theology: Evangelical Foundations*, edited by John Corrie. Downers Grove, IL: InterVarsity, 2007.

ARTICLES AND CHAPTERS, 1984–PRESENT

1984–1990

Robert, Dana L. "The Legacy of A. T. Pierson." *International Bulletin of Missionary Research* 8.3 (1984) 120–24.

Robert, Dana L., and Janice McLaughlin. "Report on Mission and Human Rights." *Mission Studies* 2.1 (1985) 70–72.

Robert, Dana L. "African Epiphany." *Anna Howard Shaw Newsletter* [Spring] (1985) 3.

Robert, Dana L., and Norman Thomas, eds. "Annotated Bibliography on Mission History." *Missiology* 14.2 (1986) 235–37.

Robert, Dana L. "The Origin of the Student Volunteer Watchword." *International Bulletin of Missionary Research* 10.4 (1986) 146–49. [Korean: *Pierson Seminary Bulletin* (1986).]

―――. "Grandmothers and the Millennium of Russian Christianity." *The Christian Century* 103 (1986) 1175–76. [Reprinted in *Focus* [Winter/Spring] (1988–1989) 8–9.]

―――. "The Legacy of Adoniram Judson Gordon." *International Bulletin of Missionary Research* 11.4 (1987) 176–81. [Reprinted in *Bringing Christ to All the World*, edited by J. Christy Wilson, 123–37. South Hamilton, MA: Gordon-Conwell Theological School, 1988; Korean: *Ministry and Theology* [April] (1991).]

―――. "Methodist Episcopal Church, South, Missions to Russians in Manchuria, 1920–1927." *Methodist History* 26 (1988) 67–83. [Reprinted in *Methodism in Russia and the Baltic States: History and Renewal*, edited by S. T. Kimbrough Jr., 70–83. Nashville, TN: Abingdon, 1995.]

―――. "Mission Study at the University-Related Theological Seminary: The Boston University School of Theology as a Case Study." *Missiology* 17.2 (1989) 193–202.

―――. "'The Crisis of Missions': Premillennial Mission Theory and the Origins of Independent Evangelical Missions." In *Earthen Vessels: American Evangelicals and Foreign Missions, 1880–1980*, edited by Joel Carpenter and Wilbert Shenk, 29–46. Grand Rapids, MI: Eerdmans, 1990.

1991–2000

Robert, Dana L. "Epilogue: Christianity in Asia, Africa, and Latin America." In *Christianity: A Social and Cultural History*, edited by Howard C. Kee et al., 757–64. New York: Macmillan, 1991.

―――. "A. J. Gordon and World Evangelization: Then and Now." In *The Vision Continues: Essays Marking the Centennial of Gordon-Conwell Theological Seminary*, edited by Garth Rosell, 3–18. South Hamilton, MA: Gordon-Conwell, 1992.

―――. "Evangelist or Homemaker?: The Mission Strategies of Early Nineteenth-Century Missionary Wives in Burma and Hawaii." *International Bulletin of Missionary Research* 17.1 (1993) 4–12. [Reprinted in *North American Foreign*

Missions, 1810–1914: Theology, Theory, and Policy, edited by Wilbert R. Shenk, 116–32. Grand Rapids, MI: Eerdmans, 2004.]

———. "Mount Holyoke Women and the Dutch Reformed Missionary Movement, 1874–1904." *Missionalia* 21 (1993) 103–23.

———. "Revisioning the Women's Missionary Movement." In *The Good News of the Kingdom: Mission Theology for the Third Millennium*, edited by Charles van Engen et al., 109–18. Maryknoll, NY: Orbis, 1993.

———. "The Legacy of A. J. Gordon." In *Mission Legacies: Biographical Studies of Leaders of the Modern Missionary Movement*, edited by Gerald Anderson, 18–27. Maryknoll, NY: Orbis, 1994.

———. "The Legacy of A. T. Pierson." In *Mission Legacies: Biographical Studies of Leaders of the Modern Missionary Movement*, edited by Gerald Anderson, 28–36. Maryknoll, NY: Orbis, 1994.

———. "From Mission to Missions to Beyond Missions: The Historiography of American Protestant Missions Since World War II." *International Bulletin of Missionary Research* 18.4 (1994) 146–62. [Reprinted in *New Directions in American Religious History*, edited by Harry Stout and Darryl Hart, 362–93. New York: Oxford University Press, 1997.]

———. "Mission." In *A Companion to American Thought*, edited by Richard Fox and James Kloppenberg, 458–60. Cambridge, MA: Blackwell, 1995.

———. "American Women and the Dutch Reformed Missionary Movement, 1874–1904." In *Mission in Bold Humility: David Bosch's Work Considered*, edited by Willem Saayman and Klippies Krtizinger, 94–112. Maryknoll, NY: Orbis, 1996.

———. "The Methodist Struggle Over Higher Education in Fuzhou, China, 1877–1883." *Methodist History* 34.3 (1996) 173–89.

———. *Evangelism as the Heart of Mission*. Mission Evangelism Series 1. New York: General Board of Global Ministries, The United Methodist Church, 1998.

———. "'History's Lessons for Tomorrow's Mission': Reflections on American Methodism in Mission." *Focus* [Winter/Spring] (1999). [Revised and republished as "History's Lessons for Methodism in Mission." *New World Outlook* New Series 59.5 (89.3) (1999) 5–9.]

———. "The Redemption of Ham." *Focus* [Fall] (1999) 23–24.

———. "Holiness and the Missionary Vision of the Woman's Foreign Missionary Society of the Methodist Episcopal Church, 1869–1894." *Methodist History* 39.1 (2000) 15–27. [Korean: Translated by Misoon Im. *Holiness and Church Theology* 11 (2004) 194–212.]

Robert, Dana L., and Norman Thomas. "Selected Annotated Bibliography: Missions: History." *Missiology* 28.2 (2000) 245–48.

Robert, Dana L. "Shifting Southward: Global Christianity Since 1945." *International Bulletin of Missionary Research* 24.2 (2000) 50–58. [Reprinted in *Focus* [Spring] (2001); Reprinted in *The Study of Evangelism: Exploring a Missional Practice of the Church*, edited by Paul Chilcote and Laceye Warner, 117–34. Grand Rapids, MI: Eerdmans, 2008; Reprinted in *Landmark Essays in Mission and World Christianity*, edited by Robert L. Gallagher and Paul Hertig, 46–60. Maryknoll, NY: Orbis, 2009; Chinese: *Zongjiao yu meiguo shehui: Dangdai chuanjiao yundong.* [*Contemporary Mission Activity*. Vol. 6 of *Religion and American Society*]. Edited by Xu Yihua et al. Beijing: Shishi, 2009; Korean: *Holiness Church and Theology* 9 (2003) 171–92.]

2001–2010

Robert, Dana L. "V. Frauen in Mission und Weltkirche." In vol. 3 of *Religion in Geschichte und Gegenwart*, edited by Hans Dieter Betz et al., 265. 4th ed. Tübingen: Mohr Siebeck, 2001.

―――. "The First Globalization: The Internationalization of the Protestant Missionary Movement between the World Wars." *International Bulletin of Missionary Research* 26.2 (2002) 50–66. [Reprinted in *Interpreting Contemporary Christianity: Global Processes and Local Identities*, edited by Ogbu Kalu and Alaine Low, 93–130. Grand Rapids, MI: Eerdmans, 2008.]

―――. "Gospel Bearers, Gender Barriers: Issues for Women and Mission Today." *Currents in Theology and Mission* 29.4 (2002) 246–57.

―――. "The Influence of American Missionary Women on the World Back Home." *Religion and American Culture: A Journal of Interpretation* 12.1 (2002) 59–89.

―――. "Changing Perceptions of Missionaries and Cultures." *Journal of Presbyterian History* 81.2 (2003) 110–11.

―――. "M. L. Daneel: Missionary as Folk Theologian." In *Frontiers of African Christianity: Essays in Honour of Inus Daneel*, edited by Greg Cuthbertson et al., 1–15. Pretoria: University of South African Press, 2003.

―――. "The Mission Education Movement and the Rise of World Christianity, 1902–2002." *Focus* [Spring] (2003) 21–23.

―――. "The Great Commission in an Age of Globalization." *Focus* [Fall] (2004) 14–19. [Reprinted in *Considering the Great Commission: Evangelism and Mission in the Wesleyan Spirit*, edited by Stephen Gunter and Elaine Robinson, 23–40. Nashville, TN: Abingdon, 2005.]

―――. "Women in World Mission: Controversies and Challenges from a North American Perspective." *International Review of Mission* 93.368 (2004) 50–61.

―――. *St. Patrick and Bernard Mizeki: Missionary Saints and the Creation of Christian Communities*. Yale Divinity School Library Occasional Publication 19. New Haven, CT: Yale Divinity School Library, 2005. [Revised and republished as "Bernard Mizeki: Missionary Saints and the Creation of Christian Communities." In *Church Beyond Walls: The Performance of Pilgrimage*, edited by Elizabeth Keopping, 154–68. Vol. 4 of *World Christianity*. Critical Concepts in Religious Studies Series. New York: Routledge, 2010.]

―――. "What Happened to the Christian Home? The Missing Component of Mission Theory." *Missiology* 33.3 (2005) 325–40.

―――. "Widows in Service." In *Faith in Action Study Bible*. Grand Rapids, MI: Zondervan, 2005.

―――. "Encounter with Christ: Luke as Mission Historian for the Twenty-First Century." In *Evangelical, Ecumenical, and Anabaptist Missiologies in Conversation: Essays in Honor of Wilbert Shenk*, edited by James Krabill et al., 19–27. Maryknoll, NY: Orbis, 2006.

―――. "The Mother of Modern Missions." *Christian History and Biography* 90 (2006) 22–24.

―――. "Protestant Women Missionaries: Foreign and Home." In vol. 2 of *Encyclopedia of Women and Religion in North America*, edited by Rosemary S. Keller and Rosemary R. Ruether, 834–43. Bloomington: Indiana University Press, 2006.

————. "Where Are We Going in Mission Today?" *New World Outlook* New Series 67.1 [96.5] (2006) 24–27.

————. "World Christianity as a Women's Movement." *International Bulletin of Missionary Research* 30.4 (2006) 180–88. [Abridged and reprinted as "Christianity's Future Will Be Shaped by Women." In *Christianity*, edited by Mike Wilson, 106–12. Introducing Issues in Opposing Viewpoints Series. Farmington Hills, MI: Greenhaven, 2008; Reprinted in *Religious Leadership, Mission, Dialogue, and Movements*, edited by Kwok Pui-lan, 165–78. Vol. 3 of *Women and Christianity*. Critical Concepts in Religious Studies Series. New York: Routledge, 2009; Portuguese: "O Cristianismo mundial como um movimento feminine." In *Missões, Religião e Cultura: estudos de história entre os séculos XVIII e XX*, edited by Carlos André Silva de Moura et al., 27–50. Curitiba: Editora Prismas, 2017.]

————. "The Great Commission in an Age of Globalization." In *The Antioch Agenda: The Restorative Church at the Margins*, edited by Daniel Jeyaraj et al., 5–22. New Delhi: Indian Society for the Promotion of Christian Knowledge, 2007.

————. "Missionaries." In *Issues and Ideas Shaping International Relations*, edited by David Levinson and Karen Christensen, 228–31. Vol. 3 of *Global Perspectives on the United States*. Great Barrington, MA: Berkshire, 2007.

————. "The Patrick Paradox." *Books and Culture* 13.4 (2007) 30–31.

Robert, Dana L., and M. L. Daneel. "Worship among Apostles and Zionists in Southern Africa." In *Christian Worship Worldwide: Expanding Horizons, Deepening Practices*, edited by Charles Farhadian, 43–70. Grand Rapids, MI: Eerdmans, 2007.

Robert, Dana L. "Foreword." In *Clio in a Sacred Garb: Essays on Christian Presence and African Responses, 1900–2000*, by Ogbu U. Kalu, xiii–xvii. Trenton, NJ: Africa World, 2008.

————. "The Ministry of Ezekiel Guti." *Books and Culture* 15.2 (2009) 34–38.

————. "A Nation in Crisis: Zimbabwe Testimony." *Focus* [Winter] (2008–2009) 49–52.

————. "Testimonies and Truth-Tellings: Women in the United Methodist Tradition." *Focus* [Spring] (2008) 34–43.

————. "Innovation and Consolidation in American Methodist Mission History." In *World Mission in the Wesleyan Spirit*, edited by Darrell L. Whiteman and Gerald H. Anderson, 127–37. Nashville, TN: Providence, 2009.

————. "Missionaries Worldwide, 1910–2010." In *Atlas of Global Christianity*, edited by Todd Johnson and Kenneth Ross, 258–59. Edinburgh: University of Edinburgh Press, 2009.

Robert, Dana L., and Douglas D. Tzan. "Traditions and Transitions in Methodist Mission Thought." In *Oxford Handbook of Methodist Studies*, edited by William J. Abraham and James E. Kirby, 431–48. New York: Oxford University Press, 2009.

2011–2020

Robert, Dana L. "Cross-Cultural Friendship in the Creation of Twentieth-Century World Christianity." *International Bulletin of Missionary Research* 35.2 (2011) 100–107.

————. "The Giants of 'World Christianity': Historiographic Foundations from Latourette and Van Dusen to Andrew Walls." In *Understanding World Christianity:*

The Vision and Work of Andrew F. Walls, edited by William Burrows et al., 141–54. Maryknoll, NY: Orbis, 2011.

———. "Historical Trends in Missions and Earth Care." *International Bulletin of Missionary Research* 35.3 (2011) 123–29. [Reprinted in *Creation Care in Christian Mission*, edited by Kapya J. Kaoma, 71–84. Oxford: Regnum, 2016.]

———. "Mission Frontiers from 1910 to 2010. Part I: From Geography to Justice." *Missiology* 39.2 (2011) 5e–16e.

———. "Mission Frontiers from 1910 to 2010. Part II: Unbelief, Unreached, and Unknown." *Missiology* 39.3 (2011) 1e–12e.

———. "Mission in Long Perspective." In *Edinburgh 2010: Mission Today and Tomorrow*, edited by Kirsteen Kim and Andrew Anderson, 55–68. Oxford: Regnum, 2011.

———. "Reconciliation as Mission." *Focus* [Winter] (2011) 32–37.

Robert, Dana L., and David W. Scott. "World Growth of the United Methodist Church in Comparative Perspective: A Brief Statistical Analysis." *Methodist Review* 3 (2011) 37–54.

Robert, Dana L. "Boston, Students, and Missions from 1810 to 2010." In *2010 Boston: The Changing Contours of World Mission and Christianity*, edited by Todd Johnson et al., 13–27. Eugene, OR: Wipf and Stock, 2012.

———. "Reflections on Historians, Historiography, and the Confessional Divide." *Fides et Historia* 44 (2012) 87–91.

———. "'Rethinking Missionaries' from 1910 to Today." *Methodist Review* 4 (2012) 57–75.

———. "Foreword." In *Bible in Mission*, edited by Pauline Hoggarth et al., ix–x. Oxford: Regnum, 2013.

———. "Gender Roles and Recruitment in Southern African Churches, 1996–2001." In *Communities of Faith in Africa and the African Diaspora*, edited by Casely B. Essamuah and David K. Ngaruiya, 116–34. Eugene, OR: Pickwick, 2013.

———. "Mission in the Global Context: Challenges and Opportunities." In *The Gift of Mission Yesterday, Today, Tomorrow: Maryknoll Centennial Symposium*, edited by James H. Kroeger, 98–105. Maryknoll, NY: Orbis, 2013.

———. "Witness and Unity in Twenty-First-Century World Christianity." *Transformation: International Journal of Holistic Mission Studies* 30.4 (2013) 243–56.

———. "Forty Years of North American Missiology: A Brief Review." *International Bulletin of Missionary Research* 38.1 (2014) 3–8. [Korean: In *Current Mission Trends* 18 (2015) 185–205.]

———. "Forty Years of the American Society of Missiology: Retrospect and Prospect." *Missiology* 42.1 (2014) 6–25.

———. "From Cooperation to Common Witness: Mission and Unity, 1910–2010." In *Called to Unity—For the Sake of Mission*, edited by Knud Jørgensen and John Gibaut, 45–58. Oxford: Regnum, 2014.

———. "Interfaith Earth Care and Dialogue in Zimbabwe." *Evangelical Interfaith Dialogue* [Fall] (2014) 31–33, 47.

———. "Women in Mission: A Protestant Tradition." *New World Outlook* New Series 74.4 [104.2] (2014) 6–9.

———. "Global Friendship as Incarnational Missional Practice." *International Bulletin of Missionary Research* 39.4 (2015) 180–84.

———. "Performing World Missions in 1911." *Harvard Divinity Bulletin* 43.1–2 (2015) 84–87.

Robert, Dana L., and Francisca Ireland-Verwoerd. "A. J. Gordon: A Major Figure in the Foreign Missionary Movement." *American Baptist Quarterly* 34.2 (2016) 210–22.

Robert, Dana L. "Christian Transnationalists, Nationhood, and the Construction of Civil Society." In *Religion and Innovation: Antagonists or Partners?*, edited by Donald Yerxa, 141–56. London: Bloomsbury, 2016.

———. "Josiah Kibira: Ecumenical Statesman." *Journal of African Christian Biography* 1.2 (2016) 5–7.

———. "One Christ—Many Witnesses: Visions of Mission and Unity, Edinburgh and Beyond." *Transformation: International Journal of Holistic Mission Studies* 33.4 (2016) 270–81.

———. "Orthodoxy and Humanitarianism: Realities, Resources and Research Agenda." *The Review of Faith and International Affairs* 14.1 (2016) 58–65.

———. "Testimony: The Task of the United Methodist Women's History." *Methodist History* 55.1–2 (2016–2017) 7–18.

———. "Afterword." In *Encyclopedia of Christianity in the Global South*, edited by Mark A. Lamport, 953–54. Lanham, MD: Rowman and Littlefield, 2018.

———. "Called and Sent: United Methodists as Missionaries." *New World Outlook* New Series 79.2 [108.4] (2018) 10–13.

———. "From 'Give Us Friends' to 'Other Sheep I Have': Transnational Friendship and Edinburgh 1910." *Interkulturelle Theologie: Zeitschrift für Missionswissenschaft* 44 (2018) 196–212; *Zeitschrift für Missionswissenschaft und Religionswissenschaft* 102 (2018) 200–14.

———. "Samuel Mutendi of the Zion Christian Church: Interpretations of a Prophet." *Journal of African Christian Biography* 3.2 (2018) 5–11.

Robert, Dana L., and Aaron Hollander. "Beyond Unity and Diversity: A Conversation with Dana Robert on Mission, Ecumenism, and Global Christianities." *Ecumenical Trends* 48 (2019) 126–33.

Robert, Dana L. "Locating *Relocating World Christianity: Interdisciplinary Studies in Universal and Local Expression of the Christian Faith*." *International Bulletin of Mission Research* 43.2 (2019) 126–33.

———. "The Founding of the Women's Foreign Missionary Society and the Beginnings of Boston University." *Methodist History* 58 (2019–2020) 40–54.

———. "Naming 'World Christianity': Historical and Personal Perspectives on the Yale-Edinburgh Conference in World Christianity and Mission History." *International Bulletin of Mission Research* 44.2 (2020) 111–28.

BOOK REVIEWS

Robert, Dana L. Review of *The World Their Household: The American Woman's Foreign Mission Movement and Cultural Transformation, 1870–1920,* by Patricia R. Hill. *Missiology* 14.2 (1986) 230–31.

———. Review of *They Went Out Not Knowing: An Encyclopedia of One Hundred Women in Mission,* by Women's Division, General Board of Global Ministries, United Methodist Church (US). *Methodist History* 25.2 (1987) 129.

—————. Review of *An Endless Line of Splendor: Revivals and Their Leaders from the Great Awakening to the Present*, by Earle Edwin Cairns. *Missiology* 15.4 (1987) 549–50.

—————. Review of *Apologia: Contextualization, Globalization, and Mission in Theological Education*, by Max L. Stackhouse. *Missiology* 17.2 (1989) 228.

—————. Review of *Guardians of the Great Commission: The Story of Women in Modern Missions*, by Ruth Tucker. *International Bulletin of Missionary Research* 13.3 (1989) 135–36.

—————. Review of *A History of Lutheranism in Korea: A Personal Account*, by Won Yong Ji. *Lutheran Quarterly* 3.4 (1989) 461–62.

—————. Review of *Countdown to 1900: World Evangelization at the End of the Nineteenth Century*, by Todd M. Johnson. *International Bulletin of Missionary Research* 14.2 (1990) 84.

—————. Review of *By My Spirit: The Story of Methodist Protestant Women in Mission, 1879–1939*, by Ethel W. Born. *Methodist History* 29.2 (1991) 127–28.

—————. Review of *Pilgrim Path: The First Company of Women Missionaries to Hawaii*, by Mary Zwiep. *International Bulletin of Missionary Research* 17.3 (1993) 134.

—————. Review of *Liberating Reformed Theology: A South African Contribution to an Ecumenical Debate*, by John W. De Gruchy. *Lutheran Quarterly* 7.3 (1993) 349–51.

—————. Review of *Toward the Twenty-First Century in Christian Mission: Essays in Honor of Gerald H. Anderson*, edited by Robert T. Coote and James M. Phillips. *International Bulletin of Missionary Research* 17.4 (1993) 174.

—————. Review of *Hyla Doc: Surgeon in China through War and Revolution*, by Elsie H. Landstrom. *Methodist History* 32.2 (1994) 141–42.

—————. Review of *A Vision Betrayed: The Jesuits in Japan and China, 1542–1742*, by Andrew C. Ross. *Studies in World Christianity* 1.1 (1995) 93–95.

—————. Review of *Missions and Ecumenical Expressions*, by Martin E. Marty. *Missiology* 23.1 (1995) 98–99.

—————. Review of *Women and Missions, Past and Present: Anthropological and Historical Perceptions*, edited by Fiona Bowie et al. *International Bulletin of Missionary Research* 19.3 (1995) 131.

—————. Review of *Justice, Courtesy and Love: Theologians and Missionaries Encountering World Religions, 1846–1914*, by Kenneth Cracknell. *Methodist History* 34.3 (1996) 195–96.

—————. Review of *Christian Mission: A Case Study Approach*, by Alan Neely. *The Princeton Seminary Bulletin* 17.2 (1996) 269–70.

—————. Review of *The Missionary Movement in Christian History: Studies in the Transmission of Faith*, by Andrew F. Walls. *Missiology* 25.4 (1997) 483.

—————. Review of *Taking Christianity to China: Alabama Missionaries in the Middle Kingdom, 1850–1950*, by Wayne Flynt. *Methodist History* 36.2 (1998) 133–35.

—————. Review of *Christianity in China: From the Eighteenth Century to the Present*, by Daniel H. Bays. *Methodist History* 36.2 (1998) 133–35.

—————. Review of *The Kingdom of Character: The Student Volunteer Movement for Foreign Missions, 1886–1926*, by Michael Parker; *The End of a Crusade: The Student Volunteer Movement for Foreign Missions and the Great War*, by Nathan D. Showalter. *International Bulletin of Missionary Research* 23.1 (1999) 38.

—————. Review of *Mary Lyon and the Mount Holyoke Missionaries*, by Amanda Porterfield. *Missiology* 27.1 (1999) 130.

———. Review of *The Conversion of Missionaries: Liberalism in American Protestant Missions in China, 1907-1932*, by Xi Lian. *The Journal of Religion* 79.1 (1999) 134–35.

———. Review of *Gendered Missions: Women and Men in Missionary Discourse and Practice*, by Mary Taylor Huber. *Missiology* 28.4 (2000) 518.

———. Review of *Gender, Religion, and "Heathen Lands": American Missionary Women in South Asia, 1860s-1940s*, by Maina Chawla Singh. *International Bulletin of Missionary Research* 25.4 (2001) 179–80.

———. Review of *Robert E. Speer: Prophet of the American Church*, by John F. Piper. *Church History* 70.4 (2001) 819–20.

———. Review of *Christianity: A Global History*, by David Chidester. *The Christian Century* 119.18 (2002) 36–37.

———. Review of *Modern Women Modernizing Men: The Changing Missions of Three Professional Women in Asia and Africa, 1902-69*, by Ruth Compton Brouwer. *International Bulletin of Missionary Research* 27.4 (2003) 182–83.

———. Review of *The Widow's Quest: The Byers Extraterritorial Case in Hainan, China, 1924-1925*, by Kathleen L. Lodwick. *Journal of Presbyterian History* 82.3 (2004) 211–12.

———. Review of *For the Glory of God: How Monotheism Led to Reformations, Science, Witch-Hunts, and the End of Slavery*, by Rodney Stark. *Church History* 73.4 (2004) 889–90.

———. Review of *Journeys That Opened Up the World: Women, Student Christian Movements, and Social Justice, 1955-1975*, by Sara M. Evans. *International Bulletin of Missionary Research* 30.1 (2006) 47–48.

———. Review of *Christian Missionaries and the State in the Third World*, by Holger Bernt Hansen. *Church History* 75.1 (2006) 240–42.

———. Review of *Christianity In Korea*, edited by Robert E. Buswell and Timothy S. Lee. *Religious Studies Review* 33.1 (2007) 86.

———. Review of *Postcolonial Imagination and Feminist Theology*, by Kwok Pui-lan. *The Asbury Journal* 62.2 (2007) 119–20.

———. Review of *Sent to Heal!: Emergence and Development of Medical Missions*, by Christoffer H. Grundmann. *International Bulletin of Missionary Research* 32.4 (2008) 215–16.

———. Review of *African Pentecostalism: An Introduction*, by Ogbu Kalu. *Church History* 78.2 (2009) 475–77.

———. Review of *The World Student Christian Federation 1895-1925: Motives, Methods, and Influential Women*, by Johanna M. Selles. *Studies in World Christianity* 18.3 (2012) 316–18.

———. Review of *Putting Names with Faces: Women's Impact in Mission History*, by Christine Lienemann-Perrin. *International Bulletin of Missionary Research* 38.1 (2014) 44.

———. Review of *Into Africa: A Transnational History of Catholic Medical Missions and Social Change*, by Barbra Mann Wall. *Church History* 87.1 (2018) 320–23.